Routledge Revivals

Marxism

First published in 1941, *Marxism: Is it Science?* was written to present the author's criticisms of Marxism and, in doing so, to further exemplify his 'Method of Instruction' first proposed in an earlier work.

The book is divided into six parts to provide six complete presentations of Marxism and why the author considers it unscientific. The six different approaches, varying in focus and complexity, work together to give the reader a detailed knowledge of Marxism and the author's critique of it.

Marxism

Is it Science?

By Max Eastman

Routledge
Taylor & Francis Group

First published in 1941
by George Allen & Unwin Ltd.

This edition first published in 2021 by Routledge
2 Park Square, Milton Park, Abingdon, Oxon, OX14 4RN
and by Routledge
605 Third Avenue, New York, NY 10017

Routledge is an imprint of the Taylor & Francis Group, an informa business

Publisher's Note
The publisher has gone to great lengths to ensure the quality of this reprint but points
out that some imperfections in the original copies may be apparent.

Disclaimer
The publisher has made every effort to trace copyright holders and welcomes
correspondence from those they have been unable to contact.

A Library of Congress record exists under LCCN: 40034929

ISBN 13: 978-0-367-75119-7 (hbk)
ISBN 13: 978-1-003-16105-9 (ebk)
ISBN 13: 978-0-367-75120-3 (pbk)

Book DOI: 10.4324/9781003161059

MARXISM
IS IT
SCIENCE?

by

Max Eastman

London
George Allen & Unwin Ltd
Museum Street

CONTENTS

6 CONTENTS

FOREWORD

A DISTINGUISHED teacher told me recently that he began his courses in political science by having his pupils read the Introduction to my *Enjoyment of Laughter*. It was gratifying to me, because I proposed there a Method of Instruction which I believe to be the correct and natural one for all subjects except perhaps mathematics. And although I exemplified it with a rather light-hearted textbook on the psychology of humor, the proposal was serious, and was based on my understanding of what the human mind is and how it acquires knowledge.

The mind—I said—should approach a body of knowledge as the eyes approach an object, seeing it in gross outline first, and then by gradual steps, without losing the outline, discovering the details. A book on American history, for instance—I mean a textbook, for I am not talking about literature, thought, argument, or education in the full sense, but only instruction—should begin by telling in a few sentences the author's conception of the significant form of that history as a whole. America was inhabited by Indians, Europe discovered it, certain phases of development were passed through, and we arrived at the Great Depression—not more than a page. Then should follow a chapter giving the history of America from the Indians to the Depression, and laying in the fundamental explanatory factors, historical, racial, geographical, and economic. Then should follow three or four chapters giving the history of America from the Indians to the Depression, and elaborating these factors. Then should come six or eight chapters giving still further fundamental factors, but some glimpse also of the more subtle elements that developed between the Indians and the Depression. Then should follow eight or ten chapters in which race, economics, and geography retire toward the fringe of consciousness, and the web of the story becomes visible—but still the full story from the Indians to the Depression. Then perhaps a book of twelve or fifteen chapters could be written, similar to those we now have, giving the history of America from the Indians to the Great Depression. This book could be read by the pupil, as it would by a well-filled mind, not only without tedium, but with active thought and understanding.

If this method were adopted, a large part of the pain of studying would disappear. Studying itself, as distinguished from attentive reading, would largely cease to darken the school hours. Instead of repeating a thing over and over to himself in the effort to nail it onto his memory, the pupil would find it repeated for him, but always with new details, from a closer view, in more intricate connection with a growing pattern. It would stay in his memory because it was entangled in that pattern. A pattern is interesting—any developing pattern is interesting when not opposed by stronger excitements. That is why it would stay.

The process of learning is mishandled because it is likened to a physical task. You are informed, for instance, that the Spanish word for *but* is *pero*, and told to "learn it." That ought to be easy, you think, because it is only one word and a short one. And if while you

are getting ready, your teacher interrupts you to remark:
"You must distinguish this from *perro*, which means
dog," you will be disposed to hold up a hand and say,
"Wait a minute—one thing at a time!" You are assuming
that the same laws which would apply to a job of lifting
or collecting apply to a job of memorizing. Up to a
certain point the opposite law applies. It is easier to
remember that *pero* means *but*, whereas *perro* means
dog, than it is to remember that *pero* means *but*. And if
while you are learning that, your teacher remarks that
you must roll the two r's in *perro* as if you were growl-
ing, but that the one r in *pero* is not rolled, the task
becomes no task at all.

Learning, in short, is a process like weaving, and not
like gathering walnuts and dropping them into a bag.
One does not have to call himself a Gestalt psychologist
in order to recognize this simple fact. And both teachers
and textbooks should be influenced by it. If there is
enough interesting overt repetition by the textbook—
repetition of general ideas that are gradually acquiring
details—the uninteresting repetition of the textbook, the
central boredom of the study hour, becomes largely
unnecessary.

I have been wanting to exemplify this Method of
Instruction in a more important field than the psychology of laughter, and Mr. Norton's suggestion of a volume
embodying my criticisms of Marxism offers a fine opportunity. There is hardly a more serious subject of study
at the present moment, one more important for all
thoughtful people, one more difficult to get hold of. If
I can enable an uninitiated person by reading one book
once over at a fair rate of speed to get a general grasp of
what Marxism is, and what I think makes it unscientific,
my Method of Instruction will be richly vindicated. That

is what I have tried to do in this book, and for the purpose I have given a complete presentation of the subject six different times.

In Part I, *The World as Escalator*, you glimpse it afar off, and I hope tantalizingly, in what is little more than an aphorism.

In Part II, *The Trouble with Marxism*, it comes nearer and should begin to touch your existing interests at a good many points.

In Part III, *The Religious Heritage*, you really begin to see and feel what this body of ideas called Marxism is, and what made it defective from the start.

In Part IV, *The Marxian System*, you examine all of its main details and trace in each the results of the original defect.

In Part V, *Marx's Effort to Be Scientific*, these many details vanish again, because our focal point of interest, the nature of science and the nature of the Marxian philosophy, is examined still more closely and carefully, and I hope with conclusive scholarship.

In Part VI, *Revolution as a Scientific Enterprise*, I have extricated from its metaphysical shell the practical hypothesis, or plan of action for building a socialist society by means of proletarian revolution, which was bound up in the Marxian religion. I have discussed the contributions made to it by anarchists and syndicalists, as well as by Lenin, and the further improvements that might have come from consciously regarding it as an hypothesis. And in Part VII, *Trotsky Defends the Faith*, I have discussed the most recent attempt to make the Marxian religion stand up in the face of scientific thinking.

By the time you finish reading these two last parts, you will find that the whole subject has been presented to you a sixth time. And you will find it, I hope, so intricately woven into your understanding as to be practically ineradicable!

In an appendix, *The Americanization of Marx*, I have placed my analysis of Sidney Hook's celebrated attempt to prove that Marx was not a Hegelian philosopher but an anticipator of the "scientific pragmatism" of John Dewey. If you can read this rather technical essay with fluent interest, you being the uninitiated person mentioned above, you may consider that you have passed a final examination in the subject-matter of this book. I award you a diploma, and one also to my Method of Instruction.

Max Eastman.

JULY, 1940

PART ONE

THE WORLD AS ESCALATOR

THE WORLD AS ESCALATOR

MARXISTS profess to reject religion in favor of science, but they cherish a belief that the external universe is evolving with reliable, if not divine, necessity in exactly the direction in which they want it to go. They do not conceive themselves as struggling to build the communist society in a world which is of its own nature indifferent to them. They conceive themselves as traveling toward that society in a world which is like a moving-stairway taking them the way they walk. Their enemies are walking the same stairway, but walking in the wrong direction. This is not a scientific, but, in the most technical sense, a religious conception of the world.

PART TWO

THE TROUBLE WITH MARXISM

THE TROUBLE WITH MARXISM

IT TOOK a revolution in Russia to wake up the English-speaking world to the importance of Karl Marx. Marx regarded England as a model of the mature workings of that capitalist system which he analyzed, and he would regard present-day America as a supermodel. Nevertheless, it is just in England and America that Marxism never found a home. It never took firm root among our radical-minded intellectuals; it never became the official philosophy of our organizations of the working class, as it has almost everywhere else in the world.

There must be some reason why in the countries most advanced economically this most advanced economic theory and program never took hold. I think the principal reason is that Marx was educated in the atmosphere of German metaphysics. He began life as a follower of Hegel, and he never recovered from that German philosophical way of going at things which is totally alien to our minds. Hegel scorned the English for speaking of Isaac Newton as a great philosopher—for regarding his discoveries, that is, as the highest kind of knowledge. We, on the other hand, regard the professorial apostle of "German thoroughness," who cannot even suggest a plan for building a dam across a creek without starting in with the creation of the world, and getting us to agree about the essential nature of being and the relations between Pure Reason and the Categories of the Understanding, as a comic type to be caricatured on the stage. In this methodological difference of opinion we are right. Our methodology, like our economic development, is the more advanced. Science in its mature forms casts loose from philosophy, just as earlier it cast loose from religion and magic. It contents itself on the theoretical side with specific solutions of specific problems, and on the practical side with methods of procedure for accomplishing specific things. If these solutions and methods *imply* some general attitude toward the universe at large, then that is conceded tentatively and with reluctance. A quick recourse to skepticism, a readiness to say "I don't know" when large general questions come up about Being and the Nature of the Universe—a readiness to say "I don't know" whenever as a simple matter of fact you *do not know*—is the surest mark of an advanced scientific mind, whether practical or theoretical.

Marx gave the world as important a gift of scientific knowledge as any man of the modern era; he is one of the giants of science. Nevertheless, he did not have this mental attitude. His approach to his problems was philosophical. It was German-professorial in the very sense that seems unnatural to us more skeptical and positivistic Anglo-Saxons. He wanted to revolutionize human society and make it intelligent and decent. He investigated its history and its present constitution with that end in view, and drew up a plan by which the thing might be accomplished. But instead of presenting his thoughts in this simple and clear form as a specific plan for the solution of a specific problem, he started in by deciding in general what the universe is made of and how it operates, and then gradually worked down toward a demonstration that by the very nature of its being and the laws of its operation this universe is inevitably going to revolutionize itself. It is going to revolutionize itself in just the manner outlined in his plan, and therefore as intelligent parts of a universe of such a kind it behooves us to get to work on the job. That method of approaching a job is alien to the Anglo-Saxon mind, especially to hard-headed and radical specimens of the Anglo-Saxon mind. That is surely one reason—and I think it is the main reason—why Marxism does not take firm root in our culture where its lessons are most neatly applicable.

In this I do not mean to boast of any inherent superiority of the Anglo-Saxon brain cells. The more advanced simplicity of logic with which Englishmen like John Stuart Mill approached social problems, however tame their solution of them, was doubtless closely associated with that more advanced industrial development of which Marx himself was so clearly aware. It is important, however, that those young Americans who wish to approach Marx as a teacher—and to some extent they all ought to—should not be "buffaloed" by his philosophical mode of approach. They are very likely to in these days, because those most interested in propagating the ideas of Marx, the Russian Bolsheviks, have swallowed down his Hegelian philosophy along with his science of revolutionary engineering, and they look upon us irreverent peoples, who presume to meditate social and even revolutionary problems without making our obeisance to the mysteries of Dialectic Materialism, as a species of unredeemed and well-nigh unredeemable barbarians. They are right in scorning our ignorance of the scientific ideas of Karl Marx and our indifference to them. They are wrong in scorning our distaste for having practical programs presented in the form of systems of philosophy. In that we simply represent a more progressive intellectual culture than that in which Marx received his education, a culture farther emerged from the dominance of religious attitudes.

For it is the relic of a religious attitude to attribute your plan for changing the world to the world itself, and endeavor to prove that the "inner law" of this world is engaged in realizing your ideals. Marx was an implacable enemy of religion, and he was also—or thought he was—in revolt against philosophy. He liked to repeat the saying of Ludwig Feuerbach that "the metaphysician is a priest in disguise"; and he expressed many times the desire to get philosophy out of the way of his revolutionary science. It was with this motive that he so vigorously insisted that the world consists of matter and not spirit. But the essence of philosophy in its kinship with religion is not to declare that the world is spirit, but to declare that this world of spirit is sympathetic to the ideals of the philosopher. Marx banished the spirit, but retained in his material world the now still more extraordinary gift of being in sympathy with his ideals. He retained, that is, the philosophical method and habit of thought. It was not that he wanted help from the universe, but he did not know how else to formulate his colossal plan for controlling social evolution except to implant it as "historic necessity" in evolution itself. The combination of affirmative and confident action in a given field with a general attitude of scientific skepticism was unknown to him.

An engineer wishing to convert a given form of society into a more satisfactory one would begin by making a very rough outline of the kind of society he proposed to build. With that rough blueprint in mind he would examine the existing society, and he would also examine all past societies, and find out what are the forces which control them and the general laws of their change. When he had finished that investigation and acquired that knowledge, he would draw up a procedure or plan of action, a scheme for getting the thing moving (supposing that his investigations had proven it possible) in the direction of his proposal. That is an engineering approach to the problems raised by Karl Marx. It separates the choice of a goal, which is primarily an act of passion, from the definition of existing facts and the discovery of their laws of motion; and it presents its plan of action as a plan of action pure and simple. It does not undertake the task of proving that the objective world is by virtue of its own inner logic destined to carry that plan out— a task impossible of accomplishment by any mortal brain. We do not know what the world is destined to do, but we know what we can in our own era try to make it do, and try with good assurance that success is possible. That is all anybody needs to know in order to act, or does indeed ever know when he acts with a hazard sufficient to make his act interesting.

Marx did not draw up any detailed plan of the future society he proposed to build. He merely made a few highly general and wholly dogmatic assertions about how wonderful it would be. Indeed his faith in the benign drift of his material universe was so great that he was for the most part ready to dispense with any plan at all. The working classes, he said in one place, "have no ideal to realize: they have only to set free the elements of the new society. . . ." And even in that sole fragment where Marx did enter with some detail into the future plans of the communists, the *Criticism of the Gotha Program*, we find him demurring against any disposition to give these plans a guiding role. He calls them "juridical conceptions," and says that they are a mere by-product of economic evolution. His goal, he permits us to know, is a society without classes and without government by force, and one in which wealth shall be distributed according to the formula: "From each according to his abilities, to each according to his needs." But he insists upon presenting the conditions which make it reasonable to strive for such a goal, and show by what stages one might move toward it, as causes of its inevitable advent.

This failure to distinguish *condition* from *cause* is the most general of those unconscious devices by which Marx and his followers keep up the attitude of a philosopher while presenting the thoughts of an engineer. But it will be obvious upon a moment's reflection that this must be so. An engineer is compelled to regard his own act as a cause, and to distinguish this from the conditions by which his act is limited—the qualities of his material, its resistance to stresses, strains, etc. The philosopher, wishing to show that his act is identical with what the universe as a whole is doing, is equally compelled to ignore the distinction. He has no other recourse, if he intends to act creatively, but to present the conditions which make his plan possible as causes which make its success inevitable. That is why Marx's blueprints of the proposed society are so sketchy, and yet are laid down as though Marx had prophetic insight and were able to write a history of the remote future of the world.

It was in examining the existing society and all past societies, and trying to find out what forces control them and in what manner they change, that Marx did his really great work. This work divides itself into two sections: first, an explanation of the dominant part played in all human culture and all its history by a gradual change and development of the technique of wealth production; and second, an analysis of our contemporary capitalist method of production—or, in other words, the Theory of History and the Marxian Economics.

The Theory of History was summarized in this way by Friedrich Engels, the close friend and cocreator of Marx's ideas:

"Marx discovered the simple fact (heretofore hidden beneath ideological overgrowths) that human beings must have food, drink, clothing and shelter first of all, before they can interest themselves in politics, science, art, religion and the like. This implies that the production of the immediately requisite material means of subsistence, and therewith the existing phase of development of a nation or an epoch, constitute the foundation upon which the state institutions, the legal outlooks, the artistic and even the religious ideas are built up. It implies that these latter must be explained out of the former, whereas the former have usually been explained as issuing from the latter."

It is impossible to exaggerate the influence of this simple idea upon the subsequent development of historic knowledge. All thoughtful men have profited by it, and they will forever. It marks a turning point in the whole art of understanding history. Here again, however, the fact that Marx conceived himself to be writing a *philosophy* of history, an explanation of the whole thing as a single process, and one which was leading up to and with necessity including his proposed plan for the future, led him to state the case in a way that is unacceptable to a modern scientific mind. The fact that men have to eat and shelter and clothe themselves before they do other things, makes the productive forces a primary factor in explaining history, a factor *conditioning* all others. That is to say that no historic phenomenon can arise and endure which *runs counter* to the prevailing mode of production. This does not mean, however, that every-

thing which arises and endures is *explained by* the prevailing mode of production. Again the idea of effective
cause is confused with that of indispensable condition.
It is confused by Engels in this most simple statement of
the Theory, and it is confused still more explicitly by
Marx in his Introduction to the *Critique of Political
Economy*, the classic passage. "The mode of production," he says, "*conditions* the social, political and spiritual life process . . ." and in the very next sentence, as
though but developing the same thought: "It is not the
consciousness of men which *determines* their existence,
but on the contrary their social existence *determines*
their consciousness." There can be no doubt here that
the limiting condition and the determining cause are
being interchanged without discrimination, and this is
true throughout the entire Marxian system.

In *Capital*, for instance, Marx turns to the investigation of our present-day method of production. He does
so because this conditions and limits the success of any
efforts that social reformers may make to improve our
society. They may talk about liberty, equality, fraternity,
and so on, but if these aims are inconsistent with the
mode of production, all their noble talk will merely ex-
pand in the air. Now Marx is, as we have seen, interested
in liberty, equality, fraternity—in all that is implied by
these abstract slogans, and more too. He is interested in
forming a society in which wealth shall be distributed
according to need, work demanded according to ability.
He sees at a glance that our system of production renders
such a dream impossible. Capitalist production involves
economic classes and the exploitation of one class by
another inherently and eternally. It involves class struggle
inherently and eternally. But there is nothing inherently
eternal about capitalist production. It was a product of

change; it evolved out of feudalism; it may not necessarily be the end of that evolution. One need not, therefore, simply abandon one's plan for a better society as impractical, and fall back upon the sad enterprise of doctoring up in small ways the one we have. One may, by further investigation and exercise of ingenuity, devise a scheme by which the mode of production can again be changed, and thus new conditions created which will not be inconsistent with the ideal of a classless society. It was this latter step that Marx took, a step that made him the intellectual father of the Russian revolution and one of the most influential men in modern history. He devised the scheme—or the science, rather, for that is what it became—of engineering with class forces. He pointed out that by organizing and directing the struggle of the working class against the capitalists and their associates, by interlinking with this struggle in certain quite possible ways the struggle of the poor peasants and tenant farmers against the landlords, and by carrying it forward to a veritable "dictatorship" of these exploited classes, it would be possible to take possession of the instruments of production and change the system.

Marx saw clearly enough that this maneuver would be possible only in a crisis, only at a moment when the system had broken down so badly that the dominant classes were unable to rule and the exploited classes were driven by suffering to forceful and imperious action—only at a moment of actual or potential civil war. He was therefore concerned to find out whether the capitalist system of production does not inevitably produce crises, any one of which may become severe enough to make such action practical. There is little doubt that he did demonstrate the inevitability under our present capitalist system of the recurrent crisis of overproduction, and bound up therewith the inevitability of imperialist wars. His contribution to the understanding of business crises and the causes of war will not often be denied today, even by the most "bourgeois" economists. And thus he completed the scientific task set by his apparently utopian aims—the task of finding out how the existing system of wealth production might be changed in such a way as to make these utopian aims possible of attainment and reasonable to strive after.

It was not necessary for him, as an engineer, to prove that this change is inevitable. It was not even necessary to prove that social evolution is tending in that direction. He might, indeed, have believed with Spengler that it is tending in an opposite direction, toward decay and disaster, and that this deliberate and informed action—this new economic engineering science—is the only thing that can save us from the fate of the older civilizations. All he had to prove was that in spite of the *limiting conditions* his method of action is practical, and the occasions for its application will arise.

That is the sum and substance of *Das Kapital* as a part of an engineering science. Owing to his philosophical mode of approach, however, and to his training in the school of Hegel, Marx felt obliged to prove that his whole scheme of salvation is involved with historic certainty in the very laws of the capitalist system which "work with iron necessity toward inevitable results." It was with this sense of his mission that he approached his studies in economics.

"As far as I am concerned," he wrote to his friend Weydemeyer in 1852, "I cannot claim to have discovered the existence of classes in modern society or their strife against one another. Petty bourgeois historians long ago described the evolution of class struggles, and political economists showed the economic physiology of the classes. I have added as a new contribution the following propositions: (1) that the existence of classes is bound up with certain phases of material production; (2) that the class struggle leads necessarily to the dictatorship of the proletariat; (3) that this dictatorship is but the transition to the abolition of all classes and to the creation of a society of the free and equal." Or to put this mode of approach in the youthful words of his friend Engels: "With the same certainty with which from a given mathematical proposition a new one is deduced, with that same certainty can we deduce the social revolution from the existing social conditions and the principles of political economy."

Such words reveal the essence of what is unscientific and untrue in the Marxian system: the reading of the desired result into the limiting conditions, the failure to realize the central role played in all science by the working hypothesis. Given these conditions, if such and such action is taken, then the conceived result will follow: that is the language of science, and that is as far as the knowledge of man can reach. The attempt of Marx to know more than is possible to know, to prove more than he needed to prove, is what makes his great book, Capital, cumbersome and obscure and something of an affliction even upon the most willing.

In prescribing the action to be taken, the mode of procedure by which it may be possible actually to pass from the conditioning facts toward the proposed goal, Marx is less troubled by his philosophical inheritance. The famous Communist Manifesto contains, to be sure, a good deal of the metaphysics of history. Its very first sentence—"The history of all hitherto existing society is a history of class struggles"—shows that disposition to

read one's own interests into the definition of facts which
distinguishes the philosopher from the scientist. "No
hitherto existing society has ever been changed fundamentally except by way of a class struggle" is all that the
author needed to say. But, on the whole, the *Communist Manifesto*, being the program of a conspiratorial
league of revolutionists who hoped it might be possible
in the approaching revolutionary disturbances in Europe
to overthrow the bourgeoisie and establish a communist
state, contains little of the phraseology of the philosopher. Historic necessity and the logic of evolution are
here pretty well forgotten. The universe is dropped out
of the picture. The Communist League declares concretely in the language of common sense and of practical science that such and such are their "views" and
such their "aims," and that these aims can be attained
only by such and such methods.

PART THREE

THE RELIGIOUS HERITAGE

1. THE WORD "DIALECTIC"

OUR LEFTWARD intellectuals let fall the word *dialectic*—the key word in the Marxian system—as lightly as though it meant nothing, and entailed nothing, but a belief in change and the possibility of successful revolutions. Few of them realize what the state of mind is which they are helping to propagate by accepting with this numb acquiescence a word so highly charged with meaning. For my part, I think there is no intellectual question of more importance to the future of American culture than the question whether we are going to conduct our social efforts in the name of science, or are going to swallow down this romantic German philosophy.

To the Greeks the word "dialectic" first meant conversation, and when in the time of the sophists argumentative conversation developed into a fashionable parlor game, the rules of this game were also called dialectic. The game consisted of someone's making an assertion, and someone else's trying to lead him into self-contradiction by asking questions to be answered yes or no. If you have ever played "twenty questions," and played it ardently, you will remember how it leads inevitably to a consideration of the fundamental categories of conception—the ways in which things can be said to "be." This game, I think, would form an excellent introduction to the study of philosophy. At any rate, that similar game of dialectic did introduce the Greeks to the main body of what became philosophy. And if you will imagine a small leisure-class society, just waking up to the joys of unsuperstitious thinking, going in for this slightly bold and improper diversion—improper because it was always leading up to irreverent conclusions about gods—and making a steady· fad of it, and then imagine some clever persons coming along and writing "scientific" books on it like Sims on Contract Bridge, you will understand how inevitably this happened. For there were earnest people there, of course, like Socrates and Zeno, who loved Truth too well to toss her back and forth quite frivolously. They took the fascinating sport of dialectic seriously, insisting that it is the very essence of the method by which a mind arrives at truth.

And then Plato came, with his mature and calmly smiling equilibrium, and without letting fall the playful humor altogether, converted these parlor games into the greatest of all works of intellectual art, his philosophic dialogues. And when he proposed—not without a hint that perhaps those who believe it are a little crazy—his famous doctrine that the general ideas arrived at and defined in this manner are alone real, and that individual things are a mere shadow, he naturally gave the name of *dialectic* to the science which knows and understands all about these ideas in their pure form. It is a science of intellectual conversation or debate, whether with another or within one's own mind, a taking of contrary positions and then slicing off what is false in each, and so arriving at a higher and better formulation—a mode of progress toward the truth by contradiction and reconciliation.

With Aristotle, who brought those Platonic ideas down into the material world and made them function as a kind of regulating norm for the growth of actual things, the word "dialectic" took a drop from its exalted position. Aristotle was interested in observing how things grow. He had, therefore, a more complete and scientific view than Plato of the method by which a mind arrives at truth. Dialectic thinking seemed merely critical to him, or "tentative," and not concerned with real or philosophic knowing.

In the Dark or Theological Ages, however, when people again believed that, with the help of an initial revelation and of Aristotle's rules for thinking, true knowledge could be spun out of man's head by a thought-process, this word regained its high position. It became, in fact, a name for all those rules of thinking which had come down from Aristotle. But now, although a sense of the importance of *disputation* still remained, the parlor game was well forgotten. The word no longer called to mind, as with Plato and his predecessors, a definite method of mental progress, a zigzag movement of the mind toward true ideas by setting two views against each other and letting them resolve their differences in a third. It meant simply logic, and was, as Abelard said, "that *doctrina* . . . whose function is to distinguish between every truth and falsity," and which "as leader in all knowledge . . . holds the primacy and rule of all philosophy."

It was man's gradual understanding that real knowledge—the kind of knowledge you can rely on in action —is neither revealed by God nor spun out of the head by Aristotle's logic, but is come at by observation and experiment, that made possible our modern world. The development of this "scientific" kind of knowledge throughout the last four hundred years has been perhaps the most momentous thing that ever happened, or could be imagined to happen, in the history of human culture. Do not be deceived about this because from time to time a fad arises to be impatient, or "skeptical," of science. Science itself is skeptical, and the high standard set by scientific knowledge is the very thing that makes us impatient of it.

With this moving up of *investigation* into the place of *disputation*, the word "dialectic" again dropped low, just as it had with Aristotle. It played no part in the minds of Copernicus, Harvey, Galileo, Newton, and it soon fell out of use entirely except among the churchy and historic-minded. Laplace, Lavoisier, Helmholtz, Maxwell, Mendelyeev, Darwin did their work without it. Science never has made use of it in any form. Only once, when Karl Marx came forward with his so-called "scientific socialism," did this word make even an appearance in a position of honor in any significant work laying claim to the title of science. It then turned up in the field of *social science* with a glory round it like that it had possessed in the Middle Ages. In the mind of the orthodox Marxist, dialectic is again the "leader in all knowledge" and "holds the primacy and rule of all philosophy," and of all science, too. It is the supreme *organon*, the ultimate and perfect instrument of understanding, an inherently revolutionary superscience to which all genuinely progressive minds must learn to conform.

How did this peculiar thing happen? And is it really true that a new Method of Thinking has been discovered, better than that upon which all modern science is built, and that this wonderful discovery is now only slowly filtering through the world along with communist propaganda? It is not true, of course. But the fable is believed in by millions, and it is well worth a strenuous mental effort to find out what *is* true, and how this fable came to be mixed up with a socialism which pretends to be, and seems to be, scientific.

2. HEGEL'S CONTRIBUTION

IN ORDER to understand this renewed apotheosis of the word "dialectic," it is necessary to realize that the whole momentous growth of matter-of-fact knowledge which we call science has had to fight its way every step against resistance from people who were not matter-of-fact. It has had to fight against people who wanted to go on holding to the old emotional beliefs which used to stand firm upon the ground of divine revelation and logical disputation. These oversoulful people have not wanted to deny science or deprive themselves of its benefits, but neither have they wanted to commit themselves to its methods of acquiring knowledge, and above all to the limitations of knowledge which those methods imply. They have used the faculty of ideation not only in order to change real things in an ideal direction, but also in order to make themselves comfortable among things-as-they-are by thinking up ideal ways of conceiving them. While matter-of-fact men, or men in their matter-of-fact moods, have been building science and trying to clarify its principles, these other men or moods of men, less based in matter and less bent on fact, have been inventing a variety of complicated intellectual machinery for keeping up the old wish-fulfilling views of the world as a whole, in spite of the disillusioning discoveries of science about each particular part of it. This wish-fulfilling machinery constitutes about one half, I suppose, of what is called modern philosophy. And it constitutes far more than one half of what is called German idealistic philosophy. That may be described almost wholesale as a disguised theology, a colossally ingenious speculative wizardry by which the old religious attitudes were maintained in the new scientific world. It was so described by Marx himself. And the most ingenious of all these disguised theologians, the "master wizard" as Marx called him, was Georg Wilhelm Friedrich Hegel, who dominated German intellectual life when Marx was young.

We need not explore all the intricacies of Hegel's wish-fulfilling machinery. It has two essential elements, or rather two legs upon which it stands, and without which it is nothing. One is an absolute conviction as to the notion put forward, somewhat tentatively I think, by Plato, that the veritable realities of this world are ideas and not things. The other is the brilliant device of conceiving these ideas, not as static entities, but as in a state of fluid logical development. Plato had said, you remember, that these real ideas, conceived as changeless, are to be studied and arrived at by a debating or dialectic process, a process of affirmation, contradiction, and reconciliation of the opposing views. Hegel declared that the ideas are themselves going through this process. This autodebating, or dialectic unfolding, of an idea is what every reality in this world consists of. And not only every particular reality, but the world as a whole is a Mind engaged in defining its content by affirmation, self-contradiction, and reconciliation of the opposites in a higher unity. It is a Divine Mind evolving with logical necessity and with intense creative emotion like a deadly serious, soulfully important, and noble and inexorable parlor game of dialectic, toward the goal of "self-realization."

Now if you are going to believe in God in a scientific age, there are decided advantages in believing in this kind of God. It enables you to be almost as "empirical" and hardheaded and unillusioned as the scientists themselves in describing any particular "phase" that this God may have to go through. It enables you to accept, and even carry forward, the discovery of science that the heavens and the earth and everything on the earth have evolved, that all is change, that nothing we care about is eternal. Next to the discovery that the earth is not the center of the heavens, that has been the most upsetting thought to soulful people. It has been the most difficult for the Eternal Being, the Unchanging, the Ancient of Days, to cope with and survive. And I think it is not too much to say that the essential function of Hegel's philosophy, what has made its ingenuity so significant, is that it saves the face of the Deity when confronted by this modern scientific world of flux and universal evolution. It saves the face of the Deity, and it saves the face of pious, conservative, optimistic morality—not shallowly but deeply optimistic—and it reestablishes with a cosmic glamour the virtues of a civil and loyally devout submission to the ordered course of events. If all the world, and human history most especially, is the mind of God moving with logical necessity through a process of affirmation and self-contradiction, and reformulation in a higher unity, toward the truth of His own being—toward that freedom which you feel when you have solved a problem and got all your definitions right—then obviously there is no use rebelling deeply against the world, or making totally disruptive efforts to reform it. The thing is to feel reverent, to feel that you are a part and member of this divine Reasoning Process, this cosmical Debating Society, and go dutifully along toward the logically inevitable solution.

It is easy, when you do not believe in any of it at all, to smile at this colossal enterprise of self-deception. But if you leave your smiles outside, and enter into it and see with what staggering sweeps and intricate ingenuities it is bewilderingly constructed, and if you remember, too, that it flourished a hundred and more years ago when our own great-grandparents were believing in the literal licks of hell's flames up the pants-legs of the sinner, you will not smile too scornfully. Remember, too, that Hegel did not wait for modern science to confront the godhead with this world of flux and universal evolution so well known to us. He got the jump on science. He foresaw this world, and had his mighty and obscure machinery of cosmic casuistics ready for the job of reinstating soulfulness before the scientists themselves quite knew what they were coming to. It is no wonder, then, that Hegel's metaphysics seemed to many Germans ultimate, and had such influence on those who learned it in their youth.

Marx learned this system in his youth, and fervently believed it all. He believed it, of course, with a "leftward" tendency, a tendency to emphasize the temporal and historic character of the divine evolution, and the importance of each forward step in the process, each "negation" of the *status quo*—and particularly the one which he felt to be about due in his own time. It requires only a shift of emphasis in Hegel's system to put God on the side of the rebels. But real rebels in the days of science have no use for God. They do not ask assistance from the cosmos, or any soul-upholding conception of it, in their attempt to overthrow a tyrant class. They ask a scientific method for going at it, and the devil take the cosmos. Indeed they see that all godly cosmic systems tend in the long run to reconcile men to oppressive conditions by cherishing illusions about the metaphysical status of those conditions. Marx himself formulated this view of religion in one of his early writings. "The abolition of religion as the illusory happiness of the people," he said, "is a demand for their real happiness"—a thought expressed with greater felicity in the I.W.W. song, "There'll be pie in the sky by-and-by." With this feeling in him, it was inevitable that Marx should throw aside Hegel's scheme for reading soul into the universe, and particularly into the bloody pages of human history, and begin talking about the world as ordinary practical-minded people talk. The world is not made out of ideas, he suddenly discovered, and much less ideas evolving with passionate logic in a benign direction. It is made out of things.

Marx was twenty-five when he arrived at this conviction which all modern radical-minded people start with. It was then that he denounced Hegel as the "master wizard," denounced his whole system as "drunken speculation," and endorsed the opinion of the so-called materialist, Ludwig Feuerbach, that all speculative philosophers are priests in disguise. Indeed, Marx went further than Feuerbach, who himself softened the hard facts of science with a sort of "anthropological philosophy," or philosophy of human love. Marx renounced all kinds of wish-fulfilling speculation whatsoever, declaring that if you adopt the attitude of a scientific investigator, no philosophy of any kind except a mere summary of your findings is either possible or necessary.

Nowhere in literature is there a more wholesale rejection of the very idea of superscientific knowledge, a more arrant declaration of independence from metaphysical conceptions of the universe, than in Marx's writings from the age of twenty-five to twenty-seven. Nevertheless, when he came to formulate his own views of what science is—a thing he did very sketchily, and that is why there is so much argument about "understanding Marxism"—it appeared that he had really got rid of but one half of Hegel's machinery of wish fulfillment, the notion, namely, that reality is made out of ideas. The notion that reality is "dialectic," which was the very kingpin in the whole soulful-consolatory apparatus of the master wizard, he never did get rid of. Reality is material, he said emphatically, and even human history can be explained in its grand outlines as an evolution of material things. But nevertheless this evolution is proceeding toward humanly ideal ends. "All successive historic conditions are only transitory steps in the endless evolution of human society from the lower to the higher," as Engels put it. And Marx himself spoke of the "higher life-form toward which the existing society tends irresistibily by its own economic development," and declared on this ground that the workers "have no ideal to realize, they have only to release the elements of the new society which the collapsing bourgeois society carries in its womb." This mysteriously "noble" and ascending movement, moreover, is taking place in the very manner proper to an apotheosis of the parlor game of dialectic. It first asserts something, and then this something passes over into its opposite, and then by its own "self-active motion," or in other words by a *logical* necessity, it reconciles or "sublates" these opposites in a higher—that is, a more desirable—unity.

3. WHAT DIALECTIC MEANT TO MARX AND LENIN

MODERN MARXISTS will hasten to assure you that the "triadic" character of the dialectic movement is not essential. And they are quite right. The essential thing is its going "from the lower to the higher"—in the direction, that is, of the Marxist's wish—and its doing this by way of conflict within a self-contradictory "totality." However, it is not difficult to find sufficiently triadic examples in both Marx and Lenin. Wealth, or private property, said Marx, is "the positive side of an antithesis"; "proletariat and wealth are opposites": it lies, therefore, in the very nature of a dialectic reality that the conflict between these two "opposites" should resolve itself in a successful proletarian revolution in which "the proletariat itself disappears no less than its conditioning opposite, private property."

To declare that "proletariat and wealth are opposites" is such loose thinking that to us it seems obvious the purpose must be other than the definition of fact with a view to verified knowledge. And yet this loose thinking forms the framework into which the mass of empirical information in *Das Kapital* has to be forced in order to make credible the historic necessity of a social revolution. This loose thinking is essential to the belief that reality is dialectic. It will be found *whenever and wherever* a downright attempt is made to explain what that belief is. Even Benedetto Croce, who wants to save all

43

that he possibly can of Hegel's philosophy because he likes it, is compelled to remark this. Hegel made an "essential error," he says, in failing clearly to conceive what he meant by "opposite"—failing, indeed, to distinguish things which are opposite from things which are merely "distinct."

"Who could ever persuade himself," he exclaims, "that religion is the not-being of art and that art and religion are two abstractions which possess truth only in philosophy, the synthesis of both; or that the practical spirit is the negation of the theoretical, that representation is the negation of intuition, civil society the negation of the family, and morality the negation of rights; and that all these concepts are unthinkable outside their synthesis—free spirit, thought, state, ethicity—in the same way as being and not being, which are true only in becoming?"

Obviously nobody could persuade himself of these fantastic propositions unless he had some reason to do so other than the desire to understand the world. Hegel's reason was that he wished to keep up, in spite of scientific understanding, a certain attitude of feeling toward the world. It was an attitude of action rather than of feeling that Marx and Lenin wished to keep up. But the thinking by which they did so was just as loose, and the lists of "opposites" which they composed just as fantastic, as those of Hegel. In fact, they merely added the class struggle—the opposition of "wealth," or bourgeoisie, and proletariat—to the old lists.

Here, for instance, is Lenin's conception of the dialectic, written in his notebook after studying Hegel's *Science of Logic*:

"Dialectic is the study of how there can be and are [how there can become] identical opposites—under what circumstances they are identical, converting themselves one into the other—why the mind of man ought not to take these opposites for dead, stagnant, but for living, conditional, moving things converting themselves one into another. . . .

"The doubleness of the single and the understanding of its contradictory parts . . . is the essence . . . of the dialectic. . . .

"In mathematics: $+$ and $-$. Differential and integral.

"In mechanics: action and reaction.

"In physics: positive and negative electricity.

"In chemistry: the combining and dissociation of atoms.

"In social science: the class struggle. . . ."

To this list he adds, in some later notes, the distinction in logic between the particular and the general: "A leaf of a tree is green: Ivan is a man: Zhuchka is a dog, etc. Here already (as Hegel's genius observed) is the dialectic; the particular is the general." And in another place, he calls the progress of the mind "from living contemplation to abstract thought and from this to practice" a "dialectic path."

The science of psychology, with all its failings, has done enough for us so that when a man makes in dead earnest such preposterous assertions as that $+$ and $-$, action and reaction, wealth and proletariat, particular and general, bear the same relation to each other—still more, that wealth and proletariat resolve their opposition in the social revolution with the same "self-active motion" with which a mind resolves in practice the "opposition" between contemplation and abstract thought —we know that he is driven, whether consciously or not, by some motive other than a wish for genuine understanding. He is not engaged in scientific investigation, but in rationalizing his motives. Just what the motive was, moreover, whose satisfaction gave a color of solid and solemn truth to this loose mixture of remarks, appears in almost every page of Lenin's notes. This, for instance, from the paragraph next following:

"Development is a 'struggle' of opposites. . . . Only [this] conception affords a key to the 'self-movement' of every existent thing; it alone offers a key to 'leaps,' to 'interruptions of continuity,' to 'transformations into the opposite,' to the destruction of the old and the arising of the new."

It is the "leaps," the "interruptions of continuity," the "destruction of the old and the arising of the new"—in short, the social revolution—that Lenin is interested in. And an underlying, always unspoken assumption that the new is going to be what he wants it to be, that the real is in harmony with the human ideal, provided it is our ideal, is just as essential to his philosophy as it was to Hegel's. As a philosopher he is using his mind not merely in order to promote the success of his action, but in order to assure himself that his action will succeed.

That this kind of thinking is not science, but is something which the "speculative thinker" *reads into* science, was clearly recognized and stated by Hegel. "The speculative science," he said, "does not in the least ignore the empirical facts contained in the several sciences, but recognizes and adopts them. . . . But besides all this, into the categories of science it introduces and gives currency to other categories." Exactly the same thing is true of the Marxian dialectic philosophy, as you may see in the assertion of Engels, who expounded it, that Marx did not use the dialectic in order to establish any fact, and also that an understanding of the dialectic nature of such a thing as a barley seed does not enable one to raise barley any better than he could if he did not understand it. What makes the Marxian philosophy so much more difficult than the Hegelian to combat, is that while Marx took over from Hegel this conception of a speculative or superscientific mental operation, he thought that he was being purely scientific, and, indeed, more purely scientific than anybody else in the field of sociology. All radically thoughtful modern minds understand that this special kind of thinking, lofty and yet loose, which stands above the best efforts of science, and is not used to prove any facts, and gives you a knowledge of the barley seed which has nothing to do with raising barley, is emotional rationalization, and what it introduces into the categories of science and gives currency to, is the wish fulfillments of the human heart.

Marx—to sum it up—rejected Hegel's divine spiritualization of the world and the historic process; he declared the fundamental reality to be solid, stubborn, unconscious, and unconsoling matter. And then he proceeded to read into that matter the very essence of the Divine Spirit as it had been conceived in Hegel's consoling system, its self-active motion by an inherent logical necessity, the necessity with which in a debating mind the conclusion follows from the premise, toward an ideal end. The end was different, and so were the actions and emotions of one who participated in the process, but the conception of the universe was essentially the same.

Hegel apotheosized a parlor game, and managed to attach pious emotions and a conservative goal and moral to a God who had nothing better to do than argue with himself about abstract ideas. Marx took the soul out of the whole fabrication, dispelled the pious emotions, and replaced the conservative with a revolutionary goal and moral, but left the apotheosis of the parlor game working away just as miraculously, just as superscientifically, as it had before. Indeed, in his mature reflections, he left it more miraculous, for now it is going through the motions of a debating society, obeying all the rules of order and arriving at the logically imposed result, without possessing reason or knowing anything about what it is doing.

"History proceeds in such a way that the end-result always issues from the conflict of many individual wills. . . . We have thus innumerable conflicting forces, an endless group of parallelograms of forces, giving a resultant—the historic event—which may itself again be regarded as the product of a force acting as a whole without consciousness and without will. For that which each individual desires, meets an opposition from every other, and the result is something which nobody desired."

It is in this blind way, according to Engels, that a material world accomplishes that "endless evolutionary progress . . . from the lower to the higher" which is its dialectic essence. And Marx, if you gather the quotations with some care, leaves equally independent of human will or consciousness the historic necessity of the dictatorship of the proletariat and its transition to the society of the free and equal.

"Man makes his own history, but he does not make it out of the whole cloth; he does not make it out of conditions chosen by himself, but out of such as he finds at hand." "It is unnecessary to add that man is not free to choose the forces of production which serve as the foundation of his entire history, for every force of production is an acquired force, the product of former activity. . . ." "By virtue of the simple fact that every generation finds at hand the forces of production acquired by an earlier generation . . . there arises a connection in human history, and the history of mankind takes form and shape." "I have added as a new contribution the following propositions: 1) that the existence of classes is bound up in certain phases of material production, 2) that the class struggle leads necessarily to the dictatorship of the proletariat, 3) that this dictatorship is but a transition to the abolition of all classes and the creation of a society of the free and equal."

Far from abandoning "all philosophy" for science, Marx did not even abandon Hegel's philosophy. He merely replaced Hegel's World Spirit with a World Robot who performs to a different purpose, and without demanding social attentions, all the work which the World Spirit was employed to perform.

"Scientific" socialism, then, *in its intellectual form*, is anything but scientific. It is philosophy of the very kind that Marx himself contemptuously denounced. A revolutionary science would study the material world with a view to changing it according to some practical plan. Marx studied the world with a view to making himself believe that it is in process of change according to his plan. In so far as his plan *is* practical, a revolutionary science is contained in his writings, tangled up in, and somewhat distorted by, an optimistic system of belief. But the belief is superscientific, metaphysical—religious in the truest sense of the term. It is a scheme for reading the ideal purpose of the communists and their plan for achieving it into the objective facts, so that their account of the changing world and their plans for changing it become one and the same thing. "It is not a question of putting through some utopian system," they cry, "but of taking a conscious part in the process of social transformation which is going on before our very eyes,"—and therefore—"All our theories are programs of action." Or, as we find it in the words of Lenin: the dialectic philosophy is "deeper and richer" than "objectivism," because it "includes in itself, so to speak, partisanship, obliging a man in every appraisal of events directly, frankly and openly to take his stand with a definite social group."

4. INCIDENTAL BENEFITS OF FAITH

TO IDENTIFY theoretic knowledge-of-fact with the program-of-action of a special social group, to regard partisanship as "deeper" than objective investigation, is so exactly *not* the attitude in which science approaches the world, whether it be pure science or applied, that you would hardly expect to find this thought surviving in the minds of educated modern men like Lenin and Trotsky. To hold your wish or purpose in suspense while you define existing facts may be said almost to be the essence of what science is. For a practical revolution-ist, however, that unscientific mental trick has, or at least has had, advantages entirely apart from its wish-fulfilling function. It has inculcated a flexibility of mind, a freedom from fixed concepts in dealing with social phenomena, a habit of constantly recurring to the facts for new starting points, new slogans, which, foreshadowed in Marx, became in Lenin the basis for as brilliant a po-litical leadership as the world has seen. It inculcated this free and fluid, and nevertheless inflexibly purposive manner of thinking, before it could have been learned from the evolutionary science of social formations and of the human mind.

It is not true, as Marxists assert, that Marx brought into the social theories of the eighteenth-century ration-alists the idea of development, and taught them to re-gard society as a totality and not just a dog-pile of individuals. Both the study of society as an organic whole, and the study of that whole as in a state of evolution, grew up out of the views of the eighteenth-century rationalists, pushed on by the general development of evolutionary science, without the slightest influence from Marx's working-class philosophy of Dialectic Materialism. It is true, however, that with his metaphysical conception of society and the mind as co-operatively evolving on a dialectic pattern toward the goal he wanted it to reach, Marx anticipated a social engineering attitude, and invented a technique of engineering with class forces, which might have been a very late result of that more purely scientific development. Just as Hegel forestalled the scientists with his conservative metaphysics, so Marx with his revolutionary metaphysics was far ahead of them in the technique of social action. That may give us a tolerant respect for Dialectic Materialism, and for the whole German romantic movement in philosophy, but it is, of course, no reason for clinging to a system that is unscientific.

There are two other facts, however, which make it hard to escape from Marx's wish-fulfilling system, and yet retain his scientific contribution and hold to his technique of class action. One is that social science, when it is applied on a grand scale, does differ from physical or mechanical or any other kind of engineering in that the scientists themselves are a part of the material they work with, and *what they think about the experiment may affect its result*. That gives to the dialectic myth bound up in scientific socialism a value similar to that at times possessed by the Christian Science myth in the eyes of a neuropathologist. True and resolutely practical science does not hesitate on that account, of course, to explode the myth and face the problem that results. It merely finds an obstacle of genuine, though limited, utility to overcome.

A similar, though still more limited, utility is the emotional ease with which this cosmic objectification of their plans enables the scientific intellectuals, the professional revolutionists as Lenin called them, to identify themselves with the spontaneous movement of the working class. The idea that the socialist thinker, who comes almost inevitably from other classes, is merely "bringing the proletariat a consciousness of its own destiny," enables him to avoid a certain appearance of patronizing, or putting something over on, the proletariat. His theory-program is a mere "mental reflection" of the proletariat's evolutionary position; his own class origin is incidental; the proletariat would, moreover, in the long run evolve its own consciousness and reach its goal without him. He can at best accelerate the inevitable. This nicety of the dialectic conception is supposed to inculcate a mood of humble co-operativeness in the intelligentsia. Nevertheless, it is just this nicety that Lenin overstepped so rudely in his book *What to Do*, and Lenin identified himself with the struggling masses more directly and with less blab than many of the more orthodox Marxists.

These subtleties of emotional equilibrium are worth nothing in the long run compared to a clear vision of the facts. And the fact is that Marx's dialectic philosophy, with all its wish to be scientific, and even to out-science the scientists, is a survival of the intellectual machinery with which oversoulful people have kept up in the face of science wish-fulfillment thoughts about the world. It is an elaborate device for reading the plans of the communists into their description of the developing objective facts. "The world is on our side," it teaches them. "The real and the motion toward our ideal are the same thing. In order to perceive with accuracy, we must conceive with prejudice."

PART FOUR

THE MARXIAN SYSTEM

1. THE BELIEF IN DIALECTIC MATERIALISM

IN PRIMITIVE culture it is possible to distinguish two quite different kinds of thinking—animistic thinking, in which one tries to adjust oneself to the external world as to a person, and the ordinary practical thinking by which the daily arts of life are carried on. Animistic thinking consists essentially in trying by some sort of hocus-pocus to transfer your own wishes into the external world, and so get them realized. It is emotional and ceremonial and soon becomes institutionalized in the religious festivals, the Mysteries, the Priests, the Church. And because of its emotional hold upon men, it is taken in charge by the ruling and exploiting classes, and becomes the guardian of custom and "good morals," and the chief cultural instrument for the maintenance of the *status quo*. It is aristocratic thinking, and makes up in elaboration and social standing for what it lacks in convincing force.

But the practical arts of life develop alongside of it, and indeed within its very temple, and the actual control of man over his environment begins to be almost as exciting as this rather montonous conjuring of the world-spirit. Moreover, these arts develop a technology which rests upon theoretic assumptions, and these theoretic assumptions begin to be formulated by creative minds in contact with the artisan class. Men appear who dare to say that the world really *is* what the artisan assumes it to be in his daily work. And they come into conflict—whether as materialists, skeptics, Sophists, Socratic exasperating questioners, or what not—with the ceremonial, soulful, socially-authoritarian world-view. They are not philosophers, except in a very agnostic sense of the word. They are people who are satisfied with the assumptions of science and the arts. And they are satisfied because their interest is in doing things with the world, rather than in establishing a comfortable relation with its spirit.

It is obvious that these people are dangerous to the ruling powers, and it is in their ranks that we find the first great martyrs of science—Anaxagoras banished, Protagoras persecuted and tried for his life, Socrates put to death protesting that true piety is obedience to the laws of the state. The crime of Socrates was deeper than disobedience to the laws of the state. It was disobedience to the laws of animistic thinking. It was asking irreverent questions about the soul of man, and the definite meaning of those large emotional ideas which have the support of custom and the priests. Indeed I can think of no more revolutionary or dangerous idea than this one of Socrates, that piety is nothing but obedience to the laws of the state. Give us an equally irreverent definition of the state, and where are we, if not on the brink of revolution? It is obvious that such matter-of-fact people must be done away with. It is obvious, moreover, since those arts and sciences from which they derive their authority are going right on developing and attracting interest, that putting them to death is not going to be enough. They must be met on their own field and refuted. And for this a new and specially honorable and arduous kind of "speculative thinking" is required.

That, it seems to me, is the principal origin of "philosophy," in what I will call the bad sense of the term.

As the practical work of the mind advances, religion weakens, the priest loses his authority. Then the metaphysician steps forward and builds a home for the soul out of the very instruments of that practical work of the mind. Those instruments are, in the main, the logical categories—being, becoming, quantity, number, and so forth. The task of the metaphysician, speaking very broadly, is to transplant into these empty abstractions that personal moral spirit, the defender of custom and established right, which is being driven out of the concrete world by the development of the scientific view. His task is to preserve animism at all costs, and to show that the "highest" function of the mind after all, and no matter what science may achieve, is still to reconcile us with the world, rather than to help us change it.

The history of philosophy shows, of course, a confusing interplay of the two attitudes, the attempt to generalize science, and the metaphysician's art of implanting animism within the assumptions of science. But there is one place in the history of philosophy where the metaphysician's art prevailed absolutely, and became like the Church a national institution, dominating the entire culture of a people from the public schools to the very laboratories of science. That is nineteenth-century Germany. German philosophy is the ultimate grandiose convulsion of animistic thought, expiring under the encroachments of the scientific point of view. And the philosophy of Hegel is the ultimate flower of German philosophy, the most adequately bold and all-comprehending and all-obscuring, the most sublimely animistic, and the most beautiful. Moreover, it is the most dexterous. Declaring that the specific motion of your mind, guided by Hegel, among the logical categories, is the universal self-active motion of those categories, and that this motion is the spirit of God in a process of self-contradiction and development, Hegel succeeded in converting logic itself, the very technique of science, into theology. And having put living movement into the divine abstractions contemplated by this logic-theology, he was able to declare that the material world, and all the science which investigates it, are a mere manifestation of these divine abstractions, and yet at the same time assert that this material world is a perpetual process of change and development. This was just what the natural scientists of his time were beginning to believe about the world, and for that reason Hegel's philosophy had an enormous vogue. It entrenched animism in the very heart and center of the advance that was made by science in the nineteenth century. It made of that science itself and of the mechanically evolving world which it revealed, a church in which God lived, and in which, in spite of its hard-seeming and cruel ways, God was but realizing Himself by His characteristic process of conflicting with Himself, and then resolving the conflict in a higher unity. In short, it declared the essence of reality to be akin to the aspirations of pious men, and hard at work upon the task of realizing them. It preached a gallant and obedient participation in the process.

"The true reason-world, so far from being the exclusive property of philosophy, is the right of every human being on whatever grade of culture or mental growth he may stand. . . . Man above all things becomes aware of the reasonable order, when he knows of God, and knows Him to be the completely self-determined. Similarly the consciousness a citizen has of his country and its laws is a perception of the reason-world, so long as he looks up to them as unconditioned and likewise universal powers, to which he must subject his individual will. And in the same sense, the knowledge and will of the child is rational when he knows his parents' will, and wills it."

That was the moral, and the most important practical meaning, of the Hegelian "Speculative Logic."

To people of revolutionary temperament, however, this wholesale doctrine of change offered an equally fine opportunity to rationalize *their* aspirations. There was no inherent reason, it seemed, why this divine Thinking-Process should be so pious and tiresome. If it really likes conflict and change, why won't It give Its sanction to the rebels, to those who really want conflict right now, and would like to see one more "higher unity" before they die? That was the mood of the "Young Hegelians," and among them Marx and Engels. Marx's childhood was less churchly-religious than that of Engels, but their educations were similar, and they approached the world in young manhood with the same mystic emotion. At the age of twenty-three, in dedicating a Doctor's Thesis to his future father-in-law, Marx wrote:

"Would that all who doubt of the Idea might be as fortunate as I, to admire an ever-young old man, who greets each advance of time with the enthusiasm and poise of the Truth, and with that conviction-deep, sun-clear Idealism, which alone knows the right word to call up all the spirits of the world, who never recoils before the shadows of reactionary spectres, before the oft-overclouded sky of the times, but with godlike energy and manly sure glance pierces always through all metamorphoses to the empyrean which burns in the heart of the world. You, my fatherly friend, have always been to me a living *argumentum ad oculos*, that Idealism is not a fancy, but a truth.

"Upon you I need not call down a bodily blessing. Spirit

is the great magical physician in whom you have put your trust."

And at the age of twenty-two Engels wrote:

"And that faith in the omnipotence of the Idea, in the victory of eternal truth, that firm certainty that it will never waver, never depart from its path, although the whole world turn against it—there you have the foundation of the real positive philosophy, the philosophy of universal history. Just that is the supreme revelation, the revelation of man to man, in which every negation of the critic becomes an affirmation. That everlasting struggle and movement of peoples and heroes, above which in the eternal world soars the Idea, only to swoop down into the thick of the fight and become the actual, self-conscious soul—there you have the source of every salvation and redemption, there the kingdom in which every one of us ought to struggle and be active at his post. . . ."

In this perfectly animistic attitude Marx and Engels developed their intellectual powers and formed their habits of thought. Their thinking consisted, up to the age of about twenty-five and twenty-three respectively, in imputing their aspirations to the Ultimate Spirit of the world, and then proceeding fervently to co-operate with that Spirit. And this animistic habit—so native to all human minds—became too strong upon them ever to be overcome. Marx was beginning to sense the harsh character of the contemporary struggle, when Ludwig Feuerbach's writings come into his hands; he must have felt already the unfitness of the Hegelian Idea to preside in such a struggle. And that is doubtless a reason why he welcomed Feuerbach's writings with such enthusiasm. Declaring joyfully that there is no Idea, no "empyrean which burns in the heart of the world," that the ultimate reality is not spirit, but matter, he went forward from that point without sentimental or confused emotion, and in what seemed an entirely matter-of-fact temper to write a science of social revolution.

But in spite of the great emotional change that had taken place in him, his writings were still, as we have seen, metaphysical, still in essence animistic. He did not examine this material world, as an artisan examines the materials of his trade, in order to determine by what means he could make something else out of it. He examined it as the priest examines the ideal world, in order to see if he could not find in it, or failing that, transplant into it, his own creative aspiration. Marxism in its intellectual form was not a step from utopian to scientific socialism—from impractical evangelical talk about a better society to a practical plan, based upon a study of the existing society, for producing a better one. Marxism was a step from utopian socialism to a socialist religion—a scheme for convincing the believer that the universe itself is producing a better society, and that he has only to fall in properly with the general movement of this universe.

"We explained," says Marx, in describing his own innovation, "that it is not a question of putting through some utopian system, but of taking a conscious part in the process of social transformation which is going on before our very eyes."

That was Marx's conception of a scientific undertaking. And that explains his dissatisfaction with Feuerbach's philosophy, his going back to Hegel to get the "dynamic principle" which he missed in the new material world. It was not merely motion that he missed, nor a particular kind of motion, but motion in a congenial direction. He wanted a world which contained his desires and would co-operate with him—a world in which "by means of all seeming accidents, and in spite of all momentary setbacks, there is carried out in the end a progressive development," "an endless ascending from the lower to the higher." It was not because of emotional dependence, I believe, but because of his intellectual habits. Marx had the dynamic principle in his own will, but being a German philosopher, he had not the least idea that practical science, like simple practical thought, might consist of defining a purpose and examining the external world with a view to its achievement.

Thus, when Marx said in his "Theses on Feuerbach" that sensation is a practical activity, he did not mean that sensation is an instrument for solving the problems of the sentient being. He meant that it is an instrument for solving problems common to the sentient being and the world that produced him. His fundamental statement in the first of those famous theses (quoted on page 180) was not that sensation is a practical activity, but that the sensible *object* is to be understood *subjectively*. And his fundamental statement in the whole of his comments on Feuerbach was this:

"The coincidence of a change of environment and human activity, or *self-change*, can only be conceived and rationally understood as revolutionary practice."

That shows what Marx meant by the word "Praxis," and it shows the direction in which his mind was traveling. He was not advancing from Feuerbach's philosophy toward the modern view of thought as in its origin an instrument for getting along in a material world. He was shrinking back from Feuerbach into the more familiar Hegelian position, in which true thought and the material world are doing the same thing, and doing it together. That statement about the simultaneous occurrence of a change of circumstances and "self-change," fulfills much the same function in the animism of Marx that is fulfilled in Christian animism by the statement, "God helps them who help themselves."

Plekhanov has a passage in which he describes the mental process by which Marx became a "scientific socialist." And it is valuable, not only as stating the animistic attitude of Marx, but as indicating how perfectly that attitude was preserved in Plekhanov himself, the founder of Russian Marxism.

"A disciple of Hegel," he says, "remaining true to the method of his teacher, could become a socialist only in case a scientific investigation of the contemporary economic structure brought him to the conclusion that its inner lawful development leads to the birth of the socialist order."

In other words, if you wish to create a socialist order, there is only one way to go about it, and that is to persuade yourself that the inner law of the objective world is creating it for you. If this attitude is remote from prayer, it is remote in the direction of its primitive origins. Dialectic Materialism rests its hope in the very sticks and stones, instead of in a spirit that is supposed to reside behind them. Otherwise it is not different from any other animistic philosophy. And whatever may have been the case with Marx, it is certain that many of his followers derive from this philosophy a support not unlike that derived by the pious from their God.

"If in spite of all the violence of its enemies," writes Rosa Luxemburg, "the contemporary workers' movement marches triumphantly forward with its head high, that is due above all to its tranquil understanding of the ordered objective historic development, its understanding of the fact that 'capitalist production creates with the necessity of a natural process its own negation—namely, the expropriation of the expropriators, the socialist revolution.' In this understanding the workers' movement sees the firm guarantee of its ultimate victory, and from this source it derives not only its zeal, but its patience, not only strength for action, but also courageous restraint and endurance."

It is not difficult to recognize in those lines the essential features of a religious psychology.

In answering those who asked the Marxians why, if socialism is the necessary product of economic evolution, they struggle to attain it, Plekhanov cited the struggle of the Puritans, the Mahometans, Calvin's Moses laboring to achieve what was predetermined by God, and the great Cromwell who always named his acts the fruit of the Divine Will.

"Here all depends," said Plekhanov, "on the question whether my own activity constitutes a necessary link in the chain of necessary events. If yes—then so much the less do I waver, so much the more decisively I act."

Plekhanov was perfectly right in relating the animistic materialism of Marx to the faith of the prophets. And he was right also in asserting that animistic faith does not put a stop to practical efforts. History would read very differently if it did. But he was wrong in thinking that it makes any difference to the impulsive man of action whether he conceives his practical activity as a necessary link in the necessary process or not. That makes a difference only to the philosopher who talks about him. And it makes a difference to the philosopher because his job is to reconcile animism with the *theo-*

retic assumptions of practical activity. And fatalism, or the idea that the result of these activities is going to be regulated externally, is too obviously in conflict with those assumptions. Therefore, he must take the idea of *causal determination*, which is one of those assumptions, and by some sort of intellectual hocus-pocus he must give it the upper hand over the idea of a *genuine alternative* in thought and action, which is another. And thus he may preserve animism for a while as a philosophy, even after it has ceased as a religion to impose upon practical minds.

The definition of freedom as *necessity become conscious* was invented by German philosophers for this express purpose. It was invented by Schelling, but greatly improved in the way of unintelligibility by Hegel, who mixed it up with his myth about everything becoming its opposite, and contrived to make his reader feel at times as though a person does really become creative when he becomes conscious. In the end, however, it appears that it is only because the cause which determines him, is also *him*, that *he* ceases, or seems to cease, to be determined when he becomes aware of the truth. Freedom is "the truth of necessity," according to Hegel. And the real significance of this statement is revealed in his philosophy of religion, when he says that a man is free when he "wants nothing but himself." He is free, that is, when he wants nothing which would involve a change in the conditions which produced him.

Marx accepted this dictum of Hegel's uncritically, and Plekhanov declared the original statement of Schelling to be "one of the most brilliant discoveries ever made by philosophic thought." Here again Plekhanov is entirely right, but it is necessary to remember just what philosophic thought is, and what its purpose is. The conception of the entire evolving variety of the world as held in the frame of an iron necessity, is not an essential part of the attempt to generalize science. The laws of science are an abstraction from the variety of nature, and that variety itself bears witness that these laws are not, and cannot be, an adequate or absolute statement of nature. The law of causation is not different from any other of these scientific laws. Moreover, the very existence of science and its development can be explained only upon the assumption that thought has a function other than the mere reflection or transmission of an already defined impulse. It has the function of defining impulse. That the future is in some degree undetermined is therefore the ineradicable assumption of all thinking. And this is nowhere more evident than in the thinking of Plekhanov about the doctrine of necessity. For his whole argument is this: *if I should cease to make efforts*, because I believe in that doctrine, I would be unreasonable. And that hypothetical proposition, *if I should*, implies a genuine alternative. It is only our acceptance of the genuineness of that alternative that gives intelligibility to the long pages Plekhanov devoted to this subject, and makes it possible to read or think them.[1] And that hypothetical proposition *if I should*, is moreover the original form of all thinking.

When Engels says that "Freedom does not consist in a fancied independence of the laws of nature, but in the knowledge of those laws and the possibility thereby created of deliberately making them function toward defined ends," he shows either a naïve innocence of the problem he is talking about, or that Hegelian sophistication which is a mockery of innocence. For the fact that my think-

[1] See Notes for some excerpts from these pages.

ing, which assumes to define ends in the future, operates with causal laws which assume that the future is already defined, is exactly the essence of the problem. The most advanced science, like the most simple practical sagacity, insists upon the validity of both those assumptions. It insists that there are, on the one hand, an adequate number of general and reliable uniformities in nature, and that there is, on the other hand, a genuine alternative in thought and action—a possibility that "I may," or "may not." These two assumptions are not absolutely contradictory, and if there is a profound mental difficulty in reconciling them, it is in the spirit of science— and especially of science as humbled by the understanding of its own origin—to leave that difficulty standing until a real solution is found. The demand that one should take his stand with Absolute Determinism and the impossibility of explaining what thought is and how it arose, or with Absolute Caprice and the impossibility of effective thinking, is a demand that comes, like other absolute demands, from the metaphysical and not the scientific mind.

Marx not only failed to escape from philosophy with his Dialectic Materialism, but he failed to escape, in the essence of the matter, from idealistic philosophy. For, if your material world has the faculty of willing the social revolution, and aspiring toward all those good things grouped by a revolutionary mind under the concept of "higher," and if it has the faculty of going after those things by a procedure that is in its essence logical, what is there left of mind that you have not surreptitiously attributed to this material world? There is left feeling only—if the attributes of mind are "will and thought and feeling"—and it was exactly and only a feeling that

Marx got rid of when he turned from Hegelian idealism to a materialism that was also Hegelian. He got rid of the ethicodeific feeling which idealistic philosophers attribute to the ultimate reality, and which makes their sense of co-operation with it sentimental and humble and conservative. Marx's ultimate reality is ascending "from the lower to the higher" cold-bloodedly and without caring anything about it. And that leaves him free, while co-operating with that reality, to have irreverent emotions, and be as hardheaded and ruthless as it is necessary for a practical revolutionist to be.

That is the extent of the "materialism" of Marx. And that explains why Marx and Engels repudiated with such violence "the materialism of natural science," "the materialism which exists today in the minds of naturalists and physicians," calling it "abstract," and "mechanical" and even "shallow and vulgar." Why should one kind of materialism describe another kind as shallow and vulgar? Whence indeed this word "vulgar" on the lips of a revolutionist? It is the Marxian way of saying *profane*. Marx and Engels were defending against scientific materialism—against that attitude which constitutes at least the simple common-sense starting point of science—a materialistic religion.[2]

And that explains, too, another thing which has troubled many critical minds attempting to enter into the Marxian system. It explains why Marx and Engels thought they could call their economic explanation of history a "materialistic" explanation. There is not the slightest logical connection between materialistic *philosophy* and the economic interpretation of history. One

[2] It is significant that Leon Trotsky, in disembarrassing himself of my views on Dialectic Materialism, revived this word "vulgar" and employed it in the same sense. I have quoted him in a Note to this page.

could believe that the course of history is entirely determined by wagging tongues, and still be a materialistic philosopher. And one could believe that it is all a matter of the instruments of production, and still believe that those instruments, like everything else, are in their ultimate reality ideas. Marx drove out of the study of history the same *feeling* that he drove out of Hegel's philosophy. That is the only connection between Dialectic Materialism and the economic interpretation of history. It was a matter-of-fact interpretation of history, and it is a matter-of-fact philosophy—so far as one can be matter-of-fact and still retain that animistic attitude which is the essence of all superscientific philosophy.

The purposive thought which explains Marx's intellectual position is contained in these sentences written in his early youth:

"The abolition of religion, the illusory happiness of the people, is a demand for their real happiness. The demand that one reject illusions about one's situation, is a demand that one reject a situation which has need of illusions."

That rejection of illusions—religious, moralistic, legal, political, aesthetic—is the immortal essence of Marx's contribution to the science of history, and to history itself. And if he did not succeed in rejecting also the illusions of philosophy, those who really esteem his life and his genius ought to carry out the process. Marx himself declared that philosophy, like law and politics and religion, and art, is subject to an economic interpretation at the hands of science. But he also declared—and within a year of the same date—that Hegel wrote the true history of philosophy. Since Hegel's history of philosophy is a history of "the self-developing reason," a "history of thought finding itself," these two statements are directly contradictory, and we have to choose between them. We have to choose between Marxism as a Hegelian philosophy and Marx's contribution to an historical science capable of explaining such philosophy.

2. THE THEORY OF HISTORY

HEGEL REGARDED history as the logical evolution of the Eternal Thinking Process in a disguised form. It was a process of advance by contradiction and the negation of the negation. And his philosophy of history consisted in seeking out in the "everlasting struggle of peoples and heroes" this necessary dialectic development, which was the one real cause and explanation of the course of that struggle, no matter what those who took part in it might be thinking or intending. Marx retained the principal assumptions of this philosophy: namely, that history is some one thing or process, irrespective of the interests of a given historian; that this process has some one cause, other than the conscious purposes of men, which explains it all; and that this cause has the property of being logical in its development, and of advancing by contradiction, and the negation of the negation. He retained this much of the Hegelian philosophy of history, but he turned that philosophy other side up. He found the ultimate one cause, not in the evolving Idea, which "soars above history in the eternal world," but in the evolving forces of production which lie underneath the soaring eloquence of history as it is usually written.

"In the social production of their subsistence men enter into determined and necessary relations with each other which are independent of their wills—production-relations which correspond to a definite stage of development of their material productive forces. The sum of these production-relations forms the economic structure of society, the real basis upon which a juridical and political superstructure arises, and to which definite social forms of consciousness correspond. The mode of production of the material subsistence, conditions the social, political and spiritual life-process in general. It is not the consciousness of men which determines their existence, but on the contrary it is their social existence which determines their consciousness. At a certain stage of their development the material productive forces of society come into contradiction with the existing production-relations, or what is merely a juridical expression for the same thing, the property relations within which they have operated before. From being forms of development of the productive forces, these relations turn into fetters upon their development. Then comes an epoch of social revolution. With the change in the economic foundation the whole immense superstructure is slowly or rapidly transformed. In studying such a transformation one must always distinguish between the material transformation in the economic conditions essential to production—which can be established with the exactitude of natural science—and the juridical, political, religious, artistic, or philosophic, in short ideological forms, in which men become conscious of this conflict and fight it out. As little as one judges what an individual is by what he thinks of himself, so little can one judge such an epoch of transformation by its consciousness; one must rather explain this consciousness by the contradictions in the material life, the conflict at hand between the social forces of production and the relations in which production is carried on. No social formation ever disappears before all the productive forces are developed for which it has room, and new higher relations of production never appear before the material conditions of their existence are matured in the womb of the old society."

In those sentences you can see all three of the Hegelian presuppositions I spoke of. You see that the whole historic life of society, and humanity in it, is regarded as one single thing or movement; that it has one general cause of which men are not conscious; and that this cause operates by a process of logical contradiction. The "productive forces" come into contradiction with the "production-relations," and this contradiction, resolving itself in a higher unity, constitutes the underlying cause of the whole movement.

To a concrete or very realistic mind, the idea of a "contradiction" between forces and relations is so abstract and undynamic as to be incapable of explaining any motion whatever. And such minds usually pass this over as merely an example of Marx's peculiar way of talking. This peculiar way of talking belongs to the essence of Marx's thought. He is not trying to explain history dynamically, but logically—or rather, with a mixture of dynamics and logic in which logic will invariably have the last word. He is seeking, not only underneath the ideologies of men for their class struggles, but also underneath their class struggles for an antithesis between two "concrete universals," whose resolution according to the principles of the Hegelian logic will necessitate the victory of the lower class. That is why he describes a social revolution as a "contradiction" between two generalities. And that is why he forgets sometimes this keyword "contradiction" and speaks of it as a conflict, or even a "rebellion" of one generality against another: "The forces of production rebel against the mode of production which they have outgrown." And the mystic perfection with which this state of affairs arises and moves to its conclusion may be seen in the dictum that "No social formation ever disappears until all the productive forces are developed for which it has room." Obviously the mere dynamics of a concrete conflict could never give us this admirable assurance. What we have to do with here is not dynamics, but "Speculative Logic."

There is no foundation in fact for any of the three assumptions which Marx borrowed from Hegel. History is no one thing or process, except as it is made so by the interests of the historian; it has no one cause, either within or without the consciousness of men, which explains it all; it does not advance by a process of dialectic contradiction and the negation of the negation. Hence it has been necessary for Marxists to qualify this concise and brilliant metaphysical statement in various practical ways. One of these ways was indicated by Marx himself in the third and fourth sentences, where he interchanges the verbs *condition* and *determine* as though they were approximately equivalent. It is obvious that if the material basis positively *determined* the superstructure, we should not have to disregard the superstructure and examine the basis, for the one could be directly inferred from the other.

Thus, the control exercised by the economic factor turns out to be in the nature of the case merely negative. And the followers of Marx, without exactly noticing this, have been content if they could show in the case of any particular historic development that economic factors *had something essential to do with it*. Lafargue, for instance, points out that if there had *not* been "systematic, rational stock-breeding" in England, Darwin could not have invented his theory of evolution. This is far, of course, from saying that economic forces caused, or determined, or "in the last analysis explain" the theory of evolution. And it is something that might be more easily proven by pointing out that if Darwin had not had anything to eat, he could not have invented the theory of evolution. Marxists defend their philosophy of history by darting back and forth between a truism and a quite fantastic assertion, and never getting caught in either the one position or the other. It is a familiar method in metaphysics, but it has nothing to do with science. A theory which ignores the difference between the verbs *condition* and *determine* cannot be called scientific, because it has not sufficient exactitude to be verified.

There are two other ideas which Marxists interchange without noticing it. At one time they present the political and cultural superstructure as a *result* of economic causes, at another time as a *reflection* of economic conditions. The Marxian explanation of law and the state, for example, may be and usually is expressed in a causal form. The development of the forces of production brings classes into conflict, and the exploiting class, in order to preserve its supremacy, creates or appropriates the state, and codifies those customs and those moral ideas and tendencies which are favorable to its supremacy. This state and these ideas and tendencies are not "reflections" of the economic process; they are nothing like it. They are results of it, and the process of their creation can be analyzed causally and scientifically understood. But when you pass into spheres which are farther away from the economic basis—religion, for instance, or art, which is half play, and therefore least of all subject to a business explanation—Marxists abandon all pretense at causal analysis, and merely assert that these things are an automatic symbolic picture of the economic conditions.

Marx dismisses the whole problem of the psychology of religion with the statement that "the religious world is merely a reflection of the real world." And Engels furnishes an example: Calvin's doctrine of predestination was the "religious expression of the fact that in the commercial world of competition success or failure does not depend upon a man's activity or cleverness, but upon circumstances uncontrolled by him." That is an interesting remark, but if you approach the doctrine of Calvin from the point of view of real causation—as Engels does, indeed, in another book—you get an opposite result. Religion is within the control of the ruling classes, and their one concern in a commercial world of competition is to keep the people convinced that their success or failure *does* depend upon their activity and cleverness. If Marxism were a science of history, it would long ago have cleared up this elementary confusion. As a philosophy of history it is vitally concerned to preserve it.

Trotsky explains futurism as a "reflection in art" of the "unheard-of industrial boom" of the last twenty years, "which overthrew old ideas of wealth and power, worked out new scales, new criteria of the possible and the impossible." That also is an interesting literary remark, but it is not a scientific explanation. How far it is from science may be seen in the observation with which Trotsky is compelled to supplement it:

"We have observed the following phenomenon, repeated more than once in history: that backward countries, which nevertheless possess a certain level of spiritual culture, reflect more clearly and more strongly in their ideology the attainments of advanced countries. Thus German thought in the eighteenth and nineteenth centuries reflected the economic achievements of the English. . . . Futurism received its clearest expression, not in America, not in Germany, but in Italy and Russia."

No mind trained in the investigation of concrete causes, trained in their accurate definition and verification, could possibly rest in this statement. By what material connection does the economic development of England produce its strongest reflection in Germany, and that of America, in Russia? And how does it happen that this reflection does not arise in Australia, or for that matter in the Polar Sea?

In order really to explain futurist art upon the basis of an economic boom, you would have to show that actual artists, or the artist class, were in a position where, in order to get a good share of the benefits of that boom, they were led to make pictures and write poems that were a "reflection" of it. And you would find it more easy to prove the opposite thesis. What artists are best paid for during an industrial boom is keeping the idle thoughts of the public occupied with Eternal Beauty, holding fast to the old ideas of wealth and power, and giving no unnecessary impetus to "new criteria of the possible and the impossible." Nevertheless, because of the mystic emotion attached by Marxists to the word "economic," and because of the complete absence in Marxism of the mere conception of a psychological science, this remark of Trotsky's is accepted by his followers as precisely what it is not, an *analytical* discussion of the causes of futurist art. And artists who read it, instead of seeing their unconscious motives explained, and profiting to the extent of their intelligence by the explanation, see themselves abstractly and mystically dominated by a strange new Deity with a scientific name. And they learn that whatever their self-knowledge may be, and whatever their effort, the work they produce can turn out nothing in the long run but an automatic image of the face of this Deity, the Economic Basis of the society in which they live. That is poison to art, but it is one of the essential ways in which Hegelian Marxists preserve their metaphysical dogma in face of the irreducible variety of the world.

Another way, and a far more promising one, if they could be held to it, is to declare that Economic Determinism is only a "principle of investigation." It is difficult to understand how anybody could make this statement, as orthodox Marxists very often do, and at the same time assert that economic determinism is an ultimate and irrefutable philosophy of history. The explanation lies in a fact already mentioned, and which the reader of this book must bear continually in mind—namely, that Marxism is not pure and natural metaphysics. Marxism is a seventy-five years' struggle between metaphysics and an instinctive practical-scientific realism, in which metaphysics carried the day. A critic is compelled to do some violence to the practically realistic side of this struggle. He is compelled to set Marxism back clearly and definitely into that metaphysical frame from which it did not in the long run escape. The idea that economic determinism is merely a "principle of investigation" was one of the momentary victories of practical science.

Another slight but highly important exception to economic determinism has to be made by all orthodox Marxists. They all have to assert that although Germany in the period of her "classical philosophy" was in a very backward economic phase, and although her political state corresponded accurately to her economic development—being, in the words of Engels, a "feudal and bureaucratic despotism"—and although her classical philosophers were "instructors of youth appointed by the state," nevertheless the speculations of these classical philosophers were the most advanced achievement of the scientific mind up to that date, and "behind their pedantically obscure utterances, and in their heavy wearisome periods . . . the revolution lay concealed." The fact is that these classical German philosophers were just as backward as the state which employed them, and they were backward in the same way. The German state patronized modern capitalism, perverting it to the support of feudal political institutions; and the German philosophers patronized modern science, perverting it to the support of animistic superstition. "The revolution," far from lying concealed in the alien and astutely reactionary speculations of these philosophers, and issuing legitimately from them, lay concealed in ideas and impulses quite apart from anything known by these philosophers. But in the process of its birth it got tangled up in their speculations, and well-nigh buried and choked to death there, and it has never completely issued from them at all, but carries along on its back a burden of "pedantically obscure utterances and heavy wearisome periods" that bear witness to its origin in a country which had not reached an advanced stage of economic development. If Marxists would apply their principle of economic determinism to the German classical philosophy, they would be relieved of the necessity of applying it to everything else under the sun. For they would see that, as a *principle of universal application*, it is nothing but a relic of the attempt of "instructors of youth appointed by the state" in an economically backward country, to prevent the youth of that country from falling into the skepticism of modern science.

Another small loophole in economic determinism was discovered by Plekhanov, who pointed out, somewhat timidly, that a man who understands Marxism may by that very fact be enabled to exercise a little special influence upon history.

"If I know," says Plekhanov, "in what direction the social relations are changing, thanks to given changes in the social process of production, then I know also in what direction the social mind is going to change. Consequently I have a chance to influence it. To influence the social mind means to influence the historic event. Thus in a certain sense, I may even make history, and not just wait for it to make itself."

It did not occur to Plekhanov that a man who understands economic determinism might change history by attacking the economic basis directly, as Lenin did when he undertook to communize Russia by means of electrification. Plekhanov approached those evolving "social relations" created by the forces of production as one approaches a living God. "The character of a personality," he exclaimed, "is a factor in social development only where, only when, and only in so far as, social relations permit it!" An exclamation which means nothing at all, unless "social relations" are personified, and the word *permit* taken to mean "give permission." Otherwise it is equally true that social relations can be a factor in development only when, only where, and only in so far as, the character of personalities permits it.

In addition to these unrecognized or unofficial ways of modifying the rigor of economic determinism, there is the official Hegelian way indicated by Marx himself—the appeal to the principle of Accident.

"World history would indeed be easy to make," said Marx, "if the struggle were always engaged only on condition of indubitably favorable chances. Nature moreover would be very mystical if 'accidents' played no role. These accidents fall quite naturally into the general course of the development, and are compensated for by other accidents. But acceleration and retardation are very dependent upon such 'accidents' among which figures such an 'accident' as the characters of the people who stand first at the head of a movement."

The reader will notice that Marx sometimes puts the word "accident" in quotation marks, but sometimes not. And this is an accurate indication of his state of mind about the problem involved. The same state of mind is indicated in Engels's use of the phrase "accidents or seeming accidents." It is a correctly Hegelian state of mind. Hegel conceived of chance, not as a mere name for our ignorance of causes, but as a genuine objective element in nature's evolution. It was only *underneath*. and *through*, and *in spite of*, chance events—events which "may or may not be"—that Hegel's divine necessity was to be found working its way to the inevitable goal. And yet at the same time Hegel believed that most apparent accidents can be proven to have been inevitable, and should be so proven by the philosophic mind.

"The problem of science," he said, "and especially of philosophy, undoubtedly consists in eliciting the necessity concealed under the semblance of contingency. That however is far from meaning that the contingent belongs to our subjective conception alone, and must therefore be simply set aside, if we wish to get at the truth. All scientific researches which pursue this course exclusively, lay themselves fairly open to the charge of mere jugglery and an overstrained precisianism."

It is this opinion of Hegel which reappears in Marx's statement that accidents fall "quite naturally" into the general course of development, but are—*quite supernaturally,* we cannot refrain from saying—compensated for by other accidents of an opposite kind. Not only the "materialism" of Marx is not materialistic, but his determinism is not the determinism of mechanical science. The ultimate historic event is necessary, according to Marx, not because all events are bound together by a perfect chain of causes, but because through a whole sea of chance happenings—some really accidental, and some only seeming so to our ignorance—the "inner laws" of history are working to their inevitable ends. The essential animism of this conception is clearly apparent in the writings of Engels, who always speaks of history as being "governed" by these mysterious laws.

"Historical events appear to be wholly controlled by chance. But even where on the surface accident plays its part, it is always governed by inner, hidden laws."

That this whole doctrine is animistic metaphysics becomes most obvious when Marxists discuss the role of their own heroes in history. This is one of the problems which trouble them the most, for having a really great hero—and two, indeed, since Lenin lived and died—they are naturally great hero-worshipers. And yet their philosophy seems to deny the essential value of heroes. Engels says that "If there had been no Napoleon, another would have taken his place," and he makes almost the same assertion about Karl Marx. He makes it a little less glibly, however, and most Marxists have sought to avoid the extreme stoicism of such a statement. They have sought to avoid also, I suppose, its extreme foolishness. For if there exists any point in all the egregious intellectual chatter of Simian man when it behooves him to say "I do not know," it is when such questions arise as "What would have happened if there had been no Napoleon?" "What would have happened if there had been no Marx?"

The orthodox way to reconcile the historic importance of Marx with the tenets of his own philosophy is that indicated in the passage which I quoted about "accidents." The leaders of a movement cannot alter the direction or outcome of the historical process, but they can alter its speed. Trotsky tries always to be orthodox, although he is a little impatient of his orthodoxy, and here is what Trotsky says:

"Of course, of course, of course, we know that the working class will triumph. We sing 'No man will deliver us' and we add 'No hero.' And that is true, but only in the last historical account. That is, in the last account of history the working class would have conquered if there had never been a Marx in the world, if there had never been a Lenin. The working class would work out those ideas which are needful to it, those methods which are needful to it, but more slowly. The circumstance that the working class on the two crests of its flood has raised up two such figures as Marx and Lenin, is a gigantic advantage to the revolution."

That is the fundamental Marxian position. But it is subject to a further slight modification in the direction of common sense and human sentiment. For upon reflection it appears that if these rather rambunctious accidents, such as Marx and Lenin, can alter the speed of the historic process, they do really play an enormous role in determining the character of history. In a world in which "everything flows," to hasten or to delay an event is to alter it. Thus, it must be assumed that when Trotsky says "in the last historical account"—and this phrase he brings directly from Engels—he means that, although the ultimate result considered abstractly is economically determined, these noneconomically determined accidents can alter the concrete details of the procedure by which we get to it. They can not only make the path longer or shorter, but they can make it more or less "thorny," as Kautsky says. Or as he formulates it more precisely: Although they cannot influence "the direction of the development," they can influence "its course, and the road by which it arrives at the inevitable result." Is it not obvious, however, that if the historic road is different, then the result also, *taken concretely*, will be different?

Indeed, in that very word "result," the animistic personification of history which lies at the bottom of this whole theory is unmistakably revealed.[1] History considered concretely and objectively, and without projecting into it the emotional interests of the historian, contains no "results." History is just a series or congeries of events, or at the best a process, and the road traveled is all there is of it. If the economic factor merely determines certain points on this road—whether a given historian chooses to call those points "results" or not—the objective question remains, just which points they are,

---

[1] Marxists will quote you in opposition to this statement an early passage in which Marx himself ridiculed the idea that "history" could do anything. "History . . . ," he said, "is nothing but the activity of man in pursuit of his own ends." This will not disturb you if you understand the ingenuity of materialist Hegelianism. History, according to this system, is directed toward human purposes by a supernatural Robot instead of a Deity, but the control exercised by this benign Robot, like that exercised by Hegel's Deity, is immanent in the activities of men, not transcendent of them. The manner in which he effects his purposes, regardless of what men think or wish, is revealed in the quotations on pages 48 and 49, but I have discussed this question more fully in *Stalin's Russia and the Crisis in Socialism*, p. 99 ff.

and how many. And that is exactly the manner in which the question is posed by those who reject economic determinism in its orthodox form, but yet "recognize the value of the idea"—Bernstein, Jaurès, Benedetto Croce, Simkhovitch, Professor Seligman—those whom orthodox Marxists despise with a kind of fear, because they insist on introducing degree into the economic determination, and asking the scientific question "How much?" The orthodox Marxists really differ from them, not in refusing to admit that history is only *in some degree* determined economically, but in personifying history, and imputing to it a goal, or a "result," or a series of "results," and declaring that *these* are determined economically. They are defending an abstract animistic philosophy of history against a concrete scientific study of historic events.

This is nowhere more apparent than in the famous letters about economic determinism written by Engels long after the death of Marx. In these letters Engels introduced such sweeping concrete qualifications and exceptions in detail to the control exercised by the economic factor in history that it seemed possible to Bernstein to declare that Engels had surrendered the essence of the Marxian theory. But at the same time Engels reasserted the ultimate and abstract control exercised by the economic factor in its most Hegelian purity, and thus enabled Kautsky to reply that he had surrendered nothing at all.

"The economic situation is the basis," wrote Engels, "but the various elements of the superstructure, the political forms of the class-struggle and its results, the system of government established by the victorious class after the battle, etc., legal forms, even the reflection of all these real conflicts in the brain of the participants, political, juridical, and philosophic theories, religious outlooks and their further development into dogmatic systems, exercise their influence upon the course of the historic struggle, and in many cases predominantly determine its forms. . . ."

And again:

"The low economic development of the prehistoric period had as its complement, and at times even as its condition and even as its cause, false representations of nature. . . . It would be pedantry to seek economic causes for all these elementary stupidities. The history of science is the history of the gradual elimination of this nonsense, or its replacement by other nonsense a little less absurd. The people who do this belong to a special sphere of the division of labor, and it seems that they are developing an independent realm. And in so far as they form a self-dependent group within the social division of labor, so far their productions, including their mistakes, exercise a *retroactive influence* upon the whole social development, even the economic."

Thus Engels went out of his way to explain that a body of ideas for whose origin it would be "absurd" to seek economic causes, and which may indeed have been itself the cause of economic processes, does nevertheless in the course of its career influence the whole social development. This seems far away, indeed, from the original drastic statement of the Marxian philosophy of history. And yet Engels has sacrificed nothing of the essence of that philosophy. Its whole heart and purpose is satisfied when he declares, in strictly Hegelian language:

The historic process "is a reciprocal action of all these factors upon each other, wherein ultimately through all the infinite number of accidents (things and events, the inner connections of which are so remote and undemonstrable, that we may count them as nonexistent and ignore them), the economic movement in the form of necessity is carried through."

Economic determinism was in its origin just as mystical and mysterious, and disposed to ignore an infinite number of things which it could not explain, as it is in this final formulation. It was simply the pious metaphysical assertion of Hegel that "Spirit is the only moving principle in history," turned into the impious but equally metaphysical assertion that the forces of production are the only moving principle in history—the only "changing element," as Kautsky explicitly puts it. Neither of these absolute statements has any basis in fact or probability. And the whole half century's discussion, so exasperating to reason, so fruitless, so destructive of all naïvely clear thinking, has value simply as a picture of the highest revolutionary intelligence trying unsuccessfully to escape from the bonds of German metaphysics.

There is only one way to escape from those bonds. That is to take the revolutionary motive back out of history, where Marx and Engels surreptitiously projected it, and locate it in the human breast where it belongs. It was Marx, and not History, that was determined to produce a social revolution, and his investigation of history was an attempt to find out the method by which it could be done. When that simple truth—as obvious to a child as it is inaccessible to a Marxist—has once been acknowledged, the whole discussion loses its mystifying character at once. History is relieved of the strait jacket of a statement wholly inadequate to express its variety, and the Marxist is relieved of the necessity of proving something that, even if it were true, is beyond the capacity of human science to prove. He has no longer any fear of a quantitative statement of the control exercised by the economic factor upon social evolution, because he is able to state clearly what quantity of control he believes to be exercised by that factor.

It is a control sufficient to render impractical and ineffectual any attempt to revolutionize society, in the direction contemplated by socialists or anarchists or early Christians, by means of operations directed against, or conducted within, the political and ideological superstructure. It is a negative control; economic determinism is like the demon of Socrates—it tells you only what you cannot do. But at the same time it is a dynamic control, whose operation can be analyzed and demonstrated in detail, and not a kind of mystic correspondence entirely incapable of verification. Its recognition is not a "philosophy of history," and it requires no patching up with special appeals to the principle of accident; no explaining away and explaining back again of the greatness of great men; no imputation to history of a personal interest in results; no concealing under mountains of pretentiously disinterested and abstract talk of the particular results in which Marxists are interested. It does not modestly profess to be a principle of investigation, and at the same time dogmatically declare itself both a metaphysical presupposition and a final result of investigations already accomplished. And, finally, it does not timidly concede that a person who understands it may "in a certain sense," and in some instances, be enabled by that very fact to "influence an historic event." It clearly states that the whole cause and purpose of its existence, like that of any other practical science, is to enable the person who understands it to control history to the fullest possible extent.

3. THE CLASS STRUGGLE

FOR MARX as a philosopher, a class struggle in its "inner" essence was not a concrete fight between people, but an abstract contradiction between generalities —between "forces of production" and "production-relations." And since all past history was but the dialectic life-story of such contradictions, Marx was able to assert that "All past history, with the exception of its primitive stages, was the history of class struggles." What is the truth under this obviously preposterous assertion?

The word "history" involves a generalization of the most loose and inclusive sort. It is a name for the whole heterogeneous agglomeration of events and developments which have caught the interest and stuck in the memories of men. The mere fact that history contains a record of the development of every explanation proves that there can be no single explanation of history. For as soon as you have explained an explanation on the basis of facts other than those contemplated in it, you have destroyed its validity. If the Copernican astronomy is subject to explanation as a result of economic motions on earth, it is not a true science of motion in the heavens. This is but one way of proving that any philosophy of history "penetrated with unity"—any single statement of the essence and essential explanation of the whole past of humanity—belongs itself to that past, which is among other things, let us hope, the grave of wish-fulfillment metaphysics. And anyone who proposes such a statement and explanation has already singled out in that past of humanity the particular development which interests him, and it is this which he designates when he uses the word "history."

The thing that most interested Marx was the effort to create a true human society. The predominating purpose of his life was to find out how to produce, and help to produce, out of the existing social materials, "an association which will exclude classes and their antagonisms, and in which there will no longer be political power properly so called"—a society which "can inscribe on its banner: 'From each according to his abilities, to each according to his needs!'" Looking over the pages of history, he observed that ever since the time of primitive communism human society has been in a state of class struggle, open or veiled, and that human relations have rarely been fundamentally changed in any way except by the victory of a new class in that struggle. Upon the basis of this historic observation, backed up by economics and a hardheaded knowledge of human nature, he felt able to assert that the only method by which our existing society can be revolutionized is the organization of the working-class struggle, and the perfection of its technique. In so far as he was a scientific engineer, and not an animistic philosopher, that is what he did assert. And that is all the truth that any person possessing the mentality of experimental science will ever find in the statement that "the history of all hitherto existing society is the history of class struggles."

*　　*　　*　　*

Marx greeted Darwin's theory of evolution as a "support from natural science." And the general Marxian opinion, expressed in numberless articles and pamphlets, is that Darwin's discovery was "a glorious corroboration and completion of the Marxian theory." Engels said, a little more temperately, that Marx's theory was "destined to do for history what Darwin's theory has done for biology."

It seems as though Engels's prediction might prove true—although not in the manner he anticipated. For if any one thing is conceded by all biologists today, it is that Darwin's theory is not an adequate explanation of the process of organic evolution. Darwin's achievement was to banish the ethicodeific out of biology, establish the fact of evolution upon a scientific basis, and point out a dominating principle of investigation and matter-of-fact explanation. And Marx made almost exactly the same contribution to the general science of history. He put in the place of moralistic and religious and poetic and patriotic eloquences a matter-of-fact principle of explanation, which has become the dominating one for all freely inquiring minds, and he established—or at least first adequately emphasized—the fact that there has been an evolution, not only in the political forms of society, but in its economic structure.

The differences between Marx and Darwin are just as significant, however, as their similarities. And the failure of Marxists to notice them is the chief cause of the weakness of their present scientific position. Darwin approached the problem of explaining evolution without any political purpose or passion. He made no pretense to foretell the future of the process. His books are a model of the pure art of inquiry, so far as that art can be attained by a mind the very forms of whose thinking are practical. And therefore they have an objective validity which Marx could have attained only if he had recognized the role played by his purpose, and separated that part of his thought which consisted of analyzing facts from that which consisted of planning for the realization of an idea.

Darwin also approached his problem of evolution without any metaphysical presupposition as to the manner in which evolution proceeds. He was not afflicted with any "universal law of motion in thought and in the external world." Therefore, he was entirely free to let the facts teach him. And they taught him something quite contrary to that view of thought and the external world which lies at the bottom of the Hegelian-Marxian conception of evolution. To Darwin—or to those who have developed the implications of his discovery—thinking is not a function belonging to Nature at large, and evolving mirrorlike in friendly and harmonious parallel with her universal evolution. Thinking is a function developed by particular organisms in mortal conflict with other organisms, and with the inclemency and indifference of Nature at large, and its character was originally determined by the requirements of success in that conflict. Its rudimentary essence is not to make pictures of the general environment in the edifying forms of the philosopher's logic, but to interpret the important parts of that environment in the practical forms of nervous and muscular attitude and adaptive action.

Instead of acclaiming Darwin as a mere support and glory of metaphysical Marxism, the thing is to replace Marxian metaphysics with a scientific methodology which will not ignore the lessons learned from Darwin.

4. THE DOCTRINE OF IDEOLOGIES

ONE FURTHER exception to the law of economic determinism, more significant than any of those I mentioned, is implied in Marx's own classical statement of it.

In studying revolutions, he says, "one must always distinguish between the material transformation in the economic conditions essential to production—which can be established with the exactitude of natural science—and the juridical, political, religious, artistic or philosophical, in short ideological, forms in which men become conscious of this conflict and fight it out."

In this statement it appears that natural science is not determined by those material changes in the conditions of production which determine the ideological forms of thinking. Natural science is "determined" by those material changes in nature which constitute the object of its study, and by no others. And it appears also that Marxism itself partakes of the independent validity of natural science. In so far as Marxism is a definition of those changes in the conditions of production which are contemporary with it, you may say that it is determined by them, and so differs from an ideology only in being conscious of its nature. But in so far as Marxism is "the law of development of human history," it obviously cannot be regarded as merely the form in which men became conscious of a transitory historic conflict, and are going to fight it out. Marx takes this for granted here, and there are other passages in which he speaks of his doctrine as a carrying-over into regions formerly dominated by economically determined ideologies, of the independent and objective methods of natural science. In practice the essence of Marxian wisdom consists, not in asserting that ideas in general are determined by changes in the conditions of production, but in knowing how to distinguish those which are so determined from those which are valid scientific findings. It consists in knowing the difference between science and ideology.

Although Marx instinctively recognized this, and spoke more than once as though natural science had independent validity and his work were akin to natural science, he never made any place for such a phenomenon in his theory of history. He never made any place there for the validity of his own opinions. He raised the problem once—in the uncompleted manuscript [1] where he and Engels first formulated their historic views—but he postponed its explicit treatment, just as he postponed everything that would have brought him face to face with the real nature of his philosophic belief. After expounding the view that all historic developments are determined by an evolution of the forces of production, the manuscript breaks off, and there occurs this annotation for future work:

"Natural science and history.
"There is no history of politics, of law, of science, etc., of art, of religion, etc."

By the remark, "There is no history of . . . science," Marx means that science, just as well as art, religion, etc., is wholly determined by the evolution of the productive

[1] *Die Deutsche Ideologie.* See p. 169.

forces. Its history is but a reflection of their history.

The question troubled him, however, and later on he mentioned it again:

"Even 'pure' natural science receives its goal, as also its material, thanks only to commerce and industry. . . ."

What science receives from commerce and industry, according to this slightly more thoughtful remark, are the *conditions* which make its general development possible. But what his former statement—that science has no independent history—demands, is that science should receive from this source *causes* determining its specific nature. We have here, then, that same confusion of *condition* with *cause* which I have mentioned as the most fundamental of those unconscious devices by which Marxism perpetuates itself as animistic philosophy while pretending to make an empirical investigation of history. Having evaded the problem in this way in early youth, Marx seems never to have reflected again that "history" is a generalization which includes the development of that "natural science" to which—in the classic passage quoted above and elsewhere—he so obviously accords an independent validity. It was his formal or philosophic opinion that natural science, like politics, art, religion, philosophy, etc., is ideological—is but the mental reflection of a "material transformation in the economic conditions essential to production." It was also his opinion that Marxism—which explains all history, and knows both its early beginning and its remote destination, and knows moreover the relation between itself and the contemporary historic process—is nevertheless nothing but a reflection of that process. Marxism differs from ideological socialism only in being "conscious" of the economic movement of which it is a "necessary reflection."

This was made perfectly clear by Engels, who did undertake some time after Marx's death to define the word *ideology* and determine its relation to science. He defined it, in effect, as follows: An ideology is a distorted reflection, which is unconscious of the fact that it is a reflection, of economic conditions. In this definition there is no trace left of the contrast between ideologies as economic reflections and natural science as independent truth, which was implied in Marx's classical statement. With Engels all ideas are economic reflections, and scientific ideas can differ from ideologies only in knowing that they are economic reflections, and being approximately correct ones. The science of astronomy, for instance, instead of being, or somehow or other *besides* being, an accurate reflection of the motion of the stars, must be also—provided it is not mere ideology—a reflection of economic motions on earth. This proposition seems absurd enough when it is applied to astronomy, and that goes to show that Engels never thought of such sciences as having a place *within* history. Their place was beside history! But Engels did think of the science of Marxism as having a place within history, and he applied that absurd proposition to the Marxism science repeatedly and explicitly. He said that Marxism is nothing but a "reflection in thought of the conflict in fact" between the existing productive forces and the capitalist relations of production.

This statement, if it is taken seriously, does not merely mean that Marx reflected this conflict at those times when he was specifically talking about it. It means that the whole general Marxian science of history is a reflection of this particular historic fact. It means that when Marx gives us an account of the primitive accumulation of capital, for instance, it is not really, or not "in the last analysis," certain material facts of past history that his thoughts are reflecting, but it is his own position, or that of the proletariat, in the society in which he lives. And when Engels writes of the Origin of the Family, it is not a reflection of the actual origin of the family, but a reflection in the form of a painstaking and classical book about the origin of the family, of the origin of a revolution in the current mode of production. And in general Marxism is not at every point a reflection of just those facts which it purports to reflect—much less a definition of them "with the exactitude of natural science"—but it is at all points a mystic and scientifically irresponsible reflection of the position of the working class in modern society, a mere "general expression" of the existing class struggle. Moreover, when the class struggle is over Marxism must lose its essential validity and give place to an entirely different science, for it is obvious that a system of ideas which merely reflects the struggles of a class can play no vital part in reflecting the evolution of a class-free society. That is the real meaning of Engels's statement about Marxism. And it is adopted with admirable boldness by Rosa Luxemburg, who says that "Marxism pretends only to temporary truth; dialectic through and through, it contains within itself the seeds of its own destruction."

Now everybody who is familiar with scientific method knows that the one thing which can verify Marxism as a science, and establish it among the indubitable and immortal conquests of human knowledge, is the triumph of the proletariat and the establishment of a class-free society. Everybody who is not familiar with scientific method, but is also innocent of metaphysics, knows the same thing. In Russia the first preliminary victory of the proletariat resulted not only in a recognition of the verified truths of Marxism, but in a codification and dogmatization and universal systematized adoration of every last letter of Marx's writing, such that, if Marx had imagined it, he would never have dared put pen to paper. It is pure mythmaking to say that Marxism will be destroyed by the triumph of the revolution, and it is arrant metaphysical nonsense to pretend that Marxism contains no other truth than the correct reflection of a contemporary change in the conditions of production. This not only contradicts the most important part of Marx's own statement—the part in which he tells us how to study revolutions—but it contradicts the simple and universal facts of human psychology. Just as everyone who thinks practically assumes that the future is in some degree undetermined, so everyone who thinks theoretically assumes that his thoughts are not ultimately determined by any facts other than those contemplated in his theory. He assumes that his thoughts are not ideology but science. They are not the forms in which men have become conscious of a material change, and are going to "fight it out," but they are the forms in which men have defined a material change and understood it.

The reason why Marxists have blurred the distinction between science and ideology, which is inextricably involved in Marx's classical statement of his theory of history, is that this distinction is inconsistent with Marx's own philosophy of Dialectic Materialism. If thought is merely a reflection of the dialectic motions of matter, there can only be right and wrong reflections, conscious and unconscious reflections. And any given thought at any given time must be, somehow or other, a reflection of dialectic motions that are contemporary with it. Science has to be an ideology, according to this system, and the very best it can do is to be a conscious and correct one. This is so obvious that Plekhanov, the unmitigated metaphysician who laid the foundations of Russian Marxism, simply dropped out the distinction between science and ideology altogether, and forgot it. In Russia today the word "ideology" retains not the slightest tincture of the meaning it had for Marx and Engels. For them it was an expert form of intellectual abuse. For Russian Marxists it is simply the name for any body of ideas held together by some common bond. Lenin speaks of "the scientific ideology as opposed to the religious." He defines Marxism as "the ideology of the proletariat instructed by capitalism." Trotsky says that "in the socialist movement ideology plays its essential and enormous role." And the Russian Bolsheviks in general regard the distinction between communism, for instance, and the principles of democracy, not as a distinction between science and ideological talk, but as a distinction between the "bourgeois" and "proletarian" ideologies.

Plekhanov carried his philosophic rectification of Marx's natural opinion about ideology and science to the point of asserting that *Das Kapital* itself is not fundamentally more scientific than the bourgeois economics. The fundamental difference between them is that the bourgeois economics reflects an earlier, and the Marxian a later stage in the historic process:

"Human society in its development passes through certain phases to which correspond certain phases of development of social science. That which we call, for example, bourgeois economics is one phase of development of economic science.

That which we call socialist economics is another phase of its development immediately following. . . .

"The bourgeois economics, in so far as it corresponds to a definite phase of social evolution, possesses scientific truth. But that truth is relative, exactly because it corresponds only to a certain phase of social development. The bourgeois theoreticians, imagining that society must always remain in its bourgeois phase, attribute absolute significance to that relative truth. In that consists their fundamental mistake, corrected by scientific socialism, the appearance of which testifies that the bourgeois epoch of social development is nearing its end."

This statement is perhaps plausible, so long as you do not remember that Plekhanov's statements themselves are scientific socialism. When you remember that, you cannot fail to ask: How does it happen that scientific socialism, which is merely the reflection of another transitory phase of social development, knows all about the whole process of social development, and all about its relation to the bourgeois phase, and in fact all about the ways and phases of the universe in general? A bourgeois ideologist could reply to Plekhanov: Your science, which declares that everything changes and progresses, is but a reflection of the position of the proletariat in capitalist society; it is a relative truth; but my science reflects the eternal relations of the bourgeoisie and the proletariat as they really are. In simple honesty there would be no answer to this.

And just this difficulty lies at the bottom of the whole structure of Russian Marxism. How can a mere proletarian ideology be a scientific account of the development of the universe and of human history? Bukharin began a textbook, which was supposed to teach the young Russian how to think, with an argument in a circle which may be summed up as follows: Everything changes; we, the proletariat, are interested in change; therefore our philosophy, which asserts that everything changes, is entitled to general belief. That is only a naïve exposure of the fallacy that Plekhanov dressed up so plausibly. And the same fallacy constitutes the deep flaw in Lenin's philosophic writings. Lenin declares that Marx and Engels were "from first to last partisan in philosophy"; that philosophy is nothing but a "partisan struggle" between idealism and materialism; that Dialectic Materialism is the ideological fortress of the working class, which "would never let petty bourgeois philistinism step over its threshold"; he declares that "in a society torn by class contradictions there can be no extra-class or super-class ideology"; and he illustrates this statement with a book which is the most embattled and violent polemic ever produced in the name of philosophy. And yet in that book he asserts that "the theory of Marx is objective truth," meaning thereby that "going by way of the Marxian theory we shall draw nearer and nearer to objective truth (never exhausting it) and going by any other road we can arrive at nothing but confusion and lies." To identify objective truth with the fighting ideology of one camp in a transitory battle between classes, and to call this truth philosophy—that is the fundamental fallacy of Russian Marxism.

But Russian Marxism is merely Marxism in its purest Hegelian-metaphysical form. And the reader must not think that this fallacy presents a difficulty out of which the Hegelian dialectic is unable to squirm. On the contrary, the Hegelian dialectic was invented for the express purpose of squirming out of such difficulties. It was invented in order to protect the right of a priesthood to identify their emotional interests, and those of the class they represent, with objective and absolute truth. And if it is able—by the simple device of standing on its head —to protect an antipriesthood, and the class they represent, in a similar right, that is but one more tribute to the expert metaphysical genius of its inventor. When you have laid it down that everything which exists is a process of self-contradiction, you are not going to be disturbed by the discovery that your own science is at the same time *objectively true* and *relative to your particular position in history*. That contradiction merely shows that it exists! And if you have also laid it down that every such self-contradictory process is destined to have its opposing elements reconciled in a "higher" unity—and if you have refrained from laying it down just when, or where, or under what circumstances, any particular part of this business takes place—then you are in a position to assert that the reconciliation between the objective and the relative in scientific truth will take place only after human experience and investigation have been extended to infinity. That infinitely distant reconciliation is Absolute Truth. But since that Absolute Truth is, by definition, a "higher" unity, and since you, who reflect the breakdown of capitalism, are farther along the road to it than your class opponent who represents capitalism rampant, it is obvious that your ideology is already absolutely true in comparison with his. In fact your ideology is able to denounce and trounce all previous ideologies, because it contains them as surmounted opposites in its own bosom, and is on its way with them to the glory goal of an Absolute that lies at the end of infinity. . . . That is the kind of semi-theological jargon by which Hegel's dialectic enables you to identify a working-class ideology with objective truth, and get along without the practical distinction which Marx drew between science and ideology. More important—that is the kind of semi-theological jargon *for the sake of which* Marx's practical distinction between science and ideology has been thrown away.

5. MARXISM AND THE PSYCHOLOGY OF FREUD

YOU HAVE only to abandon mysteries and the relics of mysteries, and introduce into Marxism the simple beginnings of a real understanding of the mind, in order to define ideology accurately, and distinguish it from science, and see that this distinction is the essence of Marx's historical wisdom. It is one of the deepest and wisest intuitions in the history of genius. Life is impulsive, and thought arises as a definition of impulse and of the means to its satisfaction. But in human society life's strongest and most universal impulses are suppressed by a standard of ideality and respectable virtue that is an automatic product of social intercourse and self-consciousness. These strong universal impulses disappear out of men's thoughts, but they do not die. They continue to function unconsciously, and the result is a falsification of the conscious thoughts wherever they touch a matter in which these suppressed impulses are concerned. Men think they are defending and pursuing such goals as Liberty, Equality, Fraternity, when in reality their concern is, as Marx put it, with Infantry, Cavalry, and Artillery. Their concern is to defend their own privileged position in a class which, in its unconscious but ultimately reliable motivation, knows nothing and cares nothing about liberty, or equality, or fraternity. That is what an ideology is. It is a thinking process which is unaware of the motive which instigated it, and toward the satisfaction of which it is directed. That a great part of written history, and of political and sociological theorizing, up to the time of Marx, was distorted with such ideological thinking, indulged in by people controlled by their own unconscious class interests, is fairly obvious. It is also obvious that this process has not ceased merely because it has been discovered. But it is certainly the ideal and the essence of scientific thinking to escape from it. Practical scientific thinking defines its real motives because it seeks a clear knowledge of the means to their satisfaction. And "pure" scientific thinking defines its motives because it wishes to abstract from them, and get a picture of the facts which will be as objective and general as the nature of the human brain permits. Both these kinds of thinking are sharply and unmistakably distinguished, exactly as Marx originally said they are, from economically determined ideologies.

In short, Marx anticipated in his doctrine of ideologies the psychoanalytic theories of Sigmund Freud. The psychoanalyist, because he is trying to cure individual disorders, emphasizes those distortions of consciousness which arise from suppressed motives of sex. The Marxist, who wishes to cure the disorders of society, emphasizes those which arise from motives of hunger and fighting egoism. It is such motives which unconsciously dominate the majority of men in those broad social and political relations which constitute so large a part of their lives. It is such motives which align them in antagonistic classes, with the result that loyalty to class takes the place of that loyalty to mankind upon which it might be possible to establish the framework of a reasonable world. Marx's word ideology is simply a name for the distortions of social and political thinking which are created by these suppressed motives. It is a general term for all that

Freudians mean when they say *rationalization, substitution, transference, displacement, sublimation*. The economic interpretation of history is nothing but a generalized psychoanalysis of the social and political mind. One might infer this from the spasmodic and unreasonable resistance it meets on the part of its patient. The Marxian diagnosis has often been regarded as an outrage rather than a science. It has been met, not with comprehension and critical analysis, but with "resistances" and "defense-reactions" of the most wild and infantile kind.

One of the most notable of these defense-reactions was contributed by the Freudians themselves. They invented the device of explaining away all revolutionary intelligence as a manifestation of the "Oedipus complex." Freud seems to have remained wisely silent upon this theme, but it is quite a fashion among his followers to dismiss any man who wants to cut under the plausibilities of existing law and government as a neurotic driven on by an unconscious fixation of infantile emotion against his father. It is a case, they say, of *substitution*, or *transference* of the libido. The answer from the Marxian point of view is obvious: Doctors are in the economic nature of things bourgeois, or petty bourgeois, and these Freudian doctors are driven on, in their attempt to explain away revolution, by unconscious motives of class-loyalty and pecuniary self-defense. It is a case of *ideological thinking*. In this exchange of amenities, the Marxian may have the satisfaction of remembering that Marx got there first. And he has this satisfaction also, that his position does not involve a snap diagnosis of some of the healthiest and most stable personalities in the world as neurotic, and it does not pretend to an expert opinion on the intimate family history of several millions of people who have never been examined. It attributes to these Freudian doctors no condition more peculiar than the most general underlying motives of all humanity and all organic life.

When I say that the doctrine of ideologies is an anticipation of the Freudian psychology, I do not mean that Marx or Engels thought of it as a psychological doctrine. I mean that, once you have put in the place of metaphysical fairy stories a science of human thought and behavior, that is what it literally and exactly becomes. This can be seen clearly in any of Engels's attempts to state what an ideology is. "An ideology," he says in one place, "is a process which is carried out, to be sure, with the consciousness of the so-called thinker, but with a false consciousness. The real motive-powers which move him remain unknown to him, otherwise it would not be an ideological process." You need only recognize that the motive-powers which move people to think are organic impulses, or "desires," and you have here all the essentials of a Freudian definition. And there are passages, indeed, where both Marx and Engels do seem to recognize this fact. In his book about the *Eighteenth Brumaire of Louis Bonaparte*, where Marx applies his theory to a piece of concrete historic action, he continually talks of the "interests" of the classes and parties concerned. He interprets their political ideas, not as an unconscious reflection of their economic position, but as an unconscious scheme for getting their economic wishes satisfied.

"As in private life we distinguish between what a man thinks and says about himself, and what he really is and does, still more in historical struggles we must distinguish the phrases and imaginations of parties from their real organism and their real interests. . . . Thus the Tories in

England long imagined that they were raving about the Kingdom, the Church, and the Beauty of the Old-English dispensation, until the day of danger snatched from them the confession that they were only raving about Ground Rent."

That this is Freudian psychology at its most brilliant needs no demonstration. Engels in his speech at the grave of Marx described the whole Marxian theory of history as a discovery of "the simple fact, heretofore concealed under ideological overgrowths, that men have first of all to eat and drink and live and clothe themselves, and only after that can they occupy themselves with politics and science and art and religion. . . ." Here again, it is simply the underlying animal motivation that explains history; Marx's theory appears as a study of human behavior, and not a searching among human "accidents" for the mysterious march of an animated generality called Forces of Production. And ideologies, in consequence, play exactly the part that is played by rationalizations in a Freudian psychology. They serve as concealments in consciousness for those crude unconscious motives which on the broad average and in the long run determine the conduct of men.

For Marx and Engels, however, these occasional analyses of human motivation were not the true, the esoteric, science of history. The true science demands that human motives should be seen as merely a specific part of that more general motor process, the Evolution of the Forces of Production, which takes the place of Hegel's Spirit. Engels describes in the following passage the relation of human motives to the historic process:

"History proceeds in such a way that the end-result always issues from the conflict of many individual wills. . . . We have thus innumerable conflicting forces, an endless group of parallelograms of forces, giving a resultant—the historic event—which may itself again be regarded as the product of a force acting as a whole without consciousness and without will. For that which each individual desires meets an opposition from every other, and the result is something which nobody desired."

That is the inscrutable way in which history operates, according to metaphysical Marxism. And it is obvious that a psychological analysis would be an awkward intrusion here. For that "result" which nobody desired is exactly the heart's desire of the Marxian metaphysician. And it is the essence of his "materialist" metaphysics to assert that the objective world is going after it and getting it for him without thought and without will—albeit by a process that is "logical," and with a "determinism" that is hard to distinguish from the most willful determination.

Thus, when Marx and Engels employ the language of human motivation in their explanation of history, it must be regarded as a temporary condescension from the abstract perfection of·the pure theory. The "inner laws" of history are not to be discovered by talking in this way. And when Engels says that the ideologist is unconscious of the forces that set his thoughts going, it must not be imagined that he means to psychoanalyze that ideologist, or say that he is not conscious of his own motives. All he means to say is that the ideologist is not conscious of a motion in the "economic conditions," which are a result of the evolution of the "productive-forces," and of which his thoughts are a mere passive reflection.

"The reflection of economic relations in the form of legal principles is accomplished in such a way that this process does not reach the consciousness of the agent. The lawmaker imagines that he is acting from a priori principles, when in reality it is all a matter of economic reflection . . . and that distortion, when it is not conscious, we call the ideological outlook."

That is the way Engels defines ideology in a more painstaking moment. And again:

"That the material conditions of life of the men in whose heads this thinking process takes place, ultimately determine the course of the process, necessarily remains unknown to these men, otherwise there would be an end of the whole ideology."

It seems a very slight and obvious correction to say *material interests* here, instead of "material conditions of life," but it is all the difference between science and mystical metaphysics. And it was nothing but mystical metaphysics which prevented Engels from saying it. Nothing but mystical metaphysics will prevent any Marxist from abandoning this philosophy of history and going forward to that more analytical scientific attitude which it anticipated. It will be objected, of course, that "psychology is in its infancy," that nobody can put his trust in these vague beginnings of a science of the mind. It is true that psychology is in its infancy; it is true that we have only the first loose principles of a science of the mind. But the philosophy of Dialectic Materialism rests upon the assumption that a hundred years ago Hegel knew all about mind, and substantially finished the science of it. The philosophy of Dialectic Materialism lives or dies with that assumption. Therefore, if the real science of the mind is in its infancy, the philosophy of Dialectic Materialism may best be described as dead. Better an infant science that is alive than a dead metaphysics.

*　　*　　*　　*

The concept of ideology not only contains the essence of Marx's contribution to the general science of history, but it reveals most exactly his innovation in the particular enterprise of revolution. Marx's word "ideology" was invented by Napoleon Bonaparte for the express purpose of deriding revolutionary idealism. "It was a nickname," to quote an early biographer, "which the French ruler used to distinguish every species of theory, which resting in no respect upon the basis of self-interest, could, he thought, prevail with none save hot-brained boys and crazed enthusiasts." That is to say, it was an epitome of the counter-revolutionary propaganda. It was a summing up in one word of what all hardheaded practical men of the world have said about social idealists from the beginning of time. And up to the time of Marx their sayings had been in a broad sense correct. Marx took the hardheaded practical realistic sagacity of these men of the world, and introduced it into the ranks of the revolution. Marx's scheme of proletarian class struggle for socialism is hardheaded idealism. It is idealism taking account of the facts. It is Napoleonic ruthlessness on the other side of the barricade. And that is why Marx instinctively adopted Napoleon's term of derision for all thinking which is detached from the facts, and which ignores those egoistical-economic motives that constitute the main driving force in history. He wanted to get the same foolish and utopian nonsense out of his way that Napoleon did, but for an opposite purpose.

Marx achieved this hardheaded condition, as we have seen, by projecting his own emotional idealism into the external world. He had been taught in a German university to regard the universe as an idealistic development, an "endless passing from the lower to the higher." He scrutinized and rejected much of what he learned in that university, but he never scrutinized this word "higher," nor endangered his entire intellectual equilibrium by asking himself what it really meant. It meant, so far as concerns human history at least, *nearer to his own emotional ideals.* Marx was able to treat these ideals with Napoleonic scorn, at the same time that he consecrated his life to them, because he regarded their appearance in his mind as merely a "symptom" of what an accommodating universe was about to do in regard to them.

"The appeal to morality and justice does not bring us forward a finger's breadth scientifically; economic science can see no proof in moral indignation, be it never so justified, but only a symptom. The task of this science is rather to explain the newly arising social evils as necessary consequences of the existing mode of production, but also at the same time as signs of its approaching dissolution, and to discover within the economic movement-form which is dissolving, the elements of the future new organization of production and exchange, which will abolish those evils."

It is easy to scorn your own ideals, treating them as mere signs of a crisis in the evolution of material forces, when you have already confided the attainment of your ideals to those material forces. That was the hardheadedness of Marx and Engels. It was only in a world which was evolving "by its own inevitable dialectic" toward something "higher," toward something "more magnificent," that they knew how to be Napoleonic and dismiss ideologies altogether. To be hardheaded in this real world, which cares nothing at all about what you consider higher, and yet at the same time be idealistic and fight to make something higher out of it, is a little more difficult. But it is the task ultimately laid on us by that course of scientific reasoning which Marx began. It is impossible, once you understand the psychology of the process, to continue this grandiose pretense at a dispassionate reflection of mere economic necessities, which is so often repeated in the writings of Marx and Engels, and so often betrayed. It is impossible, once you have defined ideology as thinking which is unconscious of its motive, to let Marxism continue to hide its motive in an animistic philosophy of the universe. Marxism as a system of dialectic metaphysics *is* ideological, just as all transcendental metaphysics is, but it is certainly the tendency and the true end of the enterprise Marx set going to become scientific.

6. MARXIAN ECONOMICS

IT IS difficult to draw a line between the ideological and the scientific element in economic theory. The subject matter here is the very essence of the egoistic struggle of men, a preoccupation of their unconscious natures. And the science is of necessity abstract and indefinite. It is a matter of formulating large groups of facts rather than accurately defining particulars, and in this act of formulation the hidden purpose of the scientist has a very free hand. However, if an economist who acknowledged a revolutionary purpose, and one who acknowledged a conservative purpose, sat down to formulate the laws upon which they could agree, we should still have something of an objective science of economics. And it is only by conceiving this science as a thing apart from the expressions of class-interest which have been bound up in it, that we can adequately describe the economic contributions of Karl Marx. He contributed certain fundamental and enduring ideas or attitudes to the science of economics, and he replaced the businessman's ideology that had been bound up in that science with a proletarian ideology.

Perhaps the most indubitable contribution of Marx to economic theory was the idea implied in our current use of the word "capitalism." Marx was the first to realize the full extent of the evolution that has taken place in human industry. He realized that many of the most fundamental of those "Laws of Political Economy," which so startled the intellectual world in the eighteenth century, were but laws of that capitalistic system of economy which had begun its existence about two hundred years before. He conceived of economics as a genuinely historical science, and traced the development of modern capitalistic business out of the previous systems of production and exchange. Viewing it in this evolutionary way, Marx was able to describe clearly certain features of "capitalism" that were not adequately perceived by previous economists. That the productive process had become co-operative, or "social," and was becoming more and more so as a result of the factory system and the invention of modern machinery, was a thing which Marx first clearly realized. And he realized the full extent to which this social process would come to be concentrated in vast organizations under the control of a few men. He "predicted the trusts," as Marxists are accustomed to say. If there is in academic circles a reluctance to acknowledge these contributions, or the source of them, that reluctance may properly be described as ideological. The contributions were scientific. They were contributions to the definition of objective facts, and they belong neither to the capitalists nor to the proletariat. They are among the common assumptions of all modern political intelligence.

But Marx not only perceived more clearly than others how profoundly the economic process has changed in the last three or four hundred years. He also perceived the essential feature in which it has not changed—the continued exploitation of the laboring masses by a possessing class. He perceived that the wageworker in our capitalist system of industry works a part of the time for himself and a part of the time for his master, just as truly as the villein did under the feudal system. Our system of "free competition" and cash payment for labor conceals this fact, and all our laws and political principles, and our most honored thoughts about the matter, are concerned to disguise it. But the fact remains. And it was a characteristic achievement of Marx's genius to lay it bare. It was an application of that distinction between science and ideology which I have described as the essence of his contribution to the study of history. Marx himself felt that this was the most original and most important thing in his system of economics. In a letter written to Engels soon after the publication of the first volume of *Capital*, he stated what were the new things of fundamental importance in it. Here is what he said:

"First, that in contrast to all former economists, who from the beginning treat the separate fragments of surplus value with their fixed forms of rent, profit, interest as something given, I treat first of all the general form of surplus value, wherein all the as yet undistinguished forms find themselves, so to speak, in solution. Second, that economists without exception ignore the simple fact that if commodities have a two-fold value, then also the labor embodied in commodities must possess a two-fold character; the mere analysis into labor *sans phrase* as with Smith, Ricardo, etc., landing us on the whole in the inexplicable. This is in fact the whole secret of the critical view. Third, that for the first time the labor-wage is expounded as the irrational phenomenal form of a relation concealed behind it."

Translated into the language of concrete intelligence, these three points all mean that the worker in our capitalist society works part of the time for himself and part of the time for the owners of the instruments with which he works, and that all of the income of the possessing classes, whether directly received in the form of rent, profit, or interest, comes ultimately, just as the wealth of the feudal nobility did, from the work which the worker does, not for himself but for his master, and not for a product but for a profit. This statement is not true in the absolute form in which Marx's philosophy compelled him to make it. But the facts upon which it is based are sufficiently general, and have been sufficiently ignored by other economists, to warrant the assertion that Marx introduced into the objective science of economics—assuming that one can find such a thing—an adequate recognition of the state of affairs designated by the term "wage slavery."

That Marx should have to write a letter to his best friend, telling what the essential proposition is, which he had just finished expounding in a volume of eight hundred pages, and that this letter in turn should require interpretation in order to make it in the least degree intelligible to a man of ordinary education, may suggest to the reader that the intellectual method adopted in the Marxian economics is not of the best. And I advise him to give free scope to the suggestion. Marx's *Capital* combines the principal vices of the classical German philosophy with the principal vices of the classical British Economy. In that sense it is indeed a classic, and has inevitably found its way, along with so many other classics, to the top shelves of a great many libraries. It contains a wealth of interesting ideas and much invaluable empirical material—a study of the development of modern industry in England that ought to be dissected out and published as one of the most significant chapters of human history. But as a "System of Economics" it must inevitably retire, along with the rest of that classical economy and that classical philosophy to whose tradition it belongs, into the position of an intellectual object of art, an ingenious and fertile historic curiosity. For it is not in its fundamental form and theoretic substance a scientific book. It is not, except incidentally, an exposition and empirical demonstration of that concrete fact about the exploitation of labor under capitalism which Marx saw so clearly. It is a flying upward from that concrete fact into the world of unreal abstractions contemplated by the classical economy, and an attempt to make it *reappear* there with an emotional glamour and a metaphysical significance greater than any simple statement of concrete facts could have.

The classical economy had settled in Marx's day upon a conception of the "value" of commodities—the rate at which they exchange on the market—as ultimately determined by the labor necessary to their production. It had also arrived at a problem of explaining according to this conception the value of labor itself, which seems to sell on the market just like any of these commodities whose value it determines. The value of labor ought also to be determined by the amount of labor necessary to produce it. But that is a useless, if not indeed a meaningless proposition, which merely reduces the given conception of value to absurdity. Marx invented a way out of this difficulty. He thought up the idea of saying that the thing which is for sale on the market is not labor, but "labor-power." The capitalist may be said to buy this commodity at a rate determined, as much as that of any other commodities, by the amount of labor necessary to produce it. But this commodity has the peculiar property of creating value, and if put into contact with machinery and raw materials it will create a value very much greater than its own. And that "surplus value" created by the laborer for the capitalist who has bought his labor-power as a commodity, will explain, with all the neatness of the classical economy, how people get rich in our society by merely producing and exchanging commodities whose value is by definition equivalent. In this way Marx succeeded in fixing up the abstract formulation of the process of capitalistic production attempted by Smith and Ricardo upon the basis of a labor explanation of value, in such a way as to make an emphasis upon the exploitation of labor just as abstract, and just as "classical," as any of their more conservative constructions.

There is no denying the ingenuity and interestingness of the idea. But it is absurd to attribute to this ingenious manipulation of abstractions a weight and significance comparable to that possessed by the simple concrete fact which made it possible—the fact that the earth and the instruments of production belong to a few people, and they get rich, on the whole, by compelling other people to work for them at approximately a living wage. The classical economy has fallen out of scientific repute, not because it was wholly at variance with the facts, but because it was not sufficiently interested in them. The principal object of its study was the relations between a set of abstract ideas. And Marx's economic system shares the fate of the classical economy because it shares the same fault. Indeed, it carries that fault to an unheard-of extreme. Marx makes it clear in his very first chapter that a "commodity" is an abstraction, that "value" in the sense in which he uses the term is an abstraction, and that the "labor" which constitutes this value is something that never existed on land or sea. It is "abstract human labor" of the "average degree of skill and intensity prevalent at the time." And nevertheless his mind is satisfied to describe commodities as the "material depositories of exchange value," to describe this value as "abstract human labor . . . in a congealed state," as, in fact, "crystals of this social substance," a "homogeneous jelly" composed of something which by definition does not exist. He treats abstract and concrete labor as two "different kinds" of labor, and declares that in a commodity which is regarded as the equivalent of another in an act of exchange, "concrete labor becomes the form under which its opposite, abstract labor, manifests itself." It would be difficult to find in the whole history of science a more mystical and unreal construction. Marx himself confessed that he "coquetted" with a Hegelian phraseology in this chapter. The fact is that only a man trained from childhood not only in this phraseology, but in the sincere conviction that the real world is composed of abstract and general ideas alienated from themselves in material objects, and who had never essentially recovered from that training, could possibly have conceived or written such a chapter, or regarded the propositions which he deduced from it, or professed in whole or in part to deduce from it, as having the character of empirical science.

That Marx's disquisitions about value and surplus value—in spite of the indubitable concrete fact out of which they are fabricated—are not scientific generalizations is practically conceded by Marx himself in the third volume of his *Capital*. At least that is my opinion about this famous subject of dispute. In this third volume Marx comes down to the question of the rates at which concrete and visible objects actually sell upon the market, and of the profits actually made by concrete and visible capitalists who employ labor. And he is compelled to concede that his laws of value and surplus value are not a definition or explanation of these actual things. They are not generalizations of fact capable of experimental verification. They are a "penetration," as he says, of the "outward disguise" constituted by these concrete facts "into the internal essence and inner form of the capitalist process of production." To an empirically and really scientific mind these words "internal" and "inner"— which come to the rescue not only here, but at every moment of critical danger in the Marxian metaphysics— mean nothing in the world but *abstract*. To such a mind, therefore, this statement is an abandonment by Marx of his own pretense to have formulated the laws of the concrete process of capitalist production. It is a confession that he is not talking about these concrete facts. The boast of Engels that "the classical economy had got lost in a blind alley—the man to find the way out was Karl Marx," is perhaps true. But Marx found his way out, as was inevitable to anyone adopting the same methods, into another blind alley. The only way to escape from these blind alleys is to abandon the deductive and rationalistic methods common to Marx and the classical economists, cease to delude ourselves that, when in the process of abstraction we draw farther away from the variety of the concrete facts, we are "penetrating" into the "inward essence" of those facts, and come back to an attitude of experimental humility before the facts themselves.

7. RELIGION IN DAS KAPITAL

THE REASON why Marxists, who are so devoted in other matters to the maxim that "The truth is always concrete," are just the last ones to give up overvaluing the abstractions of pure economics, is that there is bound up for them in that science a religious belief. They do not approach *Das Kapital* as social engineers desirous to find out the real structure and movement of the world they are working with. If they did, they would be as intolerant of its indirectness, its lumbersome, long-winded intellectualism and perfectly unnecessary obscurity, as anybody else. They come to it as adherents of a faith, desirous to be convinced that the "inner hidden laws" of this world are working with them. Obviously, then, the more "inner" these laws are, the more "hidden" they are, the better, the more convincing, the more easily defended against those who are deceived by the "visible external movement" of things.

The classical political economy had also contained an ideological element that was more than half religious. In order to formulate its laws of production and exchange, it had made the assumption that every man acts in all business relations upon a motive of reasoned self-interest. And the neatness and convincingness of the structure which it built upon this assumption were so astonishing that it did not seem absurd to tack on to it the assertion that this reasonable self-interest of every individual is a divinely fine thing, which if left to itself would automatically produce the welfare of society as a whole. This assertion was obviously not a part of the science of economics; it was the pious ideology of a thriving business class. As there is not any welfare of society as a whole, nor even any enduring welfare of the business class, this ideology did not last very long in its pure form. Various measures of social and political reform began to seem more satisfactory in its place. But the general assumption that those "laws" of capitalistic business describe what must be and ought to be, as well as what is, continues to characterize the academic science of economics even today. It is on the one hand an attempt at a scientific generalization, and on the other an ideological justification of the fundamental structure of capitalist society.

Marx put his proletarian ideology exactly in the place of that original ideology of the business class. In place of the assertion that the instinctive economic activities of men automatically produce social welfare, he put the assertion that these same activities automatically produce a social revolution. His dialectic religion had perfectly prepared him for this. His conception that when men enter into social relations an ordered development arises which is wholly independent of their consciousness and their wills, was far more dependable for this purpose than the concept of the "Economic Man." It left Marx free from that criticism from the standpoint of realism in psychology, which has spoiled the beauty, and practically broken the authority, of the classical Economics. Marx himself abandoned the Economic Man, as his defenders are careful to explain. But Marx abandoned the Economic Man not because he wished to make a closer analysis of the concrete facts, but because he wished to stay farther away from them. He abandoned the Economic Man because he had an Economic God—the self-active Dialectic Development of the Forces of Production—who was far more reliable for ideological purposes than anything so specific and dubious as a formula for human nature. The Marxian ideology consists of fitting the abstractions of the Classical Political Economy, as amended but not transcended by Marx, into Hegel's philosophy of the universe as a dialectic evolution of abstractions—this also amended, but not transcended by Marx—and thus arriving at a mystical conviction of the "iron necessity" of the revolution that he desired.

Perhaps the easiest way to see how this was accomplished is to study the thing in its origin. In *The Holy Family*, a book completed by Marx and Engels four years before they formulated their opinions in the Communist Manifesto, Marx has the following passage:

"Proletariat and wealth are opposites. As such they form a whole. They are both phases of the world of private property. It is a question of the definite position which they both occupy in the antithesis. It is not enough to declare them two sides of a whole.

"Private property as private property, as wealth, is compelled to preserve itself, and therewith its opposite, the proletariat. It is the positive side of the antithesis, private property satisfied with itself.

"The proletariat, on the contrary, as proletariat is compelled to annihilate itself, and therewith its conditioning opposite which makes it a proletariat, private property. It is the negative side of the antithesis, its dissatisfaction with itself, private property dissolved and dissolving itself . . .

"Thus within the antithesis the private property-owner is the conservative, the proletarian the destructive part. From the former comes the motion to preserve the antithesis, from the latter the motion to destroy it.

"Private property, to be sure, impels itself in its national economic movement to its own dissolution, but only through a development independent of itself, unconscious, and taking place against its will, a development involved in the nature of the case—only through the fact that it creates the proletariat as proletariat, misery conscious of its spiritual and physical misery, inhumanity conscious of its inhumanity and therefore annihilating itself. The proletariat fulfills the sentence pronounced upon itself by wage-labor in creating another's wealth and its own misery. When the proletariat triumphs, it then by no means becomes the absolute side of society, since it triumphs only in that it annihilates itself and its opposite. The proletariat itself disappears no less than its conditioning opposite, private property."

It is quite obvious in this most perfect of "dialectic constructions" that the only dynamic force—the only thing which prevents it all from standing still right where it is—is the Hegelian Logic. All existing things, or subjects of discourse, are self-contradictions, and all self-contradictions are bound by a *logical necessity* to resolve themselves in a higher unity. Therefore, when you have shown the given subject of discourse, capitalist society, to be a self-contradiction, you are under no necessity to prove that it will be resolved in a higher unity. You may show how it will be resolved, but that is merely a matter of logical deduction and not a problem in dynamics.

Of course Marx outgrew this naïve and ludicrously metaphysical way of expressing himself. He learned, as all good classical philosophers do, to mix the facts and the animistic presuppositions so intricately that it takes a lifetime to divide them. But just the same he did not move one step from his original position, so far as concerns empirically proving the dynamics of his inevitable revolution. His theorizing about the abstract idea of surplus value helped him in the conviction that class-conflict, which he saw to be from the standpoint of his practical effort the *most important* feature of capitalist society, was also from the standpoint of pure knowledge the *inward essence* of it. But it was the Hegelian philosophy, with its assertion that the inward essence of all totalities is conflict, and that all conflicts are bound to be resolved in higher unities, which assured him that his practical effort would succeed. In *Das Kapital*, as in *The Holy Family*, the force which guarantees the evolution of capitalism to the point of rupture, and the creation of the communist state, is that same logical necessity of ascending from the lower to the higher which Hegel laid on the whole universe in the name of God.

"Self-earned private property," we read, "based on a fusion, so to speak, of the separate independent working individual with the conditions essential to his work, was supplanted by capitalist private property which rests upon the exploitation of the formally free labor of others.

"As soon as this process of transformation has adequately disintegrated the old society from top to bottom, as soon as the workers are changed into proletarians, and the conditions essential to their labor into capital, as soon as the capitalist mode of production stands upon its own feet, then the further socialization of labor, and the further transformation of the earth and other means of production into socially exploited and therefore communal means of production, hence the further expropriation of the private property-owner, takes a new form. That which is now to be expropriated is no longer the self-managing worker, but the capitalist exploiting many workers.

"This expropriation is accomplished by the play of the immanent laws of capitalist production itself, by the centralization of capital. One capitalist kills many. Hand in hand with this centralization, or the expropriation of many

capitalists by a few, there develops the co-operative form
of the labor-process upon an ever-growing scale, the conscious technical application of science, the systematic exploitation of the soil, the transformation of the means of
labor into a means only to be employed in common, the
economizing of the means of production through their use
as a means of combined social labor, the entanglement of all
people in the net of the world-market, and therewith the
international character of the capitalist regime. With the
continually diminishing number of the magnates of capital, who usurp and monopolize all the advantages of this
process of transformation, the mass of misery, oppression,
slavery, degradation, exploitation increases, but there increases also the revolt of the working class, perpetually
swelling, and schooled, united, organized, by the very mechanism of the capitalist process of production. The monopoly
of capital becomes a fetter upon the mode of production
which came to its bloom with it and under it. The centralization of the means of production and the socialization
of labor reach the point where they become incompatible
with their capitalist shell. The shell bursts. The hour of
capitalist private property strikes. The expropriators are expropriated.

"The capitalist mode of appropriation, growing out of the
capitalist mode of production, and hence capitalist private
property, is the first negation of individual private property
founded upon the individual's labor. But capitalist production begets with the necessity of a natural process its own
negation. It is the negation of the negation. This does not
reinstate private property, but just individual ownership on
the basis of the achievements of the capitalist era: co-operation and the common possession of the earth and the means
of production which are themselves produced by labor."

Disregarding the empirical analysis of capitalism in
this passage—the formulation of historic and contemporary facts—ask only where is located, or whence derived,

the dynamic force which gives certainty of the motion into the future of this self-contradictory institution. That dynamic force is not to be found. Unless you have already the habit of assuming that all that group of facts denoted by the general term "mode of production" are destined by a mystical necessity to evolve upward, you find no reason here why the shell of capitalism should inevitably burst. Unless you know, through some avenue that is above the empirical determination of facts, that *all contradictions* are bound to resolve themselves in a higher unity, there is no proof in these facts that "capitalist production creates with the necessity of a natural process the negation of itself." There is no proof here, and contrary to a common belief, there is no proof anywhere in Marx's *Capital*. In this book as elsewhere, it is by conceiving the class struggle as a contradiction between two generalizations—the capitalist forces of production and the capitalist production-relations—and inferring the victory of the proletariat as a logical conclusion according to the Hegelian system, that Marx arrives at that inevitability of socialism which is supposed to rest upon the overwhelming assemblage and analysis of facts in his book. It rests upon the relics of religious metaphysics; it has no other foundation.

The Hegelian philosophy, which professed to portray an eternally fluid and evolving universe, nevertheless managed to bring that universe to a stationary goal in the knowledge of this very Hegel's philosophy, and the tempered blessings of the limited monarchy so generously and so long promised by his gracious sovereign, Frederick William the Third. And Marx's equally fluid although material universe, boasting an equally perfect and eternal evolution, comes to a dead stop when the dictatorship of the proletariat over the bourgeoisie has been resolved by the formation of "an association which excludes classes and their antagonisms." Is it a mere coincidence that Marx's economic and inward knowledge of the laws of history cannot extend a little forward toward another contradiction, or that it does not fall a little short, or lose a trifle of its iron certainty, before that perfect point is reached? Is it not quite obvious that it is not Marx's knowledge, but his purpose, that is being expressed?

Newton's law of gravitation, which can be stated in one simple sentence, and upon the verification of which the whole scientific mind of man may be said to have been working, disinterestedly and without ulterior purpose, for two hundred and fifty years, is now called into question in the light of newly discovered facts. And yet the Hegelian Marxist asks us, in the name of "natural science," to believe that this ponderous philosophico-economical construction, comprised in three enormous volumes, in no one of which is anything so clear as the political passion of its authors, is a sure and accurate statement of the exact law of development of all human history, whose "iron necessity" can be depended on up to and including that "leap from the kingdom of necessity into the kingdom of freedom," which is a perfect utopian name for the communist society. It is a stultification of the mind to believe it. Marx's *Capital* has been called "The workingman's Bible," and no more true and fundamental criticism of it can be made than that. It is a book in which the working class can find not only the "most adequate expression of its conditions and its aspirations"—to quote the phrase of Engels—but also the assurance that these have their due place in a universal scheme of evolution toward something better, and that in the due course of history, with a necessity that is absolute if not divine, they are to be satisfied and fulfilled. They are to be satisfied on this earth, and not in heaven. The God who is to satisfy them is not a Loving Father, but a Passionless Process. The mystery which surrounds him is not emotional, but intellectual. And the mode of communion with him is not prayer, but terribly confusing hard work with the brain. These are the principal distinctions between Marx's *Capital* and other kinds of Bibles, and they are not fundamental. They are not comparable to the distinction between a Bible and a textbook in Mechanical Engineering. That book tells you how to do something; it does not tell you what is going to be done.

If Marx had understood the art of practical thinking, *Das Kapital* might have been as great a book as the Hegelian Marxists think it is. And one aspect of its greatness would have been its brevity. It takes a long time to get your passionate purposes thoroughly wound up and lost in a "mental reflection" of the material world. But it does not take so long to set forth the features of that world which are relevant to the attainment of your purposes. *Das Kapital* contains the material necessary to prove that our system of production for profit through the exploitation of labor is inexpedient and uncivilized, and undesirable to anyone who takes the viewpoint of a true and free human society. And it also contains the material necessary to prove that this system is unstable, and will with practical certainty give rise to imperialistic wars and other crises of a potentially revolutionary character. Indirectly it justified the revolutionary purpose of Marx, and warranted his belief in the practical possibilities of the class struggle. Taken just as it is, however, the merit of the book lies chiefly in a certain honorific intellectual decoration that it has bestowed upon the workers' movement. It has shown that a professor of revolution can be just as erudite and irrelevant as any other professor. To offset this, it has put upon the revolutionary propagandist the task of defending a thesis unessential to his task and beyond the power of any human mind to prove.

8. THE "DIALECTIC METHOD"

ACCOMPLISHED MARXISTS, besides knowing the universe to be a dialectic process, are supposed to possess a dialectic method of thinking, which is appropriate to such a universe and which constitutes the essence of their wisdom. Let us examine this "method of thinking" in its origin and development.

The dialectic philosophy, as we have seen, was a bold maneuver in the defense of animism against science. Science has always occupied itself with changes, and animism has survived for the most part as an assertion of the Changeless which lies behind and beyond them. As science more and more invades and occupies the mind, however, this Changeless becomes more and more dubious. It becomes less and less interesting. It is a dying God. Hegel revived it by saying that it *is* Change—the one immortal, absolute, *unchanging* Principle—and that it does not dwell behind, or beyond, but *in* the subject matter of science. If he had left the matter there, however, his maneuver would not have been successful, for he would merely have transferred into the laboratories of science all the consecrated enthusiasm which he was trying to save for the Church. He had to have some mode of communion with this God, which is the subject matter of science, besides science itself, which is a matter-of-fact investigation of His various parts and modes of procedure, and a rather irreverent attempt to control them. He had to have a religious ceremony. And that was the original function of what is called "dialectic thinking."

It is obvious that real thinking, whose main function is to adjust us to the particular parts of a changing world and enable us to manage them, is not very well adapted to the task of reproducing in our minds the exact nature of this world as a whole. The only way to manage a world of change is to discover reliable uniformities and establish fixed points within it. And that is what real thinking does. It forms concepts with fixed meanings and fixed logical relations to each other, and it applies these fixed concepts to a world which is not fixed. They do some violence to the world—they falsify it to some extent—but they enable us to get along with it. And their fixity in contrast with its flux is exactly what gives these concepts their practical value.

Intellectual people, however, who live among ideas as though they were things, and may be likened in that respect to insane people, usually forget this fact. They get to imagining that logical concepts can be strung together in such a form that they will actually somehow reproduce reality, or to use the phrase of Engels, "represent the exact nature of the universe." And having devised this neat fancy, they are seriously disturbed when something reminds them that it is not so. They are disturbed when you point out, for instance, that the very fact of motion is a little illogical. A body logically "must be," you say, at any given moment either in one place or another, and therefore it logically cannot be at any given moment on its way from one to the other. An unintellectual, and as you may say, *natural* person, is not bothered by this observation, because he knows that motion is a fact, and the business of thinking is to deal with facts and not lay down laws for them. When reality slips out of the grip of logic, that is to the natural mind a joke, and not a difficulty. But to the learned intellectual who seeks to contain the universe in his thoughts, or at least put it away on the shelves of his library, the accident is serious. And so he is prepared for the assertion of some deep-voiced and obscure Philosopher of History that his very method of thinking is inadequate and elementary, and that in order to receive into his mind the exact reality of a world of change he must have a new kind of Liquefied Logic called Hegelian. . . . Or he is prepared for some more limpid but equally sonorous Philosopher of Biology, who tells him that logic must be transcended entirely and a new kind of Vital Intuition, called Bergsonian, put in its place. It makes no difference. He is prepared to be led out of the laboratory and into the temple.

Hegel availed himself of the fact that thought is not a mere reproduction of the flux of reality in order to establish in good scientific repute, and yet over and above science, his religious ceremony of "dialectic thinking," which pretends that it is a reproduction of the flux of reality. He was thus able to save the essence of animism —its peculiar mode of communion with an external world —and yet concede that the subject matter of science really is the substance of this world. He was able to combine the comforts of rationalistic religion with a hard empirical realism. He attacked the mystics, he attacked all forms of the idea of transcendent being, as harshly as any merchant-chemist would. But in proportion as he attacked the idea of transcendent being, he emphasized the idea of transcendent thinking—the ineffable logic, the mystery of the philosopher's disciplined meditation, which gives us the pure essence of that evolving God of whom science itself is but an inherent part. And he declared with noble sincerity for all who wish to know that this speculative logic—this peculiar disciplined mystery of thinking, called philosophy—"is itself a Divine Service, is a religion."

It seems strange that Marx and Engels, who were so fond of the saying of Feuerbach that "the metaphysician is but a priest in disguise," should have been hoodwinked by a metaphysician who frankly abandoned the disguise. But it is a fact which can be established by examining any one of the official expositions of the Marxian "dialectic method." It is not a method of thinking; you could not learn one definite thing about the practical art of thinking by reading these expositions. It is the relic of a religious-intellectual ceremony which has been preserved, over and above the practical business of thinking, and for a different purpose. Engels, in his chapter on the dialectic, calls the Negation of the Negation "an extremely far-reaching and important law of development of Nature. . . ." But he speaks with high scorn of the idea that Marx used this law in order to prove anything.

"It shows a complete lack of insight into the nature of the dialectic when Herr Dühring takes it for an instrument of mere proof. . . . The dialectic, besides transcending the narrow horizon of formal logic, contains the germ of a more comprehensive view of the world."

And again:

"With the mere knowledge that the stalk of barley and infinitesimal calculation fall under the law of the Negation of the Negation, I can neither successfully raise barley, nor differentiate and integrate. . . ."

Is it not rather naïve, in expounding an important and far-reaching law of nature, to confess, first, that your law of nature does not enable you to prove anything, and second, that it does not enable you to do or produce anything—and this, too, in a philosophy which declares that "in practice man must prove the truth, the reality, power, this-worldliness, of his thoughts"? A law of nature is a statement that under such and such circumstances such a thing will happen, or that if I do a certain thing, I shall get a certain result. Could Engels make it clearer that the Negation of the Negation is not a law of nature? It is a loose and not even poetically interesting analogy between certain curiosities of abstract thinking, and a way of viewing certain natural processes—a thing inconsequential to any person not in need upon emotional grounds of a superscientific mode of "knowing" the perfect Reality.

In another passage Engels declares that ordinary practical thinking is all right for "everyday purposes," but it is inadequate to the task of giving an "exact representation of the universe. . . ." It is inadequate because it draws a sharp distinction between such things, for instance, as plant and animal, alive and dead, cause and effect. Every jurist knows that you cannot determine an exact moment at which a man ceases to be alive and becomes dead. Every biologist knows that the distinction between plant and animal breaks down among the elementary forms of life. And everybody in the world knows that what is regarded in one connection as an effect has to be regarded in another connection as a cause. Nature slips out of our fixed concepts; nothing is more certain than this fact. But the thought which recognizes this fact is just the same kind of thought as any other. The inferences to be drawn from it must be drawn in the same way as other inferences. And the inference of Engels that we must try to introduce into those fixed concepts themselves the fluidity and logical unreliability of nature has no warrant whatever in the fact. Our idea of alive, he says, in effect, should also be an idea of dead, our idea of plant should include that of animal, and our antithesis between cause and effect, which "only holds good in its application to individual cases," should be abandoned in favor of a fluid conception of cause and effect as two things which are at the same time themselves and each other. Even if it were advisable, it is obviously impossible to think with such concepts, and nobody ever did so think, from Heraclitus to Lenin. But because Hegel called real thinking "metaphysical," and adopted this ingenious name of *dialectic* for his perfectly metaphysical emotional communion with Absolute Change, Marx and Engels, and every orthodox disciple of their science including Lenin himself, has been induced to *believe* that he thinks with concepts each of which logically includes its opposite.

The real inference to be drawn from the fact that our thoughts do not give us an exact representation of the universe is that we should cease putting up the pretense that they do. We should frankly acknowledge the limited and too often temporary validity of our concepts, and face the fact that whatever generality and durability certain ones may attain, the only thing they can vitally be relied upon to do is to solve specific problems. Knowledge is a thing to be found in practical good sense, and in the various sciences, and nowhere else. Not only is there no such thing as dialectic thinking, but there is no such superintellectual knowledge of the exact nature of the universe as that to which an alleged dialectic thinking pretends to give access. You can discover realities, and experience them, and convey these experiences enriched and vivified in poetry, and you can define realities, and interpret them for purposes of adjustment in practical language. You can mix poetry with practical language to make it lovable or persuasive. You can summarize your knowledge, and criticize and interrelate the different departments of it, making science itself an object of investigation. Beyond this you have the superlogical self-deception and nobly arduous nonsense of the metaphysicians, which makes you work harder, but has no other motive and no other practical significance than the sublogical and simple nonsense of the professors of occultism. Neither of them has any place in an applied science of society.

People who are the most realistic in all other spheres are just the ones most easily led away by myths in the sphere of psychology. It is because they are not introspective, and do not take any psychological statements as real statements of fact. It never occurs to them that a description of the process of thought is, or ought to be, just as specific and definite and subject to concrete verification as a description of the process of digestion. It would never occur to Lenin, for instance, that a good way to find out how a Marxist thinks is to set a Marxist down at a table and let him honestly describe the process by which he reached some simple conclusion. And a way to verify what you learn by that experiment is to set another Marxist down at another table, and let him describe the process by which he reached the same or another conclusion. After about two hours expended in that merely preliminary scientific fashion, the whole myth about negating negations, and seeking in everything for its opposite, and never resting in an affirmative statement, and studying everything in its logical self-movement, its inner hostility against itself, and remem-

bering that things can be both themselves and their opposites, and that cause and effect merge into each other,
and that quantity becomes quality, and that nature
makes jumps—this whole mixture of scientific commonplace with Hegelian higher-logical buncombe, which has
been poured out by the centers of communist education
in Russia under the guise of instruction in the art of
thinking—would go up in the air and be forgotten forever. If quantities become qualities, or if nature makes
jumps, that is a statement of fact, and it has no more
bearing upon the art of thinking than any other statement of fact. The task of thinking is to determine, if
possible, just when and just where these specific events
and others are likely to occur, and how they can be made
to occur. And there is not a word of indication in all the
literature that has been spread abroad on this subject of
dialectic method as to how that task can be fulfilled.
Psychology is indeed an infant science, but it has enough
power of fact in it to destroy this overgrown and fantastic
mythology, and it ought to be made a compulsory subject of study for every Marxist.

The fact that Lenin believed in "dialectic thinking"
will seem to a good many readers to disprove everything
that I say. Lenin was one of the most impressive political
thinkers in history, and he was one of the most adroit.
And Lenin believed that his thinking was "dialectic";
he cultivated his mind in the shadow of this belief. There
must be some value in dialectic thinking, then, besides
ceremonial communion with a God of change. And
indeed there is a value—not in dialectic thinking, for
that does not exist—but in *believing that you think dialectically*. And this value, instead of being in conflict
with what I have said, is the proof of it. Believing in

dialectic thinking is a method by which having made
false intellectualistic assumptions about the nature of
thought, you can escape from them and win back your
freedom to use thought as it was meant to be used.

If you know in the first place that thought is an instrument evolved primarily to guide a complex organism
through a world of change, then you are free to think
practically in a changing situation. You are free from
the domination of fixed ideas. You know that purpose
should dominate, and that ideas must always give way
before facts, you know that you must continually recur
to the facts, and be ready to remodel your ideas to meet
any unanticipated factual development. You know that
all general statements, and statements of what is
true "in the abstract," are subject to suspicion. In short,
there are no fixed points in thought, besides the beginning and the end of thinking, and there is no possibility
that thought, conceived as an instrument of specific
purposes, can ever arrive at anything more "absolute"
than the statement of concrete facts.

All these things you will understand and assume,
without the aid of any mythology, if you remember that
thought is an organic function. But if you imagine that
thought is a detached automatic reflection of reality and
that logical ideas are finished pictures of fact, then
there is only one way to get free from the domination
of the fixed meaning of those ideas. There is only one
way to justify yourself in changing them and subordinat-
ing them to your purpose and to the facts in a changing
situation. And that is to declare that it is the logical
nature of those ideas themselves to change. That is what
Lenin did. The "dialectic method" with Lenin was simply a declaration of independence from the domination
of fixed concepts. It was a metaphysical contraption by

which he managed to defend his right to use thoughts naturally, in spite of an unnatural conception of what thoughts are.

This may be proven, not only by examining the actual manner in which Lenin used thoughts, but by examining what he said about the dialectic itself. It is obvious that if dialectic thinking is what it pretends to be—a thinking with the self-contradictory concepts of the Hegelian speculative logic—then the first point to emphasize in teaching somebody to do it is universal self-contradiction and the negation of the negation. And it is noticeable that Lenin, in the one passage in which he really undertook to explain what the dialectic is, not only did not mention this obviously preliminary point first, but he did not mention it at all. There is just one single idea in Lenin's statement of what "dialectic logic demands," which distinctly and exclusively recalls Hegel's logic. Lenin says first that we must not imagine that any one definition of an object exhausts its nature. A tumbler, for instance, may be defined as a glass cylinder, a thing to drink from, a prison for butterflies, and in many other ways. It is the same way with a labor union. We must study "all sides" of a thing, and "all its connections." Second, we must study a thing in its change and development—and here he adds in quotation marks the word "self-movement," which is Hegelian-metaphysical. Third, "all human practice must enter into our full definition of a thing, both as criterion of truth, and as practical determiner of its connection with what is needful to mankind." And fourth, "dialectic logic teaches that 'there is no abstract truth, truth is always concrete.' "

That is the whole of Lenin's explicit instruction to his followers in the art of dialectic thinking. It was given at a moment when the question which of two groups was thinking dialectically, and which "scholastically," had been raised in connection with a critical problem in Soviet politics. And although Lenin added that "he did not of course exhaust the concept of dialectic logic," it is certain that he stated what its essential practical meaning was to him. And if you wish to see that meaning summed up in one word, you have it here, in one of his last attacks upon the leaders of the Second International:

"They call themselves Marxists, but understand Marxism to an impossible degree pedantically. The decisive thing in Marxism they completely fail to understand, namely, its revolutionary dialectic. Even the direct statement of Marx that revolutionary moments demand a maximum of flexibility, is unintelligible to them. . . ."

That is what "dialectic thinking" meant to Lenin. It meant flexibility—a maximum of flexibility, as opposed to the "pedantry" of ordinary intellectualism.

As we have seen, Marxism has been a perpetual struggle between metaphysical presuppositions and practical revolutionary realism. Lenin's thinking was simply the highest development of that practical realism. And his forgetting about the law of self-contradiction was an indispensable part of his wisdom. For that "law" is not only superfluous, but it is hostile, to the achievement of flexibility. It is a perfect example of one of those pretended abstract truths, which make impossible the concrete adjustment of ideas to the moving variety of facts. Marx did not succeed in forgetting this "abstract truth" as well as Lenin did, but even he managed to keep it usually out of the way of his practical thinking. And when it came to summarizing the dialectic in a word, he said the same thing that Lenin did. He described it as a "free movement" of the mind in the "empirical material." Engels, too, declared that "the kernel of the dialectic view" is a knowledge that nature is fluid, and that "fixity and absoluteness are the products of our own minds." [1] Plekhanov said that "the search for concrete truth constitutes the distinguishing feature of dialectic thinking"—which is but another way of saying flexibility and freedom of movement in the empirical material, for it is only "abstract truths" which deprive us of this freedom.

All these statements by great Marxists of what seems to them the essential factor in the dialectic method ignore what must obviously be the essential factor of thinking based upon Hegel's logic. They all point directly to the essential factor in thinking which understands its function, and is consciously purposive. Practical Marxists have merely used the idea of this mysterious logic in order to gain the freedom to think purposively in spite of their education. It has been a way out of intellectualistic presuppositions into the world of practical action. With Hegel it was a way out of these same presuppositions into a world of metaphysical emotion. Abandon those intellectualistic presuppositions and you destroy both of these ways out. But you find yourself in the world of practical action, for that is the real world in which the function of thinking actually developed.

[1] I call attention here to Sidney Hook's detailed and conclusive study of Engels's conception of dialectic thinking in an article in the Marxist Quarterly, Volume I, No. 2, April-June 1937, entitled "Dialectic and Nature." Nobody concerned with the subject should neglect that article.

PART FIVE

MARX'S EFFORT TO BE SCIENTIFIC

1. WHAT SCIENCE IS

SEEING THE wonders wrought by scientists in the sphere of physics, chemistry, biology, we cannot help reflecting that if the same methods could be brought to bear on social and political problems, all might be well. That is the thought behind the Brain Trust. It explains the late craze for Pareto. It is the main reason why Marxism gains such a hold upon our progressive intelligentsia. We are confronted as a society with desperate problems, and have lost our faith in untrained common sense, in magic formulas, poetic vision, prayer or pious faith, to solve them. We feel that scientific understanding and procedure, the scientific attitude of mind as a public policy, is our sole hope. It is of general importance, therefore, to be very definite about what science is. It is of special importance to us in our task of appraising the Marxian philosophy.

Science stems mainly from practical common sense, and to its major prophet, Professor Huxlcy, "trained and organized common sense" seemed an adequate definition of it. Its results aspire to be "common"—that is, accessible to, and verifiable by, everybody who has the leisure and ability to understand them; it has no kinship with privately delightful subjective beliefs. And its concept of the source and nature of knowledge is that indicated in the word "sense." Science regards all valid knowledge as derived ultimately from experience, derived by the methods of observation, experiment, and rational calculation, and subject to the practical test of action. To be sensible—if you could be sensible enough —is for a scientific mind the highest wisdom.

There is, then, little to distinguish the scientific thinker from the man of practical, or "good," common sense, except the superior system, order, scope, exactitude of his data, and his more strenuous and thoughtful discipline—in short, as Huxley said, *training* and *organization*. Common sense is amateur; science is expert.

In order to become expert, however, practical good sense had to isolate itself from certain more ingratiating preoccupations with which in its amateur condition it had often been confused: from sorcery and magic, charlatanism, pseudo science, poetry, religion, and religious metaphysics. To complete Huxley's definition, therefore, we have to distinguish science from what is centrally implied by each of these other terms.

Science and Magic

It is fairly obvious that the witch who proposed to cure cancer with a poultice of toads' knuckles and the ears of bats killed in the third phase of the moon in October, and pronouncing over it the syllables *Me mo fi fum fidoo fidoo fiducium*, was not using her mind the way a man was who, when wounded in battle, tightened a thong round his limb to stop the blood flow. And yet it is not easy, especially when the two kinds of thinking proceed in the same mind, to define this difference. It might seem sufficient to distinguish science from magic by saying that its assertions are reliable, its predictions come true, its procedures actually produce the desired result. But why is this so? The distinction between them is not one of emotional motive or general mental attitude; both the scientist and the magician attempt to change, or adjust themselves to, a world which they conceive as impersonal. The distinction lies in their attitude to the unchangeable or uncontrollable element in that world. The magician ignores this element, or reduces it in his conceptions to a minimum. The desired end plays the predominant part in his thinking; the given facts play almost no part at all. The scientist not only pays attention to those given facts, but he spends the major part of his time ascertaining their exact character and defining the relations among them that are fixed—the manner in which they invariably coexist and succeed one another. He may indeed spend all of his time that way, in clean oblivion of any wish to change or control the world. But, in any case, his efforts at change and control are based upon and guided by a definition of what is unchangeable or uncontrollable. They are based upon what is called "irreducible fact." The scientist has—to recall the words of Professor Bridgman—an attitude of almost religious humility before fact.[1]

He has also, however, a rather irreligious pride in dragging facts out into the open daylight where they can be passed around for inspection, and have their presumed relations debated and exhaustively tried out. That, too, differentiates him from the magician. He is an implacable enemy of the occult. He really wants to know; the magician wants not to know. The "numerologists," for

[1] "The fact has always been for the physicist the one ultimate thing from which there is no appeal, and in the face of which the only possible attitude is a humility almost religious" (The Logic of Modern Physics). Although Professor Bridgman offers a new "operational" interpretation of the concept of fact in physics, he will have to find in it a point of attachment for this attitude of the physicist. If he removes that, he will remove physics.

instance, a frequent survival of this type in our American leisure class, can tell you by the number and alphabetical position of the letters in your name the amount of love-genius in your soul. But they cannot point out any factual connection between the spelling of your name and the attributes of your soul. And it is of the essence of their pleasure in numerology that no such connection should be revealed. Nothing would more quickly destroy and disperse their cult than for somebody actually to discover, verify, delimit, and define a dependable relation between one's character and the number of letters in his name. Their whole doctrine would then come down from the world of mystery into the matter-of-fact world, and be no longer either of interest or profit to them.

That is what it means to say that science is an implacable enemy of the occult. It does not mean that there is any kind of phenomenon, from spirit rappings to streaks of luck, which a conscientious scientist will not investigate with an open mind. But the purpose of his investigations will be to understand how it works. The purpose of the magician is to keep its working wonderful. Houdini gained both fame and fortune playing apparently magical tricks on the public, but he always insisted they were tricks. He waged a lifelong war on the occult, as you can see in his belligerent and very interesting book, A Magician Among the Spirits. John Mulholland, the present editor of the Magician's Magazine, continues this small but not unimportant war. It is a part of the forward struggle of the scientific point of view. And the fact that men of this type have captured in our world the very name "magician" shows what progress has been made.

Charlatanism

Between the man of expert common sense and the primitive magician there stands a wavering type, also commonly identified as an enemy of science, the charlatan. Charlatanism arises in almost every branch of knowledge. It seems an inevitable by-product of the evolution of the scientific point of view, and is no such simple thing as a deliberate swindling of the public. The charlatan has often a genuine interest in knowledge, and will offer his good offices on occasion with no pecuniary motive whatever. He dwells in a mental twilight where the line between science and some magic practice is unclear. He dwells in a moral twilight which does not demand that lines be clear. He deceives himself as well as his victim; he keeps up in himself with ingenious skill a more primitive mental condition than such skill warrants. He cultivates credulity. He is a reversion rather than a perversion, and stubbornly but half-aware of his kinship with savages—often, indeed, sincerely self-convinced that he represents an outpost in the slow march of knowledge.

It is the charlatanism in Alexis Carrel's book, *Man the Unknown*, which made it so prodigiously popular—charlatanism mixed up in fatal dose with science. A purer example of the charlatan in our midst is the Georgian or Armenian, Gurdjieff, whom I had the pleasure of meeting at his institute at Fontainebleau, an institute of health made dubiously famous by the death therein of Katherine Mansfield. Gurdjieff was friendly to me because of my radicalism, and admitted me into an inner conclave where I heard readings from a manuscript which had been dictated to the world through his lips by Beelzebub. While a pale young man read the manuscript, Gurdjieff watched the auditors with a Beelzebubian expression, or the expression of a mischievously benevolent barn owl, on his dark and handsome features. When the reading was over and I asked a question, he explained—I thought very astutely—that since Beelzebub was not now present, he could not answer questions, nor enter into any discussion of the text. Notwithstanding his astuteness, and that owlish expression, and Beelzebub's commonplace thoughts and very bad literary style —perhaps in part because of this—I felt that the man possessed a certain sincerity and a genuine wish to do good. I doubt if a person so sensitive as Katherine Mansfield could have accepted his ministrations had he not. His apostle to America, A. R. Orage, one of the most cultivated and benign men of our time, was still less to be dismissed offhand as a fakir. And yet I have heard him solemnly enunciate, in a Park Avenue drawing room, beliefs literally drawn from the lore of the medicine man and the witch doctor. It was something more austere than honesty that he lacked—that humility before fact, that pride in daylight understanding, that taste for mental clarity, which has, through the long ages, completely divorced expert common sense from magic.

The Pseudo Sciences

Although thus deeply opposed to it, magic contributed to the growth of science something that common sense could not, a specialized preoccupation with the control of nature. The sorcerers, however inexpert they were, were professional. And science in many cases arose as a gradual introduction of common-sense standards of validity into the moonings and brewings of this profession. Certain sciences thus passed through a transitional period in which the occult was mixed with enough matter-of-fact knowledge to make it acceptable even to great scientific minds. Sir Isaac Newton spent about a third of his time dabbling in alchemy, and there are many relics of this halfway science in the famous book of Robert Boyle which marked the birth of modern chemistry. Astrology was mingled in the same way with the beginnings of astronomy. The astronomer engaged by Magellan to guide him round the earth abandoned the voyage because he had cast his own horoscope and found the stars unfavorable to his going. Admiral Byrd would be glad to say good-by to such an astronomer, and it may be that Magellan was too. The man was not "scientific" enough. That is to say, he was credulous of occult beliefs supported only by tradition, and not able to rest in doubt about matters upon which real knowledge was inaccessible.

This ability to rest in doubt, to withhold belief where belief is not warranted by methodical investigation—yet more, to *suspend judgment* while such investigation is in progress—is indispensable to expert common sense and it is the part most difficult for amateurs to learn. Skepticism as a mood or habitual attitude of negation is as old as belief, and is a fruitless thing. But affirmative or scientific skepticism, the ability and resolution to say "I don't know" when, and only and exactly when that is the fact, is a comparatively new thing in the world. It is the real "philosophy" of the scientist, and is so peculiar to him as to seem almost his defining trait. Still it is only the inseparable reverse side of that humility before fact and passion for clear understanding, that trained and organized practical matter-of-factness, which we have already discussed.

Science and Poetry

Besides restraining his beliefs, the scientist has largely to disregard his sensations. He has to learn to think of water not as wet, but as H_2O, a collocation of atoms in a molecule which, if he could perceive it, would not be wet at all. He has to think of colored light as a series of waves or vibrations, having scope and rapidity but no tint. This fact, first realized in modern times by Galileo, is generally supposed to be peculiar to the physical sciences, but only because there it raises more obviously the question of the ultimate nature of matter. When Freud defines love as "a transfer of ego-libido to the object"—supposing that should turn out to be science—he is treating the felt qualities of things as cavalierly as the physicist does when he calls heat molecular motion. All generalized knowledge tends to ignore perceived qualities and concentrate on conceiving things in their practically important relations. The relations are invariant, and they are what matters for prediction and control. Hence common sense as it grows expert in any field tends to assert that things "are" something more and more remote from what they always will be in experience, and likewise in imagination.

This raises many two-sided doubts, but there is no doubt whatever that it brings science into increasing contrast with poetry and poetic literature. We say contrast here, and not conflict, because, although the poet must concentrate on conveying the felt qualities of experience, he may be guided by science in the point from which he views it, the attitude he takes, the thing he has to say about it—and because science, on the other hand, although conceiving things in a manner which more and more ignores their perceived qualities, is compelled always to revert to these qualities for identification. The scientist can say that light *is* vibrations, but if you ask him: "What did you say is vibrations?" he cannot answer: "Vibrations." He has to answer: "Light."

Notwithstanding that it is limited in this way, the divergence of science from poetic literature is one of the momentous facts in human history. Their discrimination is essential to the progress, and it is essential to the definition, of the scientific attitude.

A Poetry of Science

Historically this process of discrimination has been very gradual, and, as in the case of magic, a period was passed through in which the two were reconciled in a kind of scientific poetry or poetical textbook of science. Lucretius is commonly thought of as standing alone in his effort to make a song of expert knowledge, but he was only the high point in an enterprise characteristic of the age in which he lived. Many of the greatest Greek physicists expressed their thoughts, or tried to, in poetry. Empedocles, Doctor of Medicine as well as physicist, was a poet; Xenophanes was a minstrel of science; Eratosthenes, astronomer-mathematician and founder of scientific chronology, was a poet; Solon, the lawgiver, was a poet; Homer, the historian and, as Plato called him, "educator of Greece," was a poet; Omar Khayyam was renowned in his own time as a physicist and master of algebra. It is significant that the first volume of George Sarton's *Introduction to the History of Science* is called "From Homer to Omar Khayyam." Vergil taught scientific agriculture in verse. Chaucer was an astronomer. Even in Elizabethan times poetry was still regarded as the "quintessence of knowledge," and both Spenser and Milton thought of themselves primarily as teachers. It was only in the middle of the seventeenth century that the inappropriateness of poetic language to science was clearly realized, a war was declared on "the trick of metaphor," and the Royal Society, founded in 1645, exacted from all its members "a close naked natural way of speaking, positive expressions, clear senses . . . bringing all things as near the mathematical plainness as they can."

Since that date science has made such vast rapid strides, and grown so complex, that its distinctness from poetry, both as a profession and a way of using language, is fairly obvious. And although literary men and professors of poetry are disposed to obscure it, the nature of this distinction is fairly clear to men of science. Poetry subsists primarily by making vivid in imagination the qualities of things as they arise in perception. The concern of science is to conceive things in their invariant and practically important relations—for which purpose it is compelled to disregard those very qualities which are of primary interest to the poet.

Science and Emotional Thinking

Besides restraining belief and disregarding sensation, the scientist is compelled to set aside his emotional predilections. He must not let his liking for this or that solution of a problem affect his choice. He must not let any interest of his—place, power, fortune, love, or comfortable feeling of the world—he must not let even so insidious a thing as a wish to be the solver of a problem—influence his solution. That is why the tale is so often told of how Charles Darwin well-nigh missed the

honor of introducing the theory of natural selection because he spent twenty years collecting evidence before
he would give his great idea to the public—and of Isaac
Newton waiting almost as long for similar reasons before announcing his law of gravitation. Those two inci-
dents are symbolic of what is morally most impressive
about science, its passion for an impersonal goal. A
patriot may be more or less pure in devotion to his
country; a warrior, a poet, a philanthropist may reconcile many motives in his overheated breast. But a scientist, by his very definition and in so far as he is a scientist, must be selfless in his search of truth. His very
test of truth, his litmus paper for detecting its presence,
is that it shall be capable of communication and objective verification—capable of verification by all honest
and adequate minds, no matter what their tastes and
points of view and passionate wishes in the field may be.
By taking that word "common"—so lightly spoken in
the phrase "common sense"—and raising it up into a
standard of the validity and inward respectability of his
own thoughts, the scientist has condemned himself to
a kind of sainthood that is hard to find elsewhere in this
modern world. He may be more or less of a scientist,
but in so far as he is a scientist he has singleness of purpose.

This does not mean—I hope it is obvious—that scientists are without feeling, or that their researches are pure
of all relevance to action, and supernaturally cut off from
the usual theme of the brain's labor, what to do. An
examination of the body of ideas actually called science
would show that an exceedingly small part of it is irrelevant either to man's interests or to his purposeful activities. Therefore, there is something unscientific as well
as snobbish bound up in the cult of "pure" science—the

aluminum tower attitude, as we might call it, for it is similar in texture and surface polish to the ivory tower in art. There is such a thing, of course, as pure curiosity, but it is not at all elevated or unusual. Almost anybody would be interested to know, if he could be reliably informed, what is the average number of clover stems per square mile in the region between New York and Philadelphia, taking the ocean for one boundary and the Pennsylvania Railroad for another, and what the ratio therein of four-leaved to three-leaved clovers. The knowledge would be exact, quantitative, generalized. It would meet all the requirements of the concept of "pure" science, but anyone who set out to acquire it would probably arrive in an insane asylum before he reached Newark, New Jersey.

No matter how pure science is, it chooses its subject matter under the general guidance of human aims or interests, and it orders this subject matter by means of a conceptual apparatus in the formation of which practical activities played a major part. On the other hand, no matter how practical science is, nor how passionate the purpose that motivates it and marks out the field of its inquiry, that purpose and passion must be set resolutely aside during the inquiry, and must have no influence upon its determination of the relevant facts. In that sense practical science is entirely pure. And as pure science is in the above sense inevitably practical, there is no great depth to the distinction between them. They both stand in complete contrast to that kind of thinking in which our conception of fact is in any part determined by our passion. As Bertrand Russell says:

"The kernel of the scientific outlook is a thing so simple, so obvious, so seemingly trivial, that the mention of it may almost excite derision. The kernel of the scientific outlook is the refusal to regard our own desires, tastes and interests as affording a key to the understanding of the world."

I do not know why Mr. Russell thinks this so simple and trivial a thing, unless because he himself has so spontaneous a genius for it. To the average man the main object of speculation is to get hold of some sort of belief that will sit comfortably in his breast. And certainly the most persistent and most threatening enemy of the scientific attitude is the disposition of men to think what they want to think, and of men and institutions to bend the results even of experimental investigation, and pervert its authority, to the support of their purposes and states of passion.

In celebrating the five hundred and fiftieth anniversary of the University of Heidelberg, its Nazi professor of philosophy, Dr. Ernest Krieck, declared:

"The science of a nation is a part of its total life, and is therefore bound by the necessities, direction and purposes of the national life. . . . We seek a science that forms the whole of a man's character in accordance with the great racial and political task before us."

All mature minds, in Germany and elsewhere, realize that this attempt, not merely to employ the findings of science for the purposes of the totalitarian state, but to bend these findings to the demands of totalitarian passion, will be, if successful, the end of science in Germany. It will perhaps appear in retrospect the chief of Hitler's crimes against civilization.

Science and Religion

A more ancient emotional and institutional enemy of science is religion. Religion conflicts with science not only as magic does by opposing its own occult procedure, prayer and sacrifice, to the practical way of getting things done, but still more by opposing to the general attitude of restrained emotion and suspended judgment in which scientific investigation must proceed its prior belief in an emotionally satisfying total picture of the world. I do not mean by religion, of course, a sense of the mystery of being, or the emotions which poetic people have had, and always will have, in contemplation of the concept of the unknown. I think Einstein is wrong in applying the word "religion" to his feeling of "the variety of human desires and aims, and the nobility and marvelous order which are revealed in nature and in the world of thought." Religion means, or in the interest of straight thinking ought to mean, belief that the external world, or some power in it, is interested in the interests of men. The religious believer persuades himself that the world is softer than it is, and that we know more about it than we do. The scientist has courage to face the hard facts of our human situation and abide within the limits of our slowly advancing knowledge.

Thus, the conflict between science and religion is more abrupt and violent than that between science and magic. The difference is not only one of procedure and degree of attention to fact; it is a clash of two contradictory attitudes toward the world. For this very reason it is easy to acquire the trick of keeping both science and religion alive in separate chambers of the same brain; they do not conflict because of the completeness of the separation. Until the separation is accomplished, however, science cannot flourish in any brain. The slightest admixture of piety among the motives which bring a scientist to his conclusion would vitiate the conclusion. Even those scientists who in their private or Sabbath-day selves are accustomed to commune with a Deity will accept this statement. The more astute of those whose concern is to defend the belief in the Deity also accept it. St. Augustine himself, at the beginning of the long warfare between science and Christian theology, took such a position.

"It very often happens," he said, "that there is some question as to the earth or the sky, or the other elements of this world . . . respecting which one who is not a Christian has knowledge derived from certain reasoning or observation, and it is very disgraceful and mischievous and of all things to be carefully avoided, that a Christian, speaking of such matters as being according to the Christian Scriptures, should be heard by an unbeliever talking such nonsense that the unbeliever, perceiving him to be as wide from the mark as east from west, can hardly restrain himself from laughing."

It was not difficult in those days to maintain this equilibrium, because the field occupied by science was limited and its conclusions were not in a sweeping way contrary to those of the Church. So long as it confined its question-asking and its matter-of-fact investigation to things like "the earth or the sky"—and did not disturb their relative positions as demanded by the stories in the Bible—it was just as well to allow science its sovereignty and avoid being laughed at as an ignoramus.

When, however, science began to move the earth and the sky around, and perform similarly irreverent miracles with the other elements of this world, and moreover to extend inward its matter-of-fact investigation from this world to man himself—his mind, his morals, his political and social ways and destinies, which were the peculiar sphere of operation of the Church—it was no longer possible to get out of the argument by backing out. It became necessary either to destroy the scientist, or else to reduce the cogency and conclusiveness of his views by introducing into them, or perhaps around behind them, the more credulous conceptions of man's nature and position in the universe demanded by religion.

Science and Philosophy

There thus arose, just as in the case of poetry and of magic, a mixture of religion with science, or an effort to save religious faith in the face of science—to keep going, in spite of the skepticism and austere matter-of-factness of the scientific procedure, and out of range of it, a relic of the personal relation to the world. That mixture is philosophy, in the pious and soul-upholding meaning of the term. It differs from theology in that, instead of opposing science with a contrary belief, it accepts the scientific procedure, but shows in some ingenious way— notably by demonstrating that the whole thing, facts, method, and results and all, is taking place within a "Universal Mind"—that the contrary belief is still true.

Unfortunately, there is no word in our language to distinguish philosophy in this sense from the effort of sublimely curious minds to develop the most general implications of science, to reconcile its conflicts, investigate it with its own method, and criticize it from the standpoint of its own cool search for fact. That too is called philosophy, but it is really an integral part of the development of the scientific point of view. It is a very different thing from wish-fulfillment philosophy, the philosophy which abandons doubt and clarity and austere humility before fact, and where science mutters its honest "I don't know," cries seductively, "I can tell you!" Philosophy of this kind science has had to set aside

in order to achieve its growth, and we must set it aside
in order to achieve our definition of science.

The latest of these attempts to interpret the technique
of science in such a way as to recover a sense of kinship
between man's will and the external world, is called pragmatism. The pragmatists do not accomplish this feat
by hypostatizing a Universal Mind which is imagined to
contain both knowledge and the objects known. They
are too skeptical and common-sensible for that. They declare, on the contrary, that any act of knowing is individual and concrete; it is the solution of a specific human
problem. But since human problems are set by the will,
the will participates in determining the solution. The
Truth itself, a name we give to the satisfactory solution
of problems, is something that we make in collaboration
with the external world. To put it in another way, the
pragmatists do not personify Reality with a large R, but
they declare that our knowledge of realities with a small
r is ultimately personal. It brings them the same feeling
of kinship with the objects of knowledge.

Stated so baldly, this ingenious scheme for disguising
the hard fate of human wishes in a world indifferent to
them, is not difficult to set aside. But the scheme has
been made plausible to our modern minds by being presented as a purely rational and dispassionate inference
from the findings of genetic or evolutionary psychology.
It is always on the basis of some new development in
science that the philosophers build their comforting beliefs. And in building theirs upon the evolutionary study
of the mind and brain, the pragmatists have woven it in
with certain downright facts which are of importance not
only to psychology, but to the complete understanding
of scientific method itself. Let us summarize these facts,

and try to separate the lesson they teach to scientists from the comforting belief which pragmatist philosophers have erected upon them.

Psychology and Scientific Method.

The fundamental contribution of biology to mental science is undoubtedly its conception of conscious thought as having arisen and developed primarily as a means of survival. Desire in its simple nature is undefined and unconscious, and the lower forms of life satisfy their desires by continuing in a state of random activity until they come, by chance, into bodily contact with a satisfaction. Higher forms of life develop feelers with specialized sensitivity, which enable them to explore the environment without submitting their whole body to danger. They develop organs of smell and sight and hearing which enable them to detect a satisfaction, or apprehend a danger, at a considerable distance in space and time. And it is in connection with these organs that the value of a conscious act of perception begins to be apparent. For the essence of such perception is the interpretation of a present fragment of sensation upon the basis of past experience. The smell of food is not food, and the sight of danger is not dangerous. But if by virtue of memory and imagination, the smell of food *means* food, and the sight of danger *means* danger, then the organism can satisfy itself or escape without making in each case a complete experiment.

But even here it cannot learn anything new except by the method of random experimentation—by the method, that is, of trying out in action every meaning that is suggested. And thought, in so far as it is distinguished from the mere act of perception, is distinguished by a moment of suspense during which the suggested meaning, or more than one suggested meaning, is tried out inside the head. Thought is tentative action; it is action in the process of formation. It is adjustment, delayed in order that it may perfect itself and relate itself with safety to a larger and more complex environment.[2]

Some such conception of the origin and nature of thought is forced upon the genetic psychologist, not only by the central tendency of biological science, but by an experimental study of the intelligence of infants and animals. Indeed, the very employment of experiment in these fields implies an instrumental conception of intelligence. For it is only by setting before the infant or the animal a goal of desire, and observing his efforts to attain it, that any experiment can be made.

Moreover, if we study in our own minds any simple example of thinking, we are led to a similar conception. We. button our clothes unconsciously so long as all is in order and the process goes smoothly to its end; but if a button is missing, we become conscious of the process, and we think. And our thinking takes a form corresponding to the situation in which it arose. It is an interpretation of the factual difficulty in the light of the desired end, a trying out in imagination of plans which spontaneously suggest themselves for arriving at the end on the basis of the existing facts.

[2] It is the method of some psychologists to regard all intelligent functions as completely fulfilled by the higher nerve centers, and conscious thought as a mere accidental by-product of the proceeding—or even to deny conscious thought any "scientific" existence at all. This is one of those oversimplifications of fact usually advertised as the highest blossom of the scientific spirit, but which are in reality the survival of a metaphysical taste for unity and the absolute. The fact underlying this metaphysic is that conscious thought performs a smaller function in the process of nervous adjustment, and performs it less frequently, than men have been in the habit of believing.

This instrumental interpretation of consciousness, the fruit of that biological psychology founded by Charles Darwin, has received corroboration of late years from a discipline which developed in almost complete independence of it—the psychology of the clinic. The therapeutic importance of *becoming conscious* is the heart of the discoveries made by Sigmund Freud in the sphere of functional nervous and mental disease. Such disease is, according to Freud, the result of conflicts between different powerful impulses in our nature—sexual impulses for the most part, and impulses of primitive egoism, conflicting with motives arising out of our social self-consciousness. These conflicts may never have been conscious, or they may have been conscious at one time, and been resolved by suppressing into unconsciousness the socially unacceptable impulse. That impulse does not perish by thus returning to the original condition of all life, but continues there in the organism, self-active and dynamic; and it finds expression in spite of the more acceptable motive which occupies the field of consciousness. It finds expression through rationalization and "substitution" in the first place—falsifying our conscious thought in such a way that we can pursue its ends under the guise of a more respectable motive. It finds expression in dreams, in slips and errors of everyday life, in wit and humor, in poetry and myth. And with unstable or wounded natures, it finds expression in all the innumerable symptoms of hysteria and functional nervous and mental disease.

That is the Freudian theory, relieved of certain mythological constructions that Freud's fancy reared upon it. And the Freudian treatment, psychoanalysis, consists at its best of a simple and natural effort to make the patient conscious of his own real desires. When he has become conscious of them, the ordinary process of thought and its education is the only cure that is offered. The cure is occasionally almost instantaneous, because the suppressed motive is infantile and its irrelevance to the existing situation is immédiately recognized. At other times it is very slow, and often enough it is unattainable. But, in any case, it involves nothing more mysterious than the original natural function of all conscious thought—the adjustment of a dynamic organism to a complex environment.

In treating this organism as dynamic, as a thing seeking stimuli instead of merely responding to them, Freud made a considerable departure from the traditional psychology. In the traditional psychology, thought appeared as an instrument for guiding "reactions." In the Freudian way of talking, it is an instrument for defining "desires," or resolving the conflicts between them. In both cases, however, it remains an instrument; and Freud's way of talking is only closer to the evolutionary view of organic functions in general. What survives as valid in his too highly individual, and too little verified, assemblage of opinions, supports the view that conscious thought came into being and was shaped primarily as a practical instrument.

Science can learn much by regarding itself as the skilled employment of this instrument. It can learn to be skeptical even of its own more grandiose pretenses— its recurrent delusion, for instance, that all knowledge may one day be comprised in a single formula. It can learn to distrust abstractions, even though mathematical, to remember that its ultimate subject matter is specific facts, its task to solve specific problems. It can eschew absolutes and dispense with universes. It can abandon the attempt to corral with fixed idea processes, or those elements of them, which are in a state of change. It can learn flexibility, in short, and abandon the "quest for certainty." All these wisdoms, so well taught by evolutionary students of the mind like William James and John Dewey, the scientist can well afford to ponder in his heart. They are the real lessons of the instrumental theory of knowledge, and they are in accord with the definition of science we have given. They emphasize its skepticism and restraint.

But when these same students of the mind, donning the priestlike robes of the philosopher, advise the scientist that he does not, and by implication need not, hold his wish or purpose in suspense while defining his objective facts, purpose playing a legitimate part in the very definition of fact—then they are striking at the heart of scientific method and morale. They are moreover, in my opinion, perverting the real lesson of those facts about the mind's evolution upon which they profess to base their comforting philosophy. For if thought in its rudiments is a delayed response, a suspense of action enabling memory and imagination to make a more circumspect adjustment than is possible to blind instinct, it seems obvious that in thought's expert development this suspense of action must be more, rather than less, complete. The art of valid thinking must be, as science indeed is, primarily and supremely an art of setting aside, not action only, but the whole voluntary nature, so that factual judgments may be unswerved by any influence whatever from the will. Thinking is practical—its suspension of the stream of impulse is practical—for the very reason that it guides the impulse with reference to data which are relevant to, but *not* affected by, it. In rudimentary intelligence, as in the highest range of science, that suspension of the stream of impulse is the prime essential.

The separation of thought from action is the very thing that makes thought useful to action. The pragmatists' attempt to blend the two in order to feel friendly with the world is anti-scientific.

The true inference from our knowledge that thought is in origin an instrumental function is that we must beware of any given thought's pretensions to the contrary. We must beware of this very pragmatism's pretense to give us a dispassionate account of truth, its assertion that "an interest in strictly logical analysis" is the motive to its own speculative constructions. We must beware of all similar pretenses, of all philosophies strictly so-called. We must recognize that even the most objective and "pure" science is compelled to employ concepts narrowly instrumental and valid only for specific problems and procedures. In the sciences that deal with man and his social doings these instrumental concepts will abound, and any claim they make to universal wisdom and validity must be straightly challenged. In general, the "highest" kind of thinking, and the most "scientific," is not that which makes the most grandiose pretense to universality, but that which most carefully and candidly acknowledges the specific problem out of which it arose, and the purpose which made that specific thing a problem. That is the real outcome of the influence of Darwin in the sphere of scientific method. It inculcates a more austere discipline of objectivity, a more hardy and more humble candor, than even Darwin himself exemplified. And Freud carries it a step farther by showing that this state of candor cannot be achieved by acknowledging merely those impulses of which our social dignity permits us to become conscious, but that we must be ready to suspect, in the absence of express efforts to the contrary, that our thoughts are a disguised instrument for the attainment of ends we have no knowledge of.

Conclusion

Science, then, is distinguished from common sense by its degree of system and expertness; from magic and occult ritual, no matter how systemized and expert, by its concern for uncontrollable facts and the invariant relations among them; from charlatanism and pseudo science by its austere mental honesty and its skeptical equilibrium; from poetic literature by its loyalty to the generic and practical concept as against the particular and immediate perception; from religion and metaphysical belief by its refusal to allow interest or emotion to influence its judgment of fact.

The traits of character required to develop a method and a body of results sufficient to distinguish science from these other uses of the mind are: patience in investigation and clarity in calculation; singleness of purpose; the power to suspend judgment, to remain, if need be, for a lifetime in doubt; the gift of abstraction, of thinking about things definitely but without too much intrusion of their sensuous qualities; the skill to hold in suspense one's own tastes and passions, a skill which demands discipline of the most rigorous kind. Without these traits, science as a thing distinct from common sense, from magic, pseudo science, charlatanism, poetry, religion, religious philosophy, and tendentious belief in general, could hardly have come into being. There are, however, two other traits which belong peculiarly to science in modern times. One is modesty—for science has become a co-operative enterprise in which the cranky and egotistical "genius" is more than ever out of place.

The other is open-mindedness—for scientific knowledge is in a state of fluid growth, and even its most assured hypotheses are subject to correction and development. In this connection it is well to bear in mind what Darwin, speaking of the circumstances which led him to the theory of natural selection, called his "golden rule."

"I had also during many years followed a golden rule, namely, that whenever a published fact, a new observation or thought came across me, which was *opposed* to my general results to make a memorandum of it without fail and at once."

The italics are mine, and I do not know any better phrase on which to conclude an effort to say what science is, and how different it is from less reliable ways of using the mind.

Darwin was here describing how he used his mind during the very years when Karl Marx was working up that philosophy of history and the universe which he called dialectic materialism. Let us turn back now to those years, and cross over from England to Germany, and examine this Marxian philosophy at its point of origin. We shall see with complete finality that it has no right to the name and the authority of science.

2. THE SEED OF THE MARXIAN PHILOSOPHY

THAT DISTINCTION of science from other ways of using the mind, which plays so great a part in French and Anglo-Saxon culture, was never sharply made in Germany. The German word *Wissenschaft* expresses a romantic rather than a matter-of-fact ideal, and is more tolerant both toward poetic literature and religious metaphysics than our word *science*. And the reason for this is that the Germans, notwithstanding their great achievements in the laboratory, have remained by comparison with us primitively credulous and animistic.[1] They do

[1] Hegel thought this was a virtue, and declared it the peculiar mission of Germany to cherish "philosophy" like the faith that flamed in the old pagan mysteries. St. Simon thought it was a vice. "I returned," he said after a visit to Germany, "with the conviction that learning is still in its infancy in that country because it is founded on mystical principles." Lange was inclined to smile at it. "Germany," he said in his *History of Materialism*, "is the only country in the world where the apothecary cannot make up a prescription without being conscious of the relation of his activity to the constitution of the universe." Karl Koffka, in introducing the *Gestalt Psychology*, has recently summed the matter up with favor to the German side:

"There can be no doubt that the intellectual climates of Germany and the United States are widely different. The idealistic tradition of Germany is more than an affair of philosophic schools; it pervades the German mind and appears most openly in the writings and teachings of the representatives of 'Geistes-wissenschaften,' the moral sciences. The meaning of a personality prominent in history, art, or literature seems to the German mind more important than the pure historical facts which make up his life and works; the historian is often more interested in the relation of a great man to the plan of the universe than in his relations to the events on the planet. Contrariwise, in

not like the skepticism involved in confining oneself to specific problems, and they habitually expect to taste in the solution of universal problems other satisfactions than that of having a problem solved. Although they understand the necessity of holding one's voluntary nature in suspense while ascertaining and defining concrete facts, they do not feel this to be a noble or an ultimate attitude of knowledge.

This fact, still so true in our day, was more completely so in the youth of Karl Marx, and largely explains the equivocal character of his philosophy. For that philosophy, strangely enough, was the product of an effort to get rid of philosophy altogether, to abolish it out of the world and put empirical science in its place. Without a concise concept of science and how it differs from philosophy, this was of course a forlorn attempt. It was forlorn for any mind trained in German universities and convinced, as Marx and his young friends all were, that Germans are superior to French and Anglo-Saxons in "theory," the very point where they are soft. "Theory" meant animistic speculation, and the superior "practicalness" which they attributed to the French meant scientific method. It meant the very thing that Marx was fumbling after. Dialectic Materialism, examined at its point of origin, turns out to be the rather naïve, cloudy, unsuccessful and half-finished attempt of a matter-of-fact mind to escape from German metaphysics.

America the climate is chiefly practical; the here and now, the immediate present with its needs, holds the center of the stage, thereby relegating the problems essential to German mentality to the realm of the useless and non-existing. In science this attitude makes for positivism, an over-valuation of mere facts and an under-valuation of very abstract speculations, a high regard for science, accurate and earthbound, and an aversion, sometimes bordering on contempt, for metaphysics that tries to escape from the welter of mere facts into a loftier realm of ideas and ideals." (*Principles of Gestalt Psychology*, p. 18.)

The German Ideology

The full vigor of Marx's revulsion against philosophy became known only in 1923, when the old manuscript in which he and Engels first formulated their views was deciphered and published by the Marx-Engels Institute in Moscow.[2] This manuscript, *Die Deutsche Ideologie*, revealed, at the basis of the whole edifice of Marx's intellectual life, an arrant contempt for the very name and concept of philosophy.

In *The Holy Family*, three years earlier, Marx had rejected Hegel's philosophy arrantly enough, describing it as "drunken speculation," and Hegel himself as the "master wizard." He had praised Ludwig Feuerbach for having "unveiled the mystery" of Hegel's system and "annihilated the dialectic of ideas." And he had endorsed the "vulgar and profane empiricism" of the British materialists and the philosophers of the French enlightenment, calling it "the philosophy of good sense." "It opposes philosophy to metaphysics," he had cried, "just as Feuerbach opposed reasonable philosophy to exaggerated speculation on the day when he first took a clear stand against Hegel."

That was Marx in 1843. But now in 1845—so this old and new manuscript informs us—he did not want even a reasonable philosophy or a philosophy of good sense. He did not want any philosophy at all. He was ready to pitch Feuerbach out of the window after Hegel. Feuerbach himself thought he had "found philosophy in the negation of philosophy," but nevertheless Marx now re-

[2] I did not know about this manuscript—and about one or two other things—when I wrote my book *Marx and Lenin*, and hence the first two chapters of that book are inadequate. These two chapters on *Marx's Effort to Be Scientific* are an atonement for them.

jects him as a man who never learned to "approach the world of sensation without the eyes—which is to say the eye-glasses—of the philosopher." But let us read some solid excerpts from this basic document of Marxism (the italics will be mine):

"German criticism right up to its very latest achievements has not abandoned the field of Philosophy; not only has it not examined its own general philosophical presuppositions, but on the contrary all the questions with which it is occupied have grown up out of the soil of one definite philosophical system, the Hegelian. There is mystification not only in its answers, but in the very questions it asks. . . .

"We therefore shall precede our special criticism of certain individual representatives of this movement with some general remarks (about German philosophy and *about all philosophy in general*). These remarks will be sufficient to make clear the standpoint of our criticism. . . .

"We recognize only one single science, the science of history. You can view it from two sides, and divide it into the history of nature and the history of man. . . . In direct opposition to German philosophy which came down from heaven to earth, we here intend to rise from earth to heaven —that is, we will not start from what men say, imagine, represent to themselves, nor from thought-of, represented or imagined men, in order to arrive afterward at bodily men; we will start from really acting men, and try to deduce from their actual life-process the development of these ideological images and reflections of that life-process. For these misty formations in the brains of men are necessary sublimations of their material, empirically ascertained life-process, which is bound up with material conditions. In this way morals, religion, *metaphysics*, and other forms of ideology, lose their apparent independence. They have no history, they have no development; only men, developing their material production and their material relations, change also in the course of this activity their thinking and the products of their thinking. . . .

"Thus where speculation stops, that is, at the threshold of real life, a real positive science begins, a representation of the activity, the practical process of the development of men. Phrases about consciousness disappear, their place to be occupied by real knowledge. When you begin to describe reality, then *an independent philosophy loses its reason for being*. In its place may be found, at the most, *a summary of the general results abstracted from an investigation of the historical development of man*. . . .

"We fully realize that Feuerbach . . . went as far as a theorizer could go without simply ceasing to be a theorizer and *a philosopher*. . . .

"And by the way, with this view of things, which takes them as they are in reality, *all deep-thinking philosophical problems reduce themselves to some simple question of empirical fact*. . . .

"For a *practical materialist*, that is for a communist, the thing is to revolutionize the existing world—that is, practically turn against things as he finds them, and change them."

It would seem that a more radical empiricism, a more "vulgar and profane" empiricism, is hardly to be found in philosophic literature, nor a more wholesale rejection of the idea that philosophy can be a guide or dictator of forms to science.[3]

Is it not surprising, then, that Marx should have become the founder of a new philosophy in the full sense

[3] Riazanov himself, the Russian editor of this manuscript, a sufficiently orthodox Marxist, felt compelled to acknowledge that this is the main revelation contained in it. "The manuscript permits us," he says, "to establish one fact important to any scientific investigation of the development of Marxism. The conclusion familiar to us in the Anti-Dühring was already formulated in the manuscript on Feuerbach. Philosophy as a special science of the general connections of things

of the term—a new theory of being—and that this philosophy should have become the equivalent of a state religion throughout one sixth of the habitable earth, its teaching in the schools enforced by law, and its principles propagated. throughout the world with rigid dogmatism? It is still more surprising when you learn that he founded this philosophy, or drew the outlines of it, in the very year in which he completed this contemptuous attack upon the very idea of philosophy. Engels allots *Die Deutsche Ideologie* to the year 1845-46, and it was in 1845 that Marx "hastily scribbled down," as a notation for further work along the same line, those famous "Theses on Feuerbach" in which, as Engels also tells us, he "planted the genial seed of the new philosophy."

In order, then, to complete our understanding of Marxism, we must find out why Marx planted the seed of a new philosophy in the very labor of rooting up all philosophy forever. And to this end we must recall in more detail, first the outlines of that Hegelian metaphysics in which Marx believed until Feuerbach liberated him, and then the exact nature of this liberation. After that we shall see in the "Theses on Feuerbach" themselves the reason why Marx did not succeed in getting rid of philosophy. We shall see that these Talmudic aphorisms were not a step forward from a raw materialism toward scientific method, but a step back into the shelter of German animism.

and of knowledges, a *summa summarum* of all human knowledge, becomes superfluous. Of all previous philosophy there remains only the science of the laws of thought: formal logic and the dialectic."

Riazanov's statement is inaccurate in two respects. Philosophy as a "summary" of knowledge is just what Marx in this manuscript still sanctions; anyone who seriously attacks philosophy must make allowance for a generalization and interrelating of the sciences. And, moreover, Marx makes no other exception; there is not a word here about "logic and the dialectic."

What Hegel Meant by Scientific

Hegel believed that the whole world is contained in, or made out of, Mind. And this Mind, when properly understood and arrived at in its totality by evolution, or by the thought of the philosopher, is the same thing as God. Hegel's God differs from the old Gods, however, in being active and changeful. He has his very being in the process of development. You can see this process in nature and world history, or you can see it in the way the logical categories work out their relations, the one merging into the other in a peculiar manner to which Hegel, following his predecessors, gave the name of "dialectic." It consists of an affirmative assertion, and then a passing of that over into its opposite, a negation of it by its own self-active propulsion, and then a "negation of the negation," or reconciliation of these two opposites in a higher unity which includes them both. It is astonishing how much of the change and motion in the world, as well as the relations among abstract ideas, if you examine them with a sufficiently casuistical determination to believe so, and particularly if you refrain from defining the word *opposite*, can be made to fit into this mold. For that reason, when all the emotions attending the idea of divinity and of absolute or universal being are mixed up in a description of life and the world in these terms, you have—if you can stand the hard work involved—a great philosophical poem, a great experience for the feelings and the mind. And since we really know little or nothing about the nature of life and the world as a whole, it is easy for credulous people, or people brought up in such ideas, to lend to it the added glamour of belief.

The important thing about it for us, however, is that it enabled Hegel without ceasing to be religious to be very matter-of-fact and hardheaded, indeed brutally realistic, about the "phases" that a Divine Spirit has to pass through on its dialectic pilgrimage. It enabled him to accept in the name of God the hard and bloody world of universal change and evolution that scientists were then already coming to behold, to accept and even slightly to extend the downright understanding of it. In particular, it enabled him to bridge in a new way the gap between what we know and what we want, between the "pure" and the "practical" reason as they had been separated by Kant. Kant had given a different and a firmer root in reality to the active side of our nature, our willful self, than to what our minds know. And Hegel, with his doctrine that reality is a process, and moreover a mental process, united the two. The very essence of being, he said, and therefore the highest condition of the human mind, is one in which knowledge of the real and action toward the ideal are the same thing.

"Being is Thought," according to Hegel, but Thought is a "process of becoming." "The truth is the whole. The whole, however, is merely the essential nature (thought) reaching its completion through the process of its own development. . . . What has been said may also be expressed by saying that reason is purposive activity."

Such was the flavor, and such for our purpose the essential drift, of Hegel's philosophy. The development of what he called a "scientific" consciousness was a development away from the simple condition of sense-certainty, the sensing of an object by a subject, toward a condition of pure meditation in which subject and object are both known to be thought or spirit, a condition of

"Absolute Knowledge, or spirit knowing itself as spirit."
This Absolute Knowledge is "the consummation and the
final cause of the whole process of experience"; but then
also this Absolute is not a mere goal or consummation,
it is not static, but is "the process of its own becoming."

Josiah Royce, who greately loved this Absolute Being,
or philosophic state of mind, described it thus:

"The Absolute whose expression is the world and, in
particular, the world of human life, is a being characterized
by a complete unity or harmony of what one might call a
theoretical and practical consciousness. The theoretical consciousness is a consciousness which views facts and endeavors
to apprehend them. The practical consciousness is a consciousness which constructs facts in accordance with its
ideals. The absolute consciousness is both theoretical and
practical."

For Marx, too, that must have been the great thing
in the Hegelian philosophy. We may imagine that even
in youth he accepted somewhat perfunctorily Hegel's
conception of thought, or the Idea, as "demiourgos of
the world." But Hegel's conception of *Wissenschaft*, of
the highest wisdom to which a human being can attain,
as a state of mind in which he is co-operating with, or
rather participating in, the forward and upward going
of the world toward high ends, must have meant much
to him.

Feuerbach's Revolt from Hegel

Marx believed fervently throughout his young manhood in this philosophy—or in some such philosophy as
I have described, for there is no use pretending that
Hegel's emotional imagination confined itself to saying
things with a clear meaning. And he was awakened out
of this mystical condition by Ludwig Feuerbach, who,

having been a Hegelian, became a man of relative good sense, and said that the world is not really composed of a process of thought, but is composed of objects as they appear in sense-experience. Engels describes the "rapture" with which Marx and he greeted Feuerbach. He says that no one who had not lived through it could possibly imagine the "liberating effect" that his writings had upon them. And from that you can imagine their previous state of hypnosis, the degree of their captivity to the thought-conjurings of the "master wizard."

Feuerbach's revolt against Hegel must indeed have seemed very drastic. He appears even now, at a first glance, to have sensed the animistic personification of a material world involved in regarding ideas as more completely real than objects of sense. He declared Hegelism, and indeed speculative philosophy in general, to be nothing but "theology rationalized, realized and brought home to the mind." And he seemed to strike at the heart of this whole way of thinking when he renounced Hegel's thesis that "being is thought," and that truth is arrived at by a development of consciousness away from the obvious testimony of the senses. On the contrary, he cried: "Truth, reality, sensibility are identical. Only a sensible being is a true, a real being; only sensibility is truth and reality. Only through the senses is an object in the true sense given—not through thought in itself."

As a revolt against Hegel's idealism, this was truly exciting. But, nevertheless, it was not a hearty and thorough-going materialism like that of the British and French philosophers who grew up in a native atmosphere of skeptical good sense. For them not only were sense-objects the downright reality, but man himself with his gift of perceiving them was something of an incident in a vast world of these objects. For Feuerbach "sense" was the main thing in these "objects-of-sense," and man continued to be, as with idealists, the main concern and substance of the world. "The new philosophy," he said, "makes man, including nature as the basis of man, the unique, universal, and highest object of philosophy." Indeed Feuerbach proposed to replace that speculative philosophy which he had rejected, not with the general body of the sciences, as Comte at the same time was proposing, and not with a "philosophy of good sense" as other Materialists had, but with "anthropology," regarded as a "universal science."

"In this undue prominence given to man," says Lange in his *History of Materialism*, "lies a trait which is due to the Hegelian philosophy, and which separates Feuerbach from strict Materialists. That is to say, it is only the philosophy of spirit over again that meets us here in the shape of a philosophy of sensibility. The genuine Materialist will always incline to turn his gaze upon the great whole of external nature, and to regard man as a wave in the ocean of the eternal movement of matter. The nature of man is to the Materialist only a special case of universal physiology, as thought is only a special case in the chain of the physical processes of life." [4]

And this is true, we may add, not only to the materialist, but to the modern scientific mind in general. "Lyric

[4] The Russian Marxist, Plekhanov, not interested in Feuerbach's mind, but concerned only to establish the perfect truth of dialectic materialism, exclaims against this judgment of Lange's. He insists, even against Feuerbach himself, who expressly disclaimed the title of materialist, that his philosophy was perfectly materialistic. "Feuerbach never denied," he cries, "that the nature of man 'is only a special case in the chain of the physical processes of life.'" And that is true—he never denied it. He merely permitted his feelings to forget it—or, as Lange so carefully suggests, "inclined to turn his gaze" in a different direction.

experience and literary psychology, as I have learned to conceive them," says George Santayana, for instance, "are chapters in the life of one race of animals in one corner of the natural world." How far removed Feuerbach was from this natural assumption of a mind nurtured in modern science may be seen in his statement that "Truth is only the totality of human life and being." I do not mean to say that Feuerbach, by and large, denied to nature an existence independent of man. He spoke expressly, elsewhere, of nature's independence. He was a disjointed, emotional, aphoristic thinker, and was moreover not trying to understand the world presented to him by science, but absorbed in the effort to find in it a place for the religious emotion. To isolate a sentence like the one just quoted, and impute to him all that it implies logically, would be unfair and uncomprehending. Nevertheless, it is obvious that the author of that sentence had only partially emerged from the idealistic philosophy. The "undue prominence given to man" in his system was a relic of that personification of the external world, or absorbing of it up into the mind, which is the essential heart of the romantic philosophies preceding him in Germany. He was in this respect, as was German intellectual culture at large, behind the contemporary march of the scientific point of view.

This becomes still more obvious as you read further in his *Foundations of the New Philosophy*, from which I have quoted. You learn that not only is "reality" identical with "sensibility" and "truth" with "the totality of human life and being," but that since nothing enters human life and being, or becomes an object of sensibility, unless it engages a man's interest, unless it makes some appeal to his affective nature, "reality" and "truth" are, at bottom, inseparable from human feeling. "Only that is . . ." exclaims Feuerbach at the height of his argument, "which is an object of passion." And with a little manipulation of the already obscure distinction between subject and object, he contrives to make this read: "Not to love and not to be are identical."

By reasonings of this kind, Feuerbach managed to convert his "universal science" of anthropology into a "religion of love." And although that religion was very large about accepting matters of fact, and Feuerbach's love was not afraid of physiology, nevertheless it retained the essence of all religion, and of all theology too, and of that speculative philosophy which is but "theology rationalized"—namely, the reading of man's interests into the objective reality of the world. One need only approach Feuerbach with his own formula—the speculative philosopher is "a priest in disguise"—in order to perceive that he has merely once more altered the disguise.

Marx's Revolt Against Feuerbach

And now let us see what was the nature of Marx's revolt against Feuerbach. Did he point out the essential relic of Hegel's idealism in Feuerbach's philosophy, the making of "man, including nature as the basis of man, the one universal and highest object of philosophy"? Did he say that it was not really very materialistic to talk about "sensibility," which is a mere function of the human body, as though it were identical with "reality," which to the genuine materialist lies in larger part outside of man? This was the course he must have taken in order to fulfill his wish to abandon philosophy altogether, and adopt the point of view of empirical science. He never dreamed of it. He was not himself sufficiently liberated from the "master wizard." He too, of course, in his mature reflections, would not explicitly identify "sensibility" with the objective reality of the world. But he uncritically followed Feuerbach in talking about them as identical. He based his philosophy of action, just as Feuerbach had based his philosophy of passion, upon a verbal assumption of their identity, repeating it in the very words that Feuerbach used. His single objection to Feuerbach was that he had left out of this "reality," this "object," this all-too-human "sensibility," the "active element," the element of "practical human action." He had left out of it, that is, the very essence of Hegelian metaphysics as Marx loved it—as Royce loved it—the conception that reality itself is a purposive process, and that the highest state a human being can attain, the state of *Wissenschaft*, is one in which he conceives himself as co-operating with, or participating in, the forward and upward going of that reality toward high ends.

"The chief fault of all materialism heretofore (including Feuerbach's)"—so Marx begins—"is that the object, reality, sensibility, is conceived only under the form of object or of *contemplation*: not as *sensory-human* activity, praxis, not subjectively. Hence the *active* side developed abstractly in opposition to materialism from idealism—[abstractly] since idealism naturally does not recognize real sensory activity as such. Feuerbach wants sensible objects genuinely distinguished from objects of thought; but he conceives human activity itself not as objective activity. In his *Essence of Christianity* he regards only the theoretical attitude as the genuinely human, while practice is conceived and fixed in its dirty-Jewish phenomenal form. Hence he does not grasp the significance of the 'revolutionary,' of practical-critical action."

In briefer words: The chief fault of materialism is that the object is not conceived as an active subject!

The Theses on Feuerbach

These "Theses on Feuerbach" have always presented something of a puzzle to the student of Marx, but their meaning becomes utterly clear when you realize that Marx was trying to be purely practical and scientific, and yet not abandon the animistic habits of the German idealist philosophy. He is, for that reason, saying in these theses two different kinds of things. On the one hand, he is saying things with which every skeptical scientific mind can agree. He objects, for instance, to Feuerbach's retaining an exaggerated esteem for purely theoretical thinking after he has abandoned the myth of the reality of pure thought. But, on the other hand, he is preserving the essence of a religious metaphysics, the conception of the objective world and the human mind as co-operating together in whatever tasks are worth while. Although the world is made out of material objects as given in sensation, these object-sensations are nevertheless to be "conceived subjectively"; they are to be regarded, just as Hegel regarded ideas or Reason, as "purposive activities." With Feuerbach, Marx regarded reality as human-sensory; with Hegel, he regarded it as practically active. And so he arrived at "the seed of the new philosophy," the conception that all the seemingly solid and external things in this world really are, and consist of, practical "human-sensory action." In place of Feuerbach's humanitarian philosophy, which teaches love and brotherhood by identifying it with the substance of being, this gives us a revolutionary philosophy which teaches "practical critical action" by identifying that with the substance of being. But we still have philosophy in the full religious sense. We have not taken one step from it.

In his second thesis, Marx takes up the problem of what to do with the idea or "object of thought" now that its superior reality has been abandoned for that of the "object of sense." And here he speaks again like an experimental scientist. Where thought adds something to the reality directly given in sense-experience, the validity of this something is to be tried out in action. The test of its truth, in other words, is experimental.

2. "The question whether objective truth reaches human thought is no question of theory, but a *practical* question. In practice man must prove the truth, that is the reality and power, the this-sidedness, of his thought. The dispute about the reality or unreality of thought—which is isolated from practice—is a purely scholastic question."

In his third thesis, however, Marx again speaks the language of the metaphysician who has read his own program of action into a world conceived as inherently purposive. He is now objecting not to Feuerbach, but to the materialists of the eighteenth century whom three years before he had been praising for their "profane" and "vulgar" materialism, and their insistence that men are a mere product of the environment. "It takes no extraordinary sagacity to discover," he then said, "what inevitably brings them to communism or socialism. . . . If man is formed by the environment, then we must form a humane environment." He now objects to these same profane materialists because they have not the Hegelian wisdom to embody their program in a conception of the environment as *forming itself* humanely.

3. "The materialistic teaching about the changing of the environment and education forgets that the environment

must be changed by men and the educator himself educated. It is therefore compelled to divide society into two parts, of which the one is elevated above the other.

"The coincidence of a change of environment and human activity or self-change can only be conceived and rationally understood as *revolutionary practice*."

In other words, you cannot understand why you should want to improve the world, unless you conceive the world which produced you as in process of self-improvement. Here a scientific mind would ask: But when you have so conceived the world, how do you explain those who don't want to improve it, but are steady on the job of making it worse? Marx had lived too long in Hegel's dialectics to be troubled by that question, or even to have it rise in his mind. Those ignorant miscreants are a negative and disappearing "phase," an essential part of the very "contradiction" which is being "resolved" by your own "revolutionary practice." The whole process is real, and the whole of it is truth, but your part is more real and more true because closer to the consummation of the whole.

There is a genuine problem of knowledge here, the problem of how there can be an objective science of social evolution when scientific ideas are themselves so potent a force in determining that evolution. You might call it the sociologist's fallacy to ignore this problem. But the problem is certainly not solved by this partisan personification of the whole body of the facts. We know quite well, whatever the problems involved, that no man can give a scientific account of any society without standing above it. Nor can such an account of society be applied in an effort to guide its evolution without the problem arising of how to relate those who have this scientific understanding to the blinder forces operating below—of how to relate the socialists, if you will, to the trade-unions. Marx is here merely insisting that sociology shall not cease to be philosophy and become a science.

And in a subsequent thesis, numbered 6, he insists that psychology shall not become a science. Feuerbach talks about the "essence of man," he says, "but the essence of man is not an abstraction dwelling in the separate individual." Which again sounds promising, and sounds like skeptical good sense, until he adds: The essence of man "in its reality is the ensemble of social relations"—which is pure metaphysics. Marx's modern devotees like to pretend that he is here founding social psychology. He is eliminating psychology altogether, eliminating "man" as a problem of study, in order to leave society as the sole essential object, the history of whose "practical activity" will constitute the history of man. He is making ready, in short, for the 8th thesis which reads as follows:

"All social life is essentially *practical*. All the mysteries which lead theory astray into mysticism find their rational solution in human practice and in the idea of this practice."

This Delphic utterance has literally no meaning until you realize that Marx is concerned to defend the concept of society as a single "object, reality, sensibility," having the character which all objects, realities, sensibilities have—namely, that of self-active practicality. Marx will devote his life to proving that this mysteriously unanalyzable object, social life, or society, is destined by the inner law of its being to contradict itself (the class struggle) and resolve the contradiction in a higher unity (the co-operative commonwealth). He thinks that by committing himself to this one mystical belief, and joining in the struggle of this supernaturally practical entity toward its dialectically determined goal, he can avoid all mysteries and be a purely rational and matter-of-fact mind.

It sounds too fantastic to believe, but you must remember that Marx was only "hastily jotting down" his reactions after reading an equally fantastic series of speculations which had "liberated" him. Only when you have thus understood the 8th thesis can you make any sense at all of the 9th and 10th, which read as follows:

9. "The highest point reached by contemplative materialism, that is, the materialism which does not conceive sensibility as practical activity, is the contemplation of separate individuals and bourgeois society."

10. "The standpoint of the old materialism is bourgeois society. The standpoint of the new, human society or social humanity."

What these two statements mean is that a genuine materialist, one who regards the material world as an object independent of the perceiving mind, cannot believe that it might be revolutionized, and cannot refrain from interesting himself in human nature. Only a dialectic, or pseudomaterialist, one who *conceives the object subjectively*, regarding the world and the correct or scientific perceiver of it as engaged in a mutual practical action toward revolutionary aims, can be a convinced revolutionist. Such a revolutionist will not only conceive of sensible objects in general as consisting of a practical process, but he will conceive of "society" as a single sensible object, and as therefore consisting of such a process. He will not be deceived into conceiving the individual man as also an object, or practical process, and thus getting off on schemes of moral improvement. He will understand that the individual, the "ensemble of social relations," will be taken care of incidentally when society is revolutionized.

In short, these two theses merely state succinctly that unless you read your revolutionary program into the movement of the objective facts you cannot believe in or adhere to your program. What other connection can exist between conceiving sensation as a practical activity and believing in a new human society, a social humanity? Is it not a fact that thousands of materialists have believed in a new society and in social humanity, and have adopted its standpoint, who have not had the glimmer of an idea—if indeed six hundred people have had up to this date—what Marx meant by conceiving sensibility as practical action?

The downright fact underlying all these cloudy aphorisms is both clear and brief: Feuerbach "liberated" Marx from Hegel's idealism in so far as to assert that not thought, nor ideas, but "sense experience" is the real world. And all that Marx does—all that he ever did as a philosopher—is to attribute to this world made out of "sense experience" the same "self-active motion," "dialectic" in character and proceeding "from the lower to the higher," which Hegel had attributed to his world made out of thought.

Marx concludes his theses with a brilliant epigram:

"Philosophers have interpreted the world in various ways; the thing is to change it."

In Soviet Russia this soon became the most used slogan in the whole literature of the state philosophy. And no wonder, for it epitomizes the elusive ambiguity that makes that philosophy so useful, the subtle equilibrium of one who abandons philosophy for practical scientific effort and yet preserves in that very act the essence of philosophy. On its face, it seems merely to repeat the antiphilosophical thing that Marx had said in *Die Deutsche Ideologie*:

"For a *practical* materialist, a communist, the thing is to revolutionize the existing world—that is, practically turn against things as he finds them and change them."

It did, no doubt, contain that meaning for Marx, so far as personal feeling went, for as Engels tells us he never returned to the subject of philosophy. But if that were all it meant, why mention the philosophers? Why not say "Poets have sung the world . . . painters have painted the world; the thing is to change it"? Marx in this aphorism is not only saying that we should quit philosophizing and change the world. He is saying that a true philosophy of the world and a resolute program for changing the world will be one and the same thing. And that, as we have seen, is the very soul of Hegel's metaphysics.

Marx, then, was very accurate when he said in the preface to *Capital* that he had merely turned Hegel's philosophy other side up. Hegel had been conceiving thought, or the idea, as the real thing, and the reality of the sense-object as illusory. Marx declared the sense-object to be real, and the idea a mere reflection of it. But he retained in his conception of that sense-object the essential virtue that Hegel had attributed to his Idea, the property of purposive dialectic movement toward high ends. The only radical change was that, whereas Hegel's ideal reality was traveling toward an ideal goal in the being of God, Marx's sensible reality was traveling toward a sensible goal in the organization of the communist society. Marx thought that he had thus saved the "rational kernel" and got rid of the "mystical shell" in the Hegelian philosophy. He even thought, and tried to keep on thinking, that he had achieved his aim to get rid of philosophy altogether and be scientific. But one does not get rid of philosophy by the simple device of turning an idealist philosophy other side up. One does not get rid of philosophy without clearly understanding what he means by philosophy, and how it differs from the scientific point of view.

PART SIX

REVOLUTION AS A SCIENTIFIC ENTERPRISE

1. THE PRACTICAL HYPOTHESIS IN MARXISM

THE MOTION of thought, in its origin and main development, is a motion back and forth and round about among given facts, desired ends, and plans of action for achieving the ends upon the basis of the facts. When thinking becomes very abstract and is cultivated for its own sake, or when an attempt is made to state the nature of certain facts independently of their relation to any specific end, this natural process is considerably changed, and a number of difficult problems about it arise. But these problems do not arise in connection with any thinking, no matter how "theoretical," which is concerned with the concrete practical problems of human life. Such thinking always conforms, whether consciously and with exactitude or not, to the instrumental pattern. The emphasis in any given case may be upon an accurate definition of the factual situation—but even here the end will show its influence in the facts selected and the manner of their formulation. Or the emphasis may be upon a delineation of the end, or ideal—though here still more obviously the existing facts will appear. And if the emphasis is upon a precision of the hypothesis, or plan of action, still the situation must be designated in which it is to be applied, and the end must be defined in order to put it to the test of action. These three elements are all united compactly in perception, and practical thought only separates them tentatively and imperfectly, and for the purpose of uniting them again.

Marxism, liberated from the metaphysical frame in which Marx tried to confine it, can be very easily restated in the form of a practical hypothesis. It was created by combining three intellectual disciplines: that of the classical economists, who had occupied themselves with a definition of the existing mechanism of human society; that of the utopian socialists, who had put their emphasis upon the delineation of an ideal society; and that of the young Hegelians, who were absorbed in the idea of historic process. Marxism as a practical science redefines the existing mechanism of society from the standpoint of the ends proposed by the utopian socialists; it redefines those ends from the standpoint of the facts of economics; and it points out the method of procedure by which it will be possible to take a real step from the existing situation in the direction of the desired ends.

Marx saw, to begin with, that economics does define the essential mechanism of human society. This society is predominantly neither a political nor a "civil" gathering, but a business association; and the major forces which control its operation are economic class-interests. Anyone who wants to change any human society fundamentally must attack its economic structure, and he must work with these economic forces. Approaching with this wisdom the society of our own day, Marx identified two facts of essential importance for those who want to change it in the direction suggested by the utopians—the fact that the production of wealth is becoming more and more co-operative, and the fact that the control of this process is becoming more and more centralized and concentrated in the hands of a small class. He declared that both these tendencies would increase with the further invention of machinery. He concluded that the only practical revolutionary plan for our day is to transfer this centralized control of the co-operative process of production into the hands of the producers collectively organized. And he saw that the only force capable of accomplishing this change is the revolutionary self-interest of the producers themselves, the wageworking class. The Marxian method is to accentuate the class struggle between workers and capitalists, organize it both nationally and internationally, and carry it forward, undeceived by political forms and ideologies, and in full consciousness of the ruthlessness of the forces in play, to the goal of a revolutionary dictatorship of the proletariat. Such a dictatorship could actually expropriate the owners of the land and the instruments of labor, and reduce them to the position of equal participators in the social process of production. That fundamental step having been taken, human society would begin to move, Marx thought, in the direction of freedom, and political sincerity, and international peace, and an opportunity of life for every member of it. . . . That is what the Marxian doctrine is, in outline, as a concrete scientific hypothesis, and not an abstract philosophy of the universe.

2. THE ANARCHIST CONTRIBUTION

WHEN STATED as a scientific plan of action, the Marxian doctrine bears substantially the same relation to the efforts of utopian-evangelical reformers that chemistry does to the efforts of alchemists. It examines the structure of human society and determines the forces which control it, and upon the basis of those given facts which are not changeable, it proposes a method by which human society can be changed. Revolutionary anarchism, on the contrary, clings to the attitude of the alchemists and the utopians. It merely adds the mystic act of insurrection against government to the spells of reasonable eloquence that were supposed to "call up" the ideal society. The relation of anarchists to a real science of revolution is the same as that of amateur "healers," the survivors of magic, to the science of medicine. They survive by refusing to acknowledge, or concentrate their attention upon, the unchangeable or uncontrollable elements in the given facts, to formulate these elements in "laws," and thus arrive at a systematic procedure by which the given facts can be actually and not only imaginatively changed or controlled. The procedure of the revolutionary anarchist, generally speaking, is to dwell upon the idea of a true society, and assist at moments of crisis in destroying the existing order, in the faith that this idea will be realized. That this is not the procedure of practical science is obvious, and it could be explained very simply and convincingly by Marxists, if they were themselves scientific.

But since the practical hypothesis in Marxism was misborn and crippled to fit the forms of a metaphysical religion, its relation to anarchism is by no means so simple. There are certain respects in which Marxism is the less scientific of the two. It is less scientific in its attitude toward the goal of revolutionary effort. Just as the anarchists, in their preoccupation with the goal, fail to consider the facts and the method of procedure, so the Marxists, in their apotheosis of the facts and the method, fail to consider the goal. It was possible for Marx, under the guise of a "philosophy of history," to define the relevant facts; and in the dress of "historic necessity" it was possible to present a plan of action. But Marx's religion offered no device by which he could adequately investigate the third problem essential to a scientific procedure, the problem of the possibility and appropriateness of the ideal, or objective end, of the undertaking. Instead of examining and redefining this ideal in the light of his definition of the facts, Marx merely ceased to talk about it. His dialectic religion assured him that the "contradictions" in capitalism must inevitably be "resolved" by an expropriation of the capitalists and a collective ownership of the means of production. It also declared that the state, which had arisen out of these contradictions, would "die away" after they were resolved. This was sufficient for a preliminary definition of his purpose—a determination of the general direction of activities at least up to the conquest of power. And any remaining questions Marx answered by tacking on to these two conceptions, in a very undialectic and irresponsible manner, the most utopian of all the formulas for the millennium: "From each according to his abilities, to each according to his needs." That is the extent of the Marxian science, so far as concerns drawing up a prospectus, or ground plan, of the thing to be achieved.

It was quite inevitable that Marx, imagining his own plan of action to be a description of what history was about to do, should thus leave to history the lion's share of the worry about the end to be arrived at. And it was inevitable that his followers, imagining Marx's metaphysical personification of history to be a materialistic science, should resist as "unscientific" every impulse of simple and sensible-minded people to make some inquiries about it.

"What is the value henceforth," says Plekhanov, "of those more or less laborious and more or less ingenious researches as to the best possible form of social organization? None, literally none! They can only testify to the lack of scientific instruction of those who enter upon them. Their day is past forever."

If Plekhanov had been a practical man, he could not have failed to see that if there is no need of defining the goal of your efforts, there is no need of guiding them. If the economic God is taking care of the remote future, must He not take care of tomorrow? And if not, then at what point in the unbroken flow of events does your jurisdiction end, and that of the economic God begin? A practical engineer could not fail to ask this question, for the simple reason that until it was answered he could not complete his plans—which reveals again the incompatibility of all philosophies of absolute determinism with all practical science.

The fact is that a definition of the goal of the socialist effort, while it must remain, during the early stages of the undertaking, abstract and free and subject to radical redefinition, is nevertheless indispensable to scientific procedure. Without investigating at least the abstract possibility of the society aimed at, its compatibility with the hereditary instincts of man, and thus the probability of its enduring if it were once established, no maturely scientific person would devote himself to the effort. The utopian socialists had begun such an investigation, and in abandoning it Marxism took a step backward from utopian socialism. The anarchists have continued this investigation, and that constitutes their chief contribution to the science of revolution.

"The question put by anarchism," says Kropotkin, "might be expressed in the following way: 'Which social forms best guarantee in such and such societies, and in humanity at large, the greatest sum of happiness and therefore the greatest sum of vitality?' 'Which forms of society are most likely to allow this sum of happiness to increase and develop in quantity and quality—that is to say, will enable this happiness to become more complete and more varied?' "

Kropotkin brought a vast body of biological and historical data to bear upon this important, and, in a proper scientific procedure, preliminary, question. His book *Mutual Aid* opens a question of the highest importance. He neglected, or refused to see, the relevance to his problem of the data supplied by Marx in his study of modern capitalism. And, like all modern revolutionary writers, he ignored the contributions of psychology. For these reasons his writings are inadequate; but they remain, both in their attitude and their information upon the question of the goal of revolutionary effort, a long stride in advance of Marxism.

Another matter in which the anarchists are in advance of the Marxists is their conscious renunciation of metaphysics, their unfulfilled but real aspiration toward a practical scientific attitude. Bakunin's early protest against the "everlasting theoretical insanity" of Karl Marx, runs through all the great anarchist literature, and it is essentially wise and just. It is the protest of all simple minds, with a healthy love for clarity and directness, against tangling up the real act of revolution in the unreal and awful ponderosities of German metaphysics.

Bakunin himself did not entirely escape from that theoretical insanity which he despised; he wrote his share of Hegelian higher nonsense. And Proudhon, the other founder of modern anarchism, was only saved from it by his ignorance. Nevertheless, they both represent, in their conflict with Marx, the tendency toward a more direct and natural and practical employment of the mind. Marx's famous attack upon the philosophic pretenses of Proudhon is a pitiless exposure of the philosophic infirmities of Marx.

"Let us see now," he says, "the modification to which Herr Proudhon subjects the dialectic of Hegel in applying it to political economy. For Herr Proudhon, every economic category has two sides, a good and a bad. . . .

"The *good side* and the *bad side*, the *advantage* and the *disadvantage* taken together, constitute for Herr Proudhon the *contradiction* in each economic category.

"The problem to solve: to conserve the good side, and eliminate the bad. . . .

"Hegel has no problems to put. He knows only the dialectic. Herr Proudhon has of the Hegelian dialectic nothing but the phraseology. His own dialectic method consists in the dogmatic distinction of good and evil.

"Let us for an instant take Herr Proudhon himself as a category. Let us examine his good and his bad side, his advantages and his disadvantages. . . ."

Marx is amusing in this polemic, and he successfully convicts Herr Proudhon of bombastic pretentiousness and a complete ignorance of philosophy. But ignorance of philosophy is sometimes a kind of wisdom. And it is certain that in the above passage Proudhon's naïveté is both wiser and more scientific than Marx's sophistication. Marx gave his life to an attempt to solve the problem of how "to preserve the good side while eliminating the bad side" of modern capitalism. That is the simple fact. And a person who understands psychological facts can only smile at the sophomoric assurance with which Marx asserts what he had learned at school to the contrary. Marx was not defending science here against the sentimentality of Herr Proudhon. He was defending a metaphysical rationalization of his motives against that simple recognition and definition of them, which might have been the foundation of a scientific discipline.

Thus, Proudhon's ignorance played the same part as Bakunin's impatience. It gave to anarchism a tendency away from metaphysics, and made it seem more practical and more convincing to many clear and scientific minds than Marxism. And Peter Kropotkin, himself a man of science, raised this wise tendency in his predecessors to a conscious article of faith. He rejected both the academic and the Marxian economics on the ground that they were deductive and metaphysical and ignorant of the methods of applied science.

"It is possible," he said, "that we are wrong, and they [the Marxists] are right. But the question which of us is right, and which wrong, cannot be settled by means of Byzantine commentaries as to what such and such a writer intended to say, or by talking about what agrees with the 'trilogy' of Hegel; most certainly not by continuing to use the dialectic method.

"It can be done only by studying the facts of economics in the same way and by the same methods as we study the natural sciences. . . .

"There is one point upon which without doubt anarchism is absolutely in the right. It is when it . . . parts forever with metaphysics."

In spite of this admirable and unanswerable declaration, Kropotkin did not employ the methods of applied science upon the problem of producing an anarchist-communist society. Having investigated the question, *What social forms would guarantee to humanity the greatest sum of happiness and vitality?* he did not turn round and examine the existing social forms with a view to answering the question, *What social procedure will actually move us from the one situation in the direction of the other?* Having asked, and to the best of his ability answered, the preliminary question, he abandoned the methods of applied science altogether, and adopted in its place two contrary attitudes, between which he shifted back and forth in a way that serves only the purposes of intellectual confusion.

One of his attitudes was an ineffectual pretense at "pure" science. That is to say, he objectively predicted the anarchist-communist society on the basis of "tendencies" which he professed to discover in biology and human history. It is needless to say that, in proving the predominance of these "tendencies," he did not employ those methods of accurate definition and real verification which he advocated so eloquently in his attack upon Marxism. Kropotkin's assertion on "inductive" grounds of the inevitability of the communist society has no more scientific validity than the Marxian assertion of the same thing on the ground of Hegelian Logic.

His other attitude was in the broad sense "practical,"

but it was no less utopian than that of his predecessors. It consisted of advocating evangelical miracles, and relying upon a magic supposed to reside in the mere act of revolution, to accomplish the transformation which he desired.

"For the triumph of the revolution, men must first get rid of their faith in Law, Authority, Unity, Order, Property, and other institutions inherited from past times when our forefathers were slaves.

"Without such [insurrectionary] risings, the social mind was never able to get rid of its deep-rooted prejudices. . . .

"The lessons of history tell us that a new form of economic life always calls forth a new form of political organization. . . . Consequently the chief aim of anarchism is to awaken those constructive powers of the laboring masses of the people which at all great moments of history come forward to accomplish the necessary changes. . . ."

These quotations are sufficient to show that Kropotkin did not succeed, any more than the other anarchists, in substituting the methods of applied science for Marx's metaphysical approach to the social problem. The method of revolutionary anarchism, speaking broadly and yet with technical accuracy, is to conjure up the communist society by the magical act of revolution.

3. THE SYNDICALIST EMPHASIS

REVOLUTIONARY SYNDICALISM contributed to the attempt to define an ideal society a conception of the dominating role which might be played by the labor unions—a conception which will certainly not be passed over by a mature social science. It also contributed to revolutionary method a sense of the danger involved in political activities, the necessity of unusual honesty in leaders, and the necessity of emphasizing the class character of the movement. But syndicalism did not escape from the utopian mode of thought of the anarchists to whom it owes its origin. Like them, it solved the problem presented by the enormous complexity and inevitable centralization of modern production by refusing to face it—by "believing in" decentralization. It solved the problem of the existing state by wishing it away. It solved the problem of the future state by attributing to the labor unions some mysterious property which will enable them to rule without being a government. And to the idea of a General Strike it attributed occult powers of an altogether unimagined potency. The General Strike, according to some of the syndicalist writers, will not only conjure away the existing state, and the centralization of modern industry, and transfer the direction of society to the individual labor unions, but it will regenerate man in a moral sense, and fill him with a permanent enthusiasm like that possessed by the soldiers of the French

Revolution. It is impossible not to see in this total want of proportion between cause and effect a survival of the conjuror's faith in a ritual performance.

Revolutionary syndicalism made utopian thinking seem more plausible to practical minds by associating it with references to actually existing working-class organizations, and by emphasizing the principal action which these organizations will naturally take in a revolutionary crisis. But as a practical method for revolutionizing society, it did not take one solid step away from that belief in magic which characterizes the attitude of the anarchists.[1]

On the other hand, the syndicalists took a great step backward from the anarchist position by producing a metaphysician and adding to their utopian beginnings of science all the essential faults of animistic thinking. In the writings of George Sorel, every point in which anarchism was genuinely in advance of Marxism is explicitly relinquished. The sane determination of the anarchists to discuss the possibility of a more ideal society, and the form which it ought to take, is renounced in favor of a mystic abandonment to the élan of the present moment.

"One must not hope," says Sorel, "that the revolutionary movement can ever follow a direction conveniently determined in advance, that it can be conducted according to a learned plan like the conquest of a country, that it can be

---

[1] The Industrial Workers of the World have a more businesslike way of talking than some of the European syndicalists, but the motto which they substitute for the Marxian plan of political dictatorship—"Build the new society within the shell of the old"—shows a similar disregard of the practical terms of the problem. It shows the same reliance upon magical transformations—reliance, indeed, upon a metaphor—to solve the essential problem of the transference of power.

studied scientifically otherwise than in its present. Everything in it is unpredictable."

The determination of the anarchists to be simple and intelligible, to have done with learned obscurities and the solemn casuistries of the "short-coated priests" of philosophy, is likewise abandoned by Sorel. For him, the inextricable tangle of animism and science which makes Marxism fundamentally unintelligible to clear-minded people who are honest enough to say so, is the primary virtue of Marxism.

"Socialism is necessarily a very obscure matter," he tells us, "since it treats of production, that is to say of that which is most mysterious in human activity, and since it proposes to bring a radical transformation into this region which it is impossible to describe with the clarity which one finds in superficial regions of the world. No effort of thought, no progress of knowledge, no reasonable induction can ever dispel the mystery which envelops socialism; and it is because Marxism has well recognized this character that it has won the right to serve as the point of departure for socialist studies."

The manner in which Sorel managed to introduce into an anarchist movement all the essential faults of Marxism was comparatively simple. The anarchists had got rid of Hegel; they had freed their minds of the father-fixation upon a conservative professor of religious and patriotic metaphysics. Sorel could not go back to Hegel; that would have been obviously reactionary. But he discovered in his own times another conservative professor of patriotism and religious metaphysics, Henri Bergson. He attached the anarchosyndicalist proposal to the animism of this new philosopher, and thus gave a progressive appearance to the longest backward step yet taken by any revolutionary theorist.

In place of the dialectic evolution of a determined universe in the direction of our heart's desire, Sorel gives us the "creative evolution" of a free universe in the same general direction. In place of the historic necessity of the social revolution, he gives us the *indispensability to evolution* of the social myth of the revolution. In place of the worship of dialectic, the scorn of "scientism." In place of the Hegelian-Marxian higher logic, in which "the life-process of the material receives its mental reflection," he gives us the Bergsonian vital intuition, another superior kind of intelligence in which "reason, hopes, and the perception of the particular facts seem to make but one indivisible unity." In short, he gets his own purpose transplanted into the facts, and substitutes emotional co-operation with the objective world, for the attempt to make something out of it. To preserve this religious attitude, in spite of the advance of science, is the dominating motive of Bergson's philosophy, just as it was the dominating motive of Hegel's. That is why Sorel could substitute Bergson for Hegel and yet arrive at a position not radically contrasted with metaphysical Marxism.

It is highly desirable to reconcile anarchosyndicalism with Marxism—or rather to reconcile anarchists and syndicalists to the practical hypothesis that is concealed in Marxism. But it will not be accomplished by abandoning all the virtues of anarchism and embracing all the faults of Marxism. It will be accomplished by recognizing that each has overemphasized one part of a complete act of practical intelligence to the neglect of the other part. The anarchists have neglected to define the unalterable element in the facts, and formulate a method of procedure compatible with its continued existence. The Marxists have neglected to define the ideal and bring it into working relation with their definition of fact and their method of procedure. The fault in Marxism is less serious, at least in the early stages of the undertaking, because the general direction of revolutionary effort, the outline of its ideal, is commonly agreed upon and can be taken for granted. Moreover, in recognizing and resolutely facing an unalterable element in the facts, Marxism took that one step on the road to scientific method which is the most difficult for idealistic minds to take. And under cover of its legend of dialectic thinking, Marxism unconsciously anticipated a more advanced conception of intelligence, and a more scientific employment of it, than was known to those anarchists who attacked this legend in the name of science. For these reasons, in spite of its surreptitious preservation of the animistic attitude, Marxism and not anarchism laid the foundation for that practical system of revolutionary engineering developed by Lenin.

4. THE BOLSHEVIK HERESY

NOTE

I have to warn the reader that the following chapters were written while I still believed in that system of revolutionary engineering perfected by Lenin. I believed it to be effective, not only for the seizure of power and establishment of a proletarian dictatorship, but for the development of such a dictatorship into a free and equal society. I still had hopes of that society in Russia. The direct result of Lenin's experiment, the totalitarian state of Stalin, and its by-products, fascism and Nazism, have convinced me to the contrary. The reader will find this change of opinion described in the foreword to my recent book, Stalin's Russia and the Crisis in Socialism. I have made, in view of it, certain alterations and omissions in these chapters, but I could not remove altogether the traces of the state of mind in which they were composed. They contain, I think, an exposition and partial criticism of Lenin's system that is still valid. And they still serve to show what I mean by substituting a scientific revolutionary attitude for the metaphysical socialism of Karl Marx. The reader will only have to bear in mind that, in view of the devastating results of the actual experiment, I have very much deepened my criticism of the Bolshevik procedure. I now consider it the most urgent virtue of a scientific attitude that it enables us, without relinquishing the general aim of a more free and equal society, or the hardheaded realism of the Marxian Lenin, to abandon altogether the conception of the role of the party and its relation to the masses, which he introduced. Lenin's faith in the dialectic philosophy was more vital to his thinking, and more disastrous, than I realized.

IF YOU wanted to build a bridge across a stream, it would be absurd to make your calculations upon the assumption that the properties of steel and iron are such that they are going across the stream, and that you are lending consciousness to the process. It would not require a book to demonstrate that this was a relic of animism. In creating a dictatorship of the proletariat, as a bridge toward a real human society, the absurdity of this way of calculating is less obvious, but equally great. The only difference here is that the material you work with is moving, and it is human, and you are a part of it. This does not alter the nature of thought and purposive action, or justify you in regarding yourself as a reflecting apparatus instead of an engineer. It merely gives rise to a large and altogether peculiar set of engineering problems. And it was exactly these problems which Lenin solved, and whose solution created the "Bolshevik" departure in Marxism. Lenin's fundamental contribution to the Marxian idea was a determination of the way in which engineers who use it must relate themselves to the moving human material of which they are a part.

Bolshevism, like so many other things, can best be understood by studying it at the point of origin. It was born in Lenin's attack upon a school of compromising Marxists who called themselves "Economists." Their idea was that the Marxian intellectuals in Russia ought not to alienate the workers by stressing the political aspect of the revolution, the necessity of overthrowing the czar's government, but ought simply to enter into the economic struggle with the bosses, leaving these political changes to follow in the natural course of events. They ought to subordinate themselves to the spontaneous, or as they called it "elemental," movement of the workers. Lenin destroyed this humble-casuistical tendency completely in his journal *Iskra* and his book *What to Do?* He put in its place the idea of an "organization of professional revolutionists," who, while welding themselves into a dynamic identity with the elemental movement of the workers, should nevertheless retain their own organizational identity, and their own intellectual identity—their unqualified and undissembled loyalty to the whole program of political and economic revolution. He maintained that such an organization was not only advisable, but indispensable to victory. "I assert," he said, "that no revolutionary movement can be durable without a solid organization of leaders capable of maintaining their succession."

In his further development and the development of his party, Lenin ceased to employ the concept of "professional revolutionist." It was a peculiarly Russian concept—the essential fruit, indeed, of that consecrated movement of revolt which had preceded Bolshevism in Russia. And Lenin apparently knew that it was Russian. He knew that it was out of accord with the Marxian manner of thinking as it had developed in western Europe. He always resisted the proposal to translate into other languages the book in which he had laid down the foundations of Bolshevism. But he never yielded to those in Russia who accused him of having exaggerated in that book the role of these professional revolutionists. He replied that their role *had been* indispensable, and he explained the disappearance of this concept from his writings of a later date by saying that the "professional revolutionist has done his work in the history of Russian proletarian socialism." He has succeeded, that is, in welding himself into a dynamic unity with the elemental struggle of the workers, so that the organization ultimately formed can be treated as a single unit, the "vanguard" of the revolutionary proletariat. By an adroit use of this word "vanguard," Lenin reconciled his language in later years with that of western European Marxism. But I believe no Bolshevik would deny that the professional revolutionist continued, during the growth and triumph of Lenin's party, to play the same indispensable role that was ascribed to him at its foundation. In the official *History of the Russian Communist Party*, published during Lenin's life, we read:

"If you inquire, from the standpoint of the personal staff of leaders, what our party lives by at the present time, and even our state, it will become clear that to a significant degree even now after twenty years the party, so to speak, nourishes itself upon that group of professional revolutionists, the foundations of which were laid at the beginning of the century."

The concept of professional revolutionist belongs, then, not only to the origin, but to the essence of Bolshevism. And if you will reflect how directly a person's class depends upon his profession, you will see that to make revolution itself a profession was a very real departure in a philosophy which regards revolution as an automatic outcome of the struggle of classes. To declare that the people of that profession are indispensable to the victory of the working class has the appearance of heresy. And this appearance becomes more pronounced when you learn that, in describing his professional revolutionists, Lenin repeatedly declared that "it makes no difference" whether they belong to the working class or not.

"The organization of revolutionists," he said, "ought to embrace first of all and chiefly people whose profession consists of revolutionary activity. . . . And before this general title of member of the organization, all distinction between workers and intelligentsia should be obliterated, to say nothing of distinctions between this and that separate profession."

Thus Lenin founded his Bolshevik organization upon a recognition of the *indispensable* historic function of a group of people who were not defined according to the economic class to which they belonged, but were defined according to their purposive activity and their state of mind. They were people committed and consecrated to a certain social purpose—but with this difference, from the "Narodniki," that they possessed the Marxian science and the Marxian technique for the achievement of that purpose. In short, they were revolutionary engineers.

Lenin was accused by other Marxists of "Jacobinism" and "Blanquism" on the ground of this heresy, and I think the accusation should have been accepted. Lenin was amazingly contented, or rather determined, to attribute all of his wisdom to Karl Marx. It seemed to fulfill some need of his emotional nature to do so. But a mature history of his policies would neglect neither his own contributions nor those of the great French revolutionists. Lenin corrected the error of Marx, which was a mystic faith in the proletariat as such; and he corrected the error of Blanqui, which was to trust all to the organization of revolutionists. He saw that the organization of revolutionists must be actually rooted in, and welded together with, the proletariat by a whole series of personal and organizational bonds, so that they not only assume to represent the proletariat, but also, when a revolutionary period arrives, actually do represent it. But he saw also that they must be a distinct body of men who "stand above society," and are thus able to understand it. And his arrant insistence upon centralized authority and military discipline in that body of men smacks more of the tactics of Blanqui than of the philosophy of Marx.

Moreover, in discussing the part to be played by this organization of revolutionists, Lenin contradicted the Marxian metaphysics and abandoned it absolutely. He abandoned all the confused ideological dodges of the priest of economic metaphysics, who is "bringing to the working class a consciousness of its destiny," and adopted the attitude of a practical artisan who is doing work, and doing it scientifically, and not seriously deceiving himself either about the historic destiny of his material or the essentially decorative function of his own brain and volition. It is not easy to find a formula that will flatly and absolutely contradict an animistic construction as subtle as that invented by Hegel and stood on its head by Marx, but in this book *What to Do?* Lenin succeeded in finding one. He denied both its assertion that the material elements of the world are automatically evolving toward socialism, and its assertion that the thoughts of socialists are a mere reflection of the process.

"The elemental development of the workers' movement," he said, "goes straight toward subjection to the bourgeois ideology . . . for the elemental workers' movement is trade-unionism . . . and trade-unionism means just exactly the intellectual enslavement of the workers by the bourgeoisie. For that reason our task, the task of the social-democracy consists in a *struggle with elementalness*, it consists in dragging the workers' movement away from its instinctive trade-union aspiration under the wing of the bourgeoisie, and attracting it under the wing of the social-democracy. The statement of the Economists, that no efforts even of the most inspired ideologists can distract the workers' movement from the path determined by the interaction of the material forces with the material means of production is equivalent to a renunciation of socialism. . . .

"There cannot develop among the workers a consciousness of the irreconcilable opposition of their interests to the whole contemporary political and social structure—that is, a socialist consciousness. . . . That can only be brought in from the outside. The history of all countries testifies that all by itself the working class is able to develop only a trade-union consciousness—a conviction of the necessity of combining in unions to carry on the struggle with the bosses, to extract from the Government this or that law indispensable to the workers, etc. . . . The science of socialism grew out of those philosophical, historical, and economic theories, which were developed by cultivated representatives of the possessing class. . . . This does not mean, of course, that working-men do not participate in the working out of those theories. But they participate not in the capacity of working-men, but in the capacity of socialist theorists . . . participate, in short, only when and in so far as they have succeeded to a greater or less extent in mastering the science of their age and advancing it. . . .

"Without a revolutionary theory there can be no revolutionary movement. . . . The Economists accuse *Iskra* of 'setting its program over against the workers' movement like a spirit soaring above formless chaos.' In what consists the role of the social-democracy, if not in being the 'spirit,' not only soaring above the elemental movement, but raising the latter up to its program? It certainly does not consist in dragging oneself along in the tail of the movement. . . . One must indeed confess that people, firmly determined always to follow a movement in the capacity of the tail, are once and for all absolutely guaranteed against 'minimizing the elemental factor'. . . ."

It is obvious that this is not Hegelian Marxism. This is a series of explicit and violent denials of the whole thing. For the substance of Hegelian Marxism is the assertion that the proletariat *as such*, by virtue of a dialectic necessity inherent in its elemental and material nature, is bound to fight the bourgeoisie and achieve the revolution, and that ideas and theories in the minds of socialists can be nothing but a reflection of the process. This fact was pointed out in the Party Congress of 1903 by one of the "Economists," Martinov, who arrayed against Lenin a whole series of contrary quotations from Marx and Engels, and from socialist programs of other countries. But Lenin had then the support of Plekhanov. He had the majority of the Congress. He dismissed Martinov's theoretical attack with the remark that "the Economists had bent the stick in one direction, and in order to straighten the stick it was necessary to bend it in the other." This was no answer at all, for there was no element of degree in Lenin's heresy. He had given to his superclass professional revolutionists, defined and identified by their purposive ideas and idealistic activities, an indispensable dynamic function in the historic process whch Marx's Hegelian philosophy absolutely denies to them.

Plekhanov was aware of this fact, and he said so as soon as he had decided to abandon Lenin politically. He said that he had told Lenin his book was theoretically wrong when he saw it in manuscript. He said that he had "never regarded Lenin as an able theorist, and always considered him organically incapable of dialectic thinking." He said that Lenin's popularity was due to a "departure from Marxism which made his ideas accessible to those 'practicals' who are unprepared to understand Marxism." He proved this with a quotation from Marx:

"It is not a question of what goal this or that proletarian sets himself at a given time, or even the whole proletariat. It is a question of what the class is in itself, and of what, in view of this its being, it is historically bound to accomplish."

He reminded his readers that, according to the philosophy of historic materialism, "Economic necessity gives birth to and carries to its logical end—that is, to the social revolution—that movement of the working class of which scientific socialism serves as a theoretic expression." And he excommunicated Lenin from the true church of this philosophy in these words:

"The disputed question consists in this: Does there exist an economic necessity which calls forth in the proletariat a demand for socialism, makes it instinctively socialistic, and impels it—even if left to its own resources—on the road to social revolution, notwithstanding the stubborn and continual effort of the bourgeoisie to subject it to its own ideological influence? Lenin denies this, in face of the clearly expressed opinions of all the theorists of scientific socialism. And in that consists his enormous mistake, his theoretical fall into sin."

In order to appreciate the authority of this excommunication, you must know that Lenin himself has described Plekhanov's philosophical writings as "the best in the whole international literature of Marxism." Nevertheless, Lenin never answered Plekhanov's attack. He said four years later that it "had the obvious character of empty cavil, founded on phrases torn from their connections, and upon separate phrases not entirely happy, or not accurately formulated by me, ignoring at the same time the general content and whole spirit of the book." But this also was no answer. The general spirit of the book is exactly what is heretical, and what makes it a turning point in the history of Marxism. From the first page to the last, it is the practical social mechanics of Marxism, with the metaphysics stamped under foot and ignored. Lenin's statement about the bourgeois character of the elemental movement of labor may or may not be true; it is a statement that could not be proven. But a person thinking according to the metaphysical system of Karl Marx could not possibly conceive it as true. No matter what the passing situation may be, a dialectic materialist is bound to conceive the revolution as automatically produced by the contradictions in capitalism, and the Marxian leader as "bringing consciousness" to the process, or "serving as its theoretical expression." At the most, he may permit this Marxian leader to accidentally accelerate the movement. There is not a word in Lenin's book which is even a concession to this metaphysical ideology. The book tells you "what to do," if you want to produce with the material at hand a socialist revolution. It is a textbook of practical engineering on the basis of the Marxian analysis of history. Lenin was indeed "organically incapable of dialectic thinking," in so far as dialectic thinking means attributing your own purposes to the external world. He was a practical thinker to the depth of his mind, an engineer and not a "midwife" of revolution.

5. LENIN AS AN ENGINEER OF REVOLUTION

LENIN HAD no sooner formed his party round a nucleus of "professional revolutionists"—defined and selected according to the purposive ideas in their minds—than he proceeded to split it upon the question whether people of a certain type should be allowed to consider themselves members. And these people again were not defined according to their economic class. They were defined according to their attitude to these purposive ideas. They were the people who talk revolution, and like to think about it, but do not mean business. They were the "soft" as opposed to the "hard," the "reasoners" as opposed to the "fighters," the "talkers" as opposed to the "workers." Lenin proposed to eliminate them by demanding that every party member should work under the orders of the conspirative organization, accepting the full risk and discipline involved. Martov proposed a "more elastic" definition of a party member. Upon this issue the party split into "Bolsheviks" and "Mensheviks." Thus, the very meaning of these words "Bolshevik" and "Menshevik" is to be found in that sharp psychological distinction made by Lenin at the beginning of his career.

"Better that ten workers should not call themselves members of the party (real workers are not so eager for position) than that one talker should have the right and the opportunity to be a party member. There is the principle which seems to me irrefutable, and which compels me to fight against Martov."

Lenin subsequently fought these Mensheviks upon a great variety of questions, and he attempted to define them in ways more in accord with the economic metaphysics. But the one element in their position as he conceived it which never changed, and which alone makes it possible to define his conception, is this psychological one: they were always seeking a formula which would enable them to talk revolution without incurring the danger of realizing it.

Thus, Lenin's first innovation was to recognize the indispensable function of the man of ideas, his second innovation was to divide men of ideas into two camps, and expel without mercy those in whom ideas do not mean action. It is plain, then, that Lenin did not regard revolutionary ideas as a mere reflection of the evolution of the forces of production. A talker is just as good a reflecting apparatus as a worker. Indeed, the very use of the word "work," in order to make this all-important distinction, is a denial of the philosophy according to which revolution is an automatic product of nature's development. For work, according to the definition of Marx himself, is "a process between man and nature, in which man through his own act adjusts, regulates and controls his material intercourse with nature. He opposes himself to nature as one of her own forces. . . ." A Bolshevik, then, according to the distinction originally made by Lenin, is a man of Marxian ideas who opposes himself to nature with a view to regulation and control; a Menshevik a man of Marxian ideas who is willing to let nature regulate and control him, so long as he is allowed to express and cherish these ideas.

In forming his revolutionary party, Lenin identified and excluded another type of revolutionist whose attitude he described as the "Infantile Disease of Leftism." This distinction was also fundamentally a psychological one, as the name implies. But, unlike the distinction between Menshevik and Bolshevik, it was originally formulated by Lenin in terms of economic class, and only received this more concrete definition in later years. At the time when Lenin formed his party, practically all the Infantile Leftists in Russia were opposed to Marxism itself. They found their natural place in the terrorist wing of the Narodniki, and the Narodniki denied, along with the entire Marxian system, the importance of the industrial proletariat. They believed in "the people"; and the people, numerically speaking, were quite obviously the small peasant proprietors. For this reason, it was possible at that time to identify and define the Infantile Leftist in orthodox Marxian fashion as a "petty bourgeois revolutionist." Later on, when this same psychological phenomenon appeared in Lenin's own proletarian party, the economic designation gave place more and more to the psychological. The name "revolutionists of the phrase" became a very important one with Lenin. And in 1908 a whole group was expelled from his party for the merely tactical crime of refusing to sit in a bourgeois parliament. They were described at that time as "Leftists." And in 1920, when as a result of the successful revolution in Russia this same phenomenon made its appearance throughout the whole Bolshevik International, Lenin wrote his famous pamphlet defining it as "The Infantile Disease of Leftism," and denouncing it almost exclusively in psychological terms.

I say "almost exclusively," because Lenin began his

pamphlet with a recollection of the origin of the distinction in Russia, and an orthodox Marxian definition of it.

"It is not sufficiently known abroad," he wrote, "that Bolshevism grew up, formed and hardened itself in long years of struggle against *petty bourgeois revolutionism*, which resembles or borrows something from anarchism. . . . For Marxians it is well established theoretically . . . that the small owner . . . who under capitalism is constantly oppressed and suffering, and whose conditions of life often take a sharp and rapid turn for the worse, moves easily when faced with ruin to extreme revolutionism, but is incapable of displaying consistency, organization, discipline and firmness. The petty bourgeois 'gone mad' from the horrors of capitalism is a social phenomenon which, like anarchism, is characteristic of all capitalist countries. The weakness of such revolutionism, its futility, its liability suddenly to transform itself into obedience, apathy, phantasy, and even into a 'mad' infatuation with some bourgeois 'fashionable' tendency—all this is a matter of common knowledge."

Thus Lenin states at the beginning of his pamphlet the orthodox Marxian philosophy of Leftism. Then he departs from that philosophy, which he describes as "an abstract theoretical recognition of the truth," into the concrete psychological investigation and definition of what Leftism in a proletarian party really is, and he never comes back to the orthodox position at all. From that point on to the last word in the last sentence—"childishness"—his pamphlet is a demonstration, not that Leftism is petty bourgeois, but that Leftism is *infantile*.

He shows these Leftists that, while they may be emotionally sincere, they are intellectually immature. They do not know how to think practically. He describes them at various points as "abstract," "sectarian," as substituting "purity of principle" for practicality of tactics, as following a "tactic of mere negation," of "opposition on principle," satisfying themselves with "mere words," with "revolutionary moods and dispositions." He demonstrates the impracticality of their characteristic policies, *no compromise, down with leaders, abstention from bourgeois parliaments and reactionary trade-unions, individual terrorism, illegality-for-its-own-sake,* and the like. In short he explains to them, not as a representative of the proletariat talking to representatives of the petty bourgeoisie, but as a teacher talking to his pupils, what practical thinking is, and how to do it. The real definition of Infantile Leftism, as it is implied throughout the body of Lenin's pamphlet, seems to me to be this: It is an attitude of immature revolutionary minds, who judge ideas and policies as an expression of the revolutionary motive and emotion rather than as a means of achieving the revolution.

After Leftism has been defined in this way, the inference is obvious that it will appear *more often* and more characteristically among small owners "faced with ruin" and temporarily "driven mad" by the horrors of capitalism than among proletarians systematically exploited by capitalism. To proletarians the very problem of everyday existence takes the form of a class struggle which is potentially revolutionary. And toward the problem of daily existence all healthy minds are practical, and they are capable of displaying "consistency, organization, discipline. . . ." I believe that anyone who reads Lenin's pamphlet without metaphysical predispositions will concede that such a statement of the relation between Leftism and the economic classes is more true to his mental attitude—as it is certainly more true to the facts—than the orthodox Marxian statement.

After the formation of his organization, the next distinctive feature of Lenin's policy was the manner in which he determined its relation to the working class. And the essence of his policy here, as it seems to me, was that instead of attempting to enlighten or "convert" the working class as a whole to socialism, permitting socialism to lose in this process a certain amount of its scientific clarity and revolutionary extremism, he stressed the necessity of staying with the working class personally no matter how far they wandered from the path of socialism, and yet remaining intellectually distinct from them, and loyal at all times to the extreme program. This principle is best illustrated in Lenin's policy toward the trade-unions. It seems a natural inference from the Marxian theory of socialism, as an automatic result of the class struggle between labor and capital, that these organizations of labor should be or become socialistic. It seemed the natural business of Marxian agitators to "express" or "accelerate" this process. Lenin took the opposite view.

"Every socialist," he said, "ought so far as possible to co-operate with and actively work in these organizations. That is true, but it is not at all in our interest to demand that only socialists should be members of the 'trade' unions. That would narrow the extent of our influence upon the mass. . . . The broader these organizations, the broader will be our influence, an influence manifested, not only through the elemental development of the economic struggle, but through the direct conscious action of the socialist members of the union upon their companions."

This is merely the common sense of a man who is completely free from the intellectualistic view of the relation of social ideas to the movement of labor. When Lenin says "our interest," "our influence upon the mass," he refers to an organization of people with a purposive idea, people who are trying to do something in company with the working class, and by means of it, and not merely bringing the working class a consciousness of what it is doing. Other Marxians had frequently adopted this attitude of Lenin; no active person can be perfectly loyal to an animistic philosophy. But Lenin adopted it completely and continually, and carried it to its ultimate conclusion. His language seemed so different at first from that of the accredited priests of Marxism, that he was seriously attacked on the ground that "he never used the word proletariat in the nominative case." Lenin had a more perfect feeling of identity with the proletariat than those who attacked him, but he could not pretend that the proletariat was doing what he was doing. A proletarian party is not worthy of the name, he said, until it has "united leaders, class, masses into one single uninterrupted whole." But he never lost sight of the fact that this uniting is a conscious act to be performed by men of revolutionary ideas.

The same thing appears in Lenin's determination of the policy of his party toward the general mass of the population. He demanded that socialists should go among the masses of the people and give expression to all their natural protests and discontent. He demanded that they should become "veritable tribunes of the people," organizing an "all-popular indictment" of the existing regime. And when he was reproached with anti-Marxism, and asked wherein, then, will consist the class character of the movement, he replied: "Just in this, that we who organize this all-popular indictment are socialists; that the explanation of all the agitational questions raised will be given in an inflexibly socialist spirit, without any conscious or unconscious distortions of Marxism. . . ." Another emphatic assertion of the separate identity of the Marxian engineer, and the dynamic function of his ideas.

Lenin is alleged to have profoundly modified Marxism as a theory by recognizing the peasants and the oppressed colonial peoples as "allies" of the working class in its struggle. And yet this assertion always has to be accompanied by the remark that Marx also recognized the peasants and the colonial peoples as allies of the working class. What then is the modification introduced by Lenin? Simply this, that being profoundly indifferent to the metaphysical picture of the revolution as automatically produced by a resolution of "contradictions" involved in the development of industrial capitalism, Lenin was able to see the industrial proletariat, the peasants, and the colonial peoples, in their *practical* proportions. Marx saw them in the proportions determined by a dialectic construction of which the peasants and the colonial peoples are not a perfectly integral part. Therefore, his recognition of them as "allies" was incidental and inadequate in comparison with Lenin's. Marx was a metaphysician accommodating his metaphysics in a parenthesis to the demands of practical science; Lenin was a practical engineer, ignoring altogether the metaphysics in which he believed. That is the essential difference between Lenin and Marx, so far as concerns the peasants and the colonial peoples.

The most striking feature of Lenin's political tactics was the "policy of sharp turns." Lenin would adopt a program, or a slogan, sufficiently fundamental to serve among ordinary politicians as the cornerstone of a republic, or the motto of a "Grand Old Party" through several generations, and then he would appear some morning a short while later and say: "The situation has changed, our program has no further value, the slogan for the present period is as follows. . . ." Nothing like this had ever been seen before. It makes most of the great liberators appear a little wooden, a little out of gear with reality, in comparison with Lenin. It contributed more than anything else to make his political power seem occult and almost magical. And yet it was the opposite of magic; it was the essence of scientific engineering introduced into the sphere of politics. I have shown that the distinction between scientific engineering and the practice of magic, whether in the matter of producing gold or in the matter of producing a true society, lies in the scientists' recognition and definition of an unchangeable or uncontrollable element in the given facts. There is, however, this great difference between an engineer of human history, applying the principles of Marxism, and a chemical or physical engineer: the engineer of history works with a material which is itself spontaneously changing, and he with it, in ways not irrelevant to his purpose. He cannot define once for all, except in the most general terms, the factual conditions limiting and prescribing his action. He cannot keep these conditions constant. He must, therefore, continually revert to the conditions, and continually redefine them, amending his procedure according to the new elements which are beyond his control. That is the significance of the "policy of sharp turns." It is a proof that in Lenin the conjurer survived no more than the priest.

Lenin's Marxian eulogists usually point to the soviet form of government as the essential expression of his creative genius. The superficiality of this judgment becomes apparent when you know that during the months preceding the October revolution, pursuing his essential policy of sharp turns, Lenin was once on the point of abandoning altogether the slogan "All power to the soviets!" The essential expression of Lenin's genius was the creation of an organization of purposive revolutionists capable of standing above and outside all such specific forms and formulations, using them or discarding them according to their transitory relation to a more general social purpose. Lenin left to "history" the decision whether the revolution should flow in the channel of the soviets or not. But he did not leave to history the decision whether the revolution should be led by the Bolshevik party. He did not leave to history the creation of that party, nor the maintenance of its entirely extraordinary character and policy. If he had, there would have been no Bolshevik revolution, as Trotsky in his *Lessons of October* has very effectively shown. Lenin's party was an organization of a kind which never existed before. It combined certain essential features of a political party, a professional association, a consecrated order, an army, a scientific society—and yet was in no sense a sect. Instead of cherishing in its membership a sectarian psychology, it cherished a certain relation to the predominant class-forces of society as Marx defined them. And this relation was determined and progressively readjusted by Lenin, with a subtlety of which Marx never dreamed.

It seems obvious that this unique organization, with its scientifically determined equilibrium in the society surrounding it, and that unique "policy of sharp turns" successfully applied by it through a quarter of a century, was the essential expression of Lenin's creative genius. And yet the very members and heads of the party, paus ing to write a tribute to Lenin, and enumerate his creative contributions to Marxism and to human history, relegated the party to a secondary position. They rarely mentioned its delicately adjusted relation to society, and almost never that peculiar policy which it applied with triumphant success. The reason for this is that the nature of the party, its position, and its policy of sharp turns, were all alike inconsistent with the philosophy of historic determinism. The whole situation, the whole history of the Russian revolution as it was actually lived by the members of the Bolshevik party, involved at every point a distinction between what was historically determined and what might be done with history by this purposive organization. All practical scientific efforts involve this same distinction between what is determined and what is not. And for that reason, again, all philosophies of absolute determinism are in disaccord with all applied science. The inability of Russian Marxists to state the reality about Lenin, and about their own lives, is but a further example of the one-eyed character of such philosophies.

It is not only the essential genius of Lenin which is distorted to meet the demands of Marxian metaphysics, but also the essential nature of the government which he founded. It was called a soviet government, and the soviets did indeed play a vital part in it. But it would be mere academic formalism to pretend that "soviet rule" was the essence of the governmental institution established by Lenin in Russia. Its essence was the rule, within and through a soviet structure, of a disciplined and centralized organization of several hundred thousand people sworn to the purpose and trained in the science of revolution, and so placed in society in relation to the dominant forces of class interest, as Marx defined them, that their sovereignty was unshakable. The most significant administrative change in Russia during Lenin's life was a gradual shifting of the center where decisions were really made from the Soviet of People's Commissars, the highest organ of the soviet structure, to the Politburo, the highest organ of the Communist party. And this change was nothing but the actual reality of the situation gradually breaking through the forms in which, out of loyalty to the Marxian philosophy, Lenin attempted to confine it.

"The dictatorship of the proletariat is a relentless struggle, bloody and bloodless, violent and peaceful, military and industrial, pedagogical and administrative, against the forces and traditions of the old society. The force of habit of millions and tens of millions is a most formidable force. Without a party of iron, tempered in struggle, without a party possessing the confidence of all that is honest in the class in question, without a party able to detect the moods of the mass and influence it, it is impossible to wage such a struggle with success. . . .

"Not one important political or organizational question is decided by any state institution in our republic without the governing instruction of the central committee of the party."

In those sentences you have the essence of the new kind of sovereignty established by Lenin in Russia. And you have the measure of his distance from the Marxian metaphysics. Marx declared the dictatorship of the proletariat to be an *inevitable* result of the material nature and economic situation of the proletariat. Lenin declared that without a party whose characteristics are defined in psychological and social terms, the dictatorship of the proletariat is *impossible*. And he was not deterred by considerations of metaphysical propriety, any more than by considerations of democratic ideology, from giving into the hands of the party so defined, and so constituted, a position in the new state not unlike that occupied by the personal sovereign in the old.

Lenin's crowning heresy was to create this proletarian republic in a country in which capitalism was relatively undeveloped. Because of the practicality of his methods, and the fundamental truths contained in the Marxian system, he succeeded in producing that change which is metaphysically supposed to result from a "ripening" of the "contradictions" in capitalism, in a society in which those contradictions were entirely unripe. The October revolution was a violation of Hegelian Marxism, and every genuine success of Lenin's effort after the revolution was a disproof of it. For this effort was, on the one hand, to make fast in Russia a political superstructure and a way of thinking which were in advance of her economic development, and, on the other hand, to make her catch up in economic development to this way of thinking and this political superstructure. No person who means what he says seriously, and concretely, could possibly declare that the political forms set up by Lenin in Russia, and the ideas propagated by his party, were a reflection of existing economic conditions. Never did a reflection put forth such gigantic efforts to produce its likeness in the object reflected.

This fact was too flagrant to escape the attention of Lenin's orthodox Marxian critics, and he therefore found himself engaged at the end of his career, just as he had been at the beginning, in a polemic which compelled him to give expression to his fundamental intellectual attitude. He found himself compelled to choose between metaphysical Marxism and the thoughts of a practical mind. And he chose, as always, the thoughts of a practical mind.

Accusing his critics of "slavish imitation of the past," he wrote:

"How utterly mechanical is that idea which they learned by heart during the development of western European social democracy, that we in Russia have not yet grown up to socialism, that we lack—as various learned gentlemen among them express it—the objective economic premises for socialism. And it does not come into anybody's head to ask himself: Might not a people, encountering a revolutionary situation such as was created during the imperialist war, under the influence of the hopelessness of its situation, throw itself into such a struggle as opened to it even the barest chance of some slightly unusual conditions for the further growth of civilization? . . .

"If the creation of socialism demands a definite level of culture (although nobody can say just exactly what that definite level is) then why can we not begin by winning with a revolution the premises for that definite level of culture, and then afterward, on the basis of the workers and peasants' power and the soviet structure, set out to catch up to the other peoples?"

There was little here to which a practical revolutionist having an experimental attitude could object. But for a Marxian metaphysician, taught to believe that the world-process is logical, and that its motor force is a dialectic necessity of self-resolution in the contradictions inherent in the capitalist system of industry when they have reached their full development, there is not a syllable of satisfaction.

"No social formation ever disappears," says Marx, "before all the productive forces are developed for which it has room, and new higher relations of production never appear before the material conditions of their existence are matured in the womb of the old society."

"The organization of the revolutionary elements as a class presupposes the finished existence of all the productive forces which can be developed in the bosom of the old society."

"Law can never be on a higher level than the economic conditions and the degree of social civilization corresponding to it."

"The industrially more developed country reveals to the less developed the image of its own future."

That is Dialectic Materialism. That is history proceeding according to the logic of the metaphysician.

Why can we not "begin" by organizing the revolutionary elements as a class, says Lenin, and not only that, but by winning the revolution and establishing higher relations of production, and passing laws that are on a level above our economic condition, and showing the industrially more advanced nations an image of their own future, and then "afterward set out to catch up to the other peoples" in the matter of developing the productive forces?

That is Bolshevism. That is history as it was made in a certain concrete situation by an organization of men who took the ideas of Karl Marx as instrumental science, and not as animistic philosophy.[1]

[1] Trotsky did not always fall behind Lenin in his ability to ignore the Marxian philosophy of history. He said in a discussion in Pravda, Feb. 2, 1926: "The social form of our industry is immeasurably higher than that of the United States. There a mad capitalist exploitation and the most terrible inequality of classes; here a form of industry such as opens the road to full equality of living conditions for the whole people. But in America in the frame of the capitalist form, there exists the highest technique. With us in the frame of the socialist or transitional form, an extremely backward technique. And the extent of that backward-

A further quotation from the same article will reveal the precise method by which Lenin managed to "believe in" this philosophy, while completely ignoring it in his practical thoughts and actions. He managed this by making its meaning more abstract and general in proportion as, taken concretely and specifically, it got in his way.

"What if the complete hopelessness of their situation, multiplying ten-fold the strength of the workers and peasants, opened to them the possibility of a different transition to the creation of the basic premises of civilization from that of all western European nations? . . . Would that change the general line of development of world history?"

In other words, what if the events in Russia directly contradict the dogmas of Dialectic Materialism? Can we not interpret those dogmas in a more *general* sense, a sense general enough, indeed, and loose enough, and inconsequential enough, so that they will include the events in Russia, and thus enable us to retain our metaphysical belief over and above our real thoughts and actions?

This is the way in which every believer in animistic religion reconciles his belief with the concrete realities which contradict it. Cardinal Manning lays down the following dogma: "Ask in faith and perfect confidence

ness we ought to keep constantly before our eyes: not in order to drop our hands in despair, but in order to double our efforts in the struggle for technique and culture. . . . The technique of America combined with the soviet social regime would give us not only social-ism—it would give us communism, or at least it would bring very close those conditions of life in which each would work according to his abilities and receive according to his needs."

A more perfect contradiction of the Marxian philosophy of history, according to which social forms are "determined" by the evolving technique of industry, could hardly be imagined—nor a more sensible attitude to the actual problem.

and God will give us what we ask." And when the crude facts fall out to the contrary he says:

"God has said that He will give you whatsoever you ask; but the form in which it will come, and the time in which He will give it, He keeps in His own power. . . . Sometimes it may be a chastisement, or a loss, or a visitation against which our hearts rise, and we seem to see that God has not only forgotten us, but has begun to deal with us in severity. Those very things are the answer to our prayers."

The purpose is different, but the mental process is the same. Cardinal Manning generalizes the idea of an answer to prayer in order to cover all possible contingencies. Lenin generalizes the idea of history as determined by the development of the forces of production, in order to cover the Russian revolution. And there is not the slightest doubt that if Lenin had happened to be able to produce a Communist revolution all over Europe and Asia and Africa and America and in the islands of the South Sea—a revolution which contradicted in no matter what fashion this Hegelian philosophy—he would have pushed the philosophy still farther up into the sky, and perhaps ended by forgetting it altogether. For he had no real interest in it. He was interested only in the freedom it gave him to use his mind instrumentally in a perpetually changing situation. He was interested in the one wisdom which Hegelism did contribute to a real science of thinking, the maxim that "truth is always concrete." And it is just that maxim that he violated when he tried to maintain that Marxism, although not applicable to the concrete "transition" effected in Russia, remained true to the "general line of development of world history."

To me the fundamental difference between Marx and Lenin is visible throughout a great amount of what they wrote. It is not a contradiction, but a difference of mental attitude. And it is not a complete difference, because Marx had in him the practical scientist as well as the metaphysician, and Lenin never consciously abandoned metaphysics for the scientific attitude. But it is a difference of profound and many-sided importance. It may be summed up in the following two quotations about the dictatorship of the proletariat:

Marx says: "The new thing that I did consisted in demonstrating . . . that the class struggle inevitably leads to the dictatorship of the proletariat."

Lenin says: "Marx's teaching about the class struggle leads inevitably to a recognition . . . [that] the overthrow of the bourgeoisie is attainable only through the transformation of the proletariat into a ruling class."

Marx states that such a thing will happen in such a way. Lenin states that such is the only way to make it happen. Marx attributes his purpose to the external world, and tries to convert the facts and methods of action which make its realization possible into a proof of its certainty. Lenin assumes that the revolutionary purpose exists in revolutionary people, and shows them those facts in the external world, and those methods of action, which make its realization possible. In Marx the Hegelian metaphysician was dominant over the practical scientific thinker; in Lenin the scientific thinker gained the victory. And that victory is the theoretical foundation of Bolshevism. Bolshevism is an unconscious, and therefore incomplete, substitution of a practical revolutionary hypothesis for that revolutionary philosophy of the universe which Marx created.

6. LENIN'S PHILOSOPHY

LENIN COMPENSATED for his practical betrayals of the Marxist philosophy by asserting it theoretically with extreme and violent dogmatism. He is far more rigid in his "belief" in Dialectic Materialism than Marx and Engels were. "How young is all human history," says Engels, "and how ridiculous it would be to wish to ascribe any absolute validity to our present views. . . ." Lenin says: "From that philosophy of Marxism, poured from a single chunk of steel, you cannot withdraw one fundamental premise or one essential piece, without departing from objective truth, and falling into the arms of the bourgeois-reactionary lie."

In this extreme spirit Lenin defended in philosophy exactly the opposite proposition from that which rests at the bottom of his politics. His politics is founded upon a belief in the dynamic function of revolutionary ideas, and of the men who make it a profession to realize them.

"Without a revolutionary theory there can be no revolutionary movement. . . . The statement that no efforts even of the most inspired ideologist can distract the workers' movement from the path determined by . . . material forces, is equivalent to a renunciation of socialism. . . . In what consists the role of the social-democracy, if not in being the 'spirit' . . . raising the elemental movement up to its program?"

That is the foundation of Lenin's politics. And here is his philosophy:

"The world is an ordered movement of matter, and our knowledge, being the highest product of nature, is able only to reflect that movement. . . . Social consciousness reflects social existence, there is the substance of Marx's teaching."

Doubtless many volumes of Hegelian higher nonsense may be written in the effort to reconcile these statements, but in the end the statements will remain contradictory. Lenin defended in philosophy a position inconsistent with his fundamental attitude in politics. And although his attention was called to it, he never attempted to resolve this inconsistency. He instinctively ignored it, or chose to leave it standing. Why? Because, for a revolutionist lacking the conception of a genetic science of the mind, that was the most practical thing to do.

Lenin defended the assertion that ideas are the mere automatic reflection of things, not because he had thought about ideas, and examined them, and decided that that is what they are. He would have been the last man to be deluded by so unreal an account of anything he had examined. He defended that assertion because he saw no alternative except to say that ideas are the reality, and that material things are secondary and a delusion. He regarded the question "How can mind know matter?" as a real question which has but two answers: Either mind is the reality, and matter a kind of illusory product or predicate of it; or matter is the reality and mind an automatic reflection of it. And he knew that of these two answers the latter is more akin to the scientific view, the view of anybody who seriously intends to change the world. The former leads directly into religion and the disposition to get into a comfortable relation with the world as it is. He chose the more hardheaded, practical, and scientific of those two answers to the question, "How can mind know matter?"

But if you adopt the scientific point of view thoroughly, and as it really exists in the minds of scientists at work, the question "How can mind know matter?" is a meaningless question. It is a question that was asked for the sole purpose of giving the idealistic answer. It has the same significance for a science of psychology that the question, "How can a hen lay an egg?" has for a science of physiology—namely, none at all. In permitting themselves to be led into the discussion of a meaningless question, the dialectic materialists deserted the scientific point of view, and they never got back to it. They never got back to the real question "How *does* a mind know matter—and *why?*" And hence Lenin, educated as a dialectic materialist, remained unaware of the existence of a natural science which would have supported his assertion of the dynamic function of ideas.

The conception of conscious thought as an instrument of adaptation produced by material nature in the evolution of living organisms, just as other organic functions are produced, is a product and a continuation of that hardheaded confrontation of scientific facts which Lenin tried to defend in his philosophy. And it is the very thing that he asserted in his politics. With this conception Lenin could have escaped from the inconsistency between his philosophy and his politics. He could have got rid of the Marxian metaphysics which tended to impede him as an engineer, without falling into the idealistic metaphysics which would impede him as a revolutionist. He could have got rid of all metaphysics, and become consciously and theoretically what he was in actual fact—a revolutionary engineer.

If there is a "philosophy" involved in recognizing the origin and biological function of human intelligence, it consists in dismissing as meaningless a number of questions which are meaningless, and learning to say "I do not know" in response to all those questions of which you do not know the answer. It is a method rather than a philosophy, a method which I have described as affirmatively skeptical, because it is skeptical of philosophy and of the attempts of philosophy to prescribe forms or limits to science, but it affirms the validity and believes in the development of science. In my opinion this philosophy, that is a method, would have been far more grateful to Lenin's temperament than that surreptitiously animistic materialism in which he felt compelled to believe. One thing is certain, and that is that Lenin did not depend for the strength of his purpose upon a metaphysical conviction that the material world was co-operating with him. "The elemental workers' movement goes straight toward subjection to the bourgeoisie," he said. "Our task is to drag it away." Intellectually you may insist that this was but a temporary lapse from the Marxian ideology; but a person emotionally dependent upon that ideology could not possibly have committed this lapse. The idea expressed by some of our *literati* who visited Lenin, that he derived his heroic force from a metaphysical conviction of the certainty of the future communist state, is in my opinion erroneous. Certainty of success is the natural accompaniment of a gigantic will, but metaphysics seems to me to have been merely a weapon in Lenin's hand.

The most original thing about his book of philosophy

is the startling way in which he asserts this very fact.
He asserts that all philosophy is a weapon of "party
struggle," and Marx's philosophy no exception. "From
first to last Marx and Engels were partisan in philosophy," he says, and they made no pretense to the contrary, and that is their merit. For such a thing as a
nonpartisan philosophy does not exist. "The newest
philosophy is just as partisan as the philosophy of two
thousand years ago."

I have already discussed the semi-theological tricks by
which Hegel enabled Lenin to assert that his philosophy
is an instrument for winning a temporary struggle, and
at the same time assert that it is objectively true. In
that he was merely orthodox. And yet in the abandon
with which he asserts that the whole thing is "partisan"
—the Russian word is "party" rather than partisan, and
actually belongs to the political arena—he is to my feeling unlike Marx and Engels. And he is unlike them in
the manner in which he lives up to this statement. He
blends together all through his book the question
whether Dialectic Materialism is true, and the question
whether it is revolutionary. He shows, or attempts to,
that it is the unconscious assumption of the "immense
majority of natural scientists," and he shows at the same
time that it is an instrument delicately and most adroitly
adjusted for winning the victory of the working class.
He does these two things in the same breath, in the
same sentence, and without any apparent sense of the
difference. Marx and Engels envisaged these two questions separately. They believed that the objective truth
is revolutionary, but they inferred this from a system of
philosophy which they attempted to establish, as other
philosophies are established, on objective grounds. I cannot imagine Marx and Engels contrasting objective truth

with *bourgeois-reactionary* falsity, as Lenin does in that sentence I quoted: "You cannot withdraw one fundamental premise . . . without departing from objective truth and falling into the arms of the bourgeois-reactionary lie." Marx and Engels were too well schooled in the ways of philosophy to write a sentence like that. The difference is doubtless one of degree. You may say that Lenin was more enthusiastic about being partisan, and less concerned about being philosophic, than Marx and Engels were.

And that is an extremely significant difference. For if you dismiss Hegelian theological tricks altogether, and come back to your own natural intelligence, what does it mean to say that all philosophy is partisan, and your own no exception? Does it not mean that you do not believe in philosophy? It is obvious to anybody but a superlogician that in order to have an authentic existence, and be capable of definition, philosophy must be nonpartisan. It must rise above the interests of either side in a temporary struggle. If Lenin never made a statement which was nonpartisan and did rise above the interests of his side in the class struggle, we might perhaps accept this partisan thing called Dialectic Materialism as his nearest approach to philosophy. But when he says that this thing is an instrument of temporary struggle, when he says that all philosophy is partisan, he has uttered a nonpartisan opinion. That opinion is his real philosophy. And it is not a philosophy of Dialectic Materialism. It is a philosophy of affirmative skepticism —an intellectual attitude which denies the validity of philosophy, while affirming the validity of the science which understands it. It is exactly the attitude which is forced upon a man who knows the biological origin and function of his own intelligence, the attitude of a scientist who includes genetic psychology in his equipment. That is why I think this attitude would have been more grateful to Lenin's mind than the animistic metaphysics which he felt compelled to assert, and which he asserted with excessive and unnatural dogmatism.

7. MERITS OF THE SCIENTIFIC ATTITUDE

THE CONSCIOUS substitution of scientific skepticism for the Hegelian philosophy of Marx would have deprived Lenin's followers of a religious certainty of success which may have made good soldiers of some of them. "Trust God and keep your powder dry" is the slogan with which soldiers have usually been led into battle. "Trust Economic Determinism and keep your powder dry" fits the same way into the mind. "Keep your powder *dry*" is more heroic. It is easy to exaggerate the emotional importance of these mental attitudes, however. When Rosa Luxemburg said that the workers' movement derives its strength, zeal, patience, courageous restraint, and endurance from a conviction of the objective necessity of the social revolution, she undoubtedly expressed a genuine emotion, but that does not prove that her statement is true. Nothing could be more improbable than that the workers' movement, or she herself, or any other great revolutionist, ever derived these attributes from a philosophical conviction.

Psychology and Other Sciences

Whatever might be lost in getting rid of the relics of animism would be more than compensated by the advantages of a consciously practical and scientific attitude. Aside from the general advantage of basing oneself upon fact, and living in the real world, unloading a mountain of cant and conscientious sophistry, and becoming clear-minded and capable of unlimited growth, there are certain specific advantages to radicals in abandoning metaphysical habits of thought. For one thing, it removes from them a certain fear of the developments of science. It is not impossible that the achievements of psychology in this century, basing itself upon the physiology of the nervous system, will compare in their interest with those of the physical sciences in the nineteenth century. It is certain that they will attract increasing attention, and this science will have nothing but ridicule for Marx's antiquated theory of the mind. Marxists will thus find themselves, not "in the forefront of the science of their day" as they have always boasted of being, but in the backwash, clinging to an abandoned piece of intellectual baggage.

Dialectic Materialism declares that the world is essentially material, and that mind evolved out of matter in connection with the complex organization of the central nervous system in animals and men. But it does not, and dare not, go and say that the motions of this mind are a continuation of the motion of matter in that central nervous system, adaptive motions, to be studied primarily from the standpoint of biology and physiology rather than logic. For, studied from this standpoint and in their actuality in concrete cases, these motions will be found to be not essentially logical—much less "dialectic"—and the whole mystic-intellectual legend of Hegel will fall to the ground altogether. As Hegel himself said, "To see that thought in its very nature is dialectical" is a "lesson of logic." And the moment logic is cast down from its position as a factual account of what thought in its "inner essence" really is, and recognized to be a

set of rules which men have made for the better employment of their thoughts, that moment this "lesson of
logic" will lose its validity.

It will not lose its validity, for it never had any. But
it will lose the possibility of obscuring and confusing
the boldest political minds of five generations of mankind with an unintelligible mixture of emotional mysticism and psychological half-truth. Certainly nobody
will contend that a dialectic philosophy of the universe
could survive without Hegel's Logic, upon the sole basis
of his Philosophy of Nature and History, and of such
desultory empirical observations as he and his disciples
occasionally bring to the support of it. A dialectic philosophy of the universe, whether materialistic or idealistic, stands or falls with Hegel's fundamental science of
the mind. It stands or falls with the belief that "the principle and very unadulterated self of the mind" is to be
found, not by examining its simple beginnings, but by
winding oneself all up in its most complicated and hyper-
cultivated manifestation, where it has become an end in
itself, and where its end is "to reach and get hold of itself and liberate itself to itself," whatever in honest fact
that may mean. Marx's philosophy of Dialectic Materialism is inextricably bound up with this old-fashioned way
of studying the mind.

It is not impossible that if Marx had devoted his mature mind to a restatement of Hegel's logic, as he once
contemplated doing, he might have arrived at a real science of human intelligence, which would have swept the
last vestiges of Hegelism out of him. He devoted himself
to economics instead, and he left to Engels the task of
formulating their common philosophy. Engels had
neither the inventive genius nor the depth of intellectual
conscience that Marx had. All the forms of conscious-

ness are for Engels mere automatic portraits of material reality, and their practicality is not a quality in them—it is merely an evidence that they are pictorially accurate. The motion of consciousness is to him not a dynamic, but a rational motion, factually described by the rules of the Hegelian logic; and this motion also is but a "reflection" of the motion of nature.

That is the extent of the Marxian psychology as it appears in the writings of Engels. And up to the time of the Russian revolution this psychology took no single step forward. The greatest theorists of Marxism seem to have been as unaware of the development of a genetic and experimental science of the mind as though it had taken place on another planet. Lafargue, in an essay on "The Origin of the Ideas of Justice and the Good," draws his authority from no psychologist later than Hobbes and Locke. Plekhanov, four years after the publication of James's *Psychology*, dismissed with a derisive phrase the idea of a science of human nature. Kautsky, assigning to Marx his position among the sciences, mentions the existence of a natural science of psychology, but only in order to run away from it and forget it. Lenin, although he was the incarnation of purposive thinking, was satisfied to describe all the dynamic activities of his mind as an automatic "reproduction," "copy," "reflection"—and in one place he even says "photograph"—of the self-active motions of the material world. Never was the "spectator theory" of knowledge reduced to a more perfect absurdity than on the lips of Lenin. Never was it expressed in a nakeder form. "Consciousness in general reflects existence . . . social consciousness reflects social existence"—that is the extent of Lenin's psychology.

The Russian revolution set free a great body of Marxian theorists, and theorists willing to become Marxian,

if only from the pure love of theory. It supplied them
with publishing facilities, and encouraged them to take
possession of the whole field of science in the name of
Dialectic Materialism. Naturally the science of psychology did not escape this invasion. It was approached—
with somewhat the same mixture of caution and contempt with which one approaches a poisonous reptile—
and a certain preliminary investigation was begun. The
absurdity of the whole operation was foreshadowed by
a communist professor, K. Kornilov, who took up what
he called the fundamental problem of the Stream of
Consciousness. He said that the theory of the Association of Ideas had been inadequate to explain the motion
of this stream, and that this problem remained to be
solved by the dialectic method. "The fundamental principle of the movement of psychic life may yet be discovered," he exclaimed, "and just by way of applying the
dialectic method in the sphere of psychic life." Forgetting that the dialectic *is* the fundamental principle of
the movement of psychic life—forgetting that Hegel has
already discovered and decreed that all mental activities
are only "a mode of expression of the forms of pure
thought," and that "we have but to let the thought-
forms follow the impulse of their own organic life" in
order to see that every one "naturally veers round into
its opposite"—forgetting that this complete analysis and
revelation by Hegel of the fundamental principle of the
movement of psychic life is the sole ground and reason-
for-being of the "dialectic method," this Marxian psychology would now proceed to employ the "dialectic
method" in order to investigate the unsolved problem
of how the psychic life moves!

There was more good sense in the extremists of Lenin's
party who denounced the very word "psychology" as

counterrevolutionary. For that is the sole tenable position if you are going to defend the Marxian adaptation of Hegel's philosophy. Hegel himself had a well-founded phobia of an empirical, and especially a genetic, science of psychology. He insisted with continual anxiety upon the vast abyss between the rational faculties of man and the intelligence of "brutes," as though knowing in advance that this universal evolution, the child of his logic, might prove capable of devouring its mother. And Marx, as we remember, removed all psychological questionings from the path of the triumphal march to the millennium of his Forces of Production, by saying that man is nothing but a "complex of social relations." Both these attitudes of obscurantism inhere in any dialectic philosophy, and make alarming to its adherents a genuine science of the mind and brain.

It is not only psychology that Marxists fear, however, but they fear any perfectly objective investigation into the nature of anything whatever. Having projected their purpose into a description of things in general, they are compelled, in order to defend that purpose, to defend this description. In a preface to his *Anti-Dühring*, Engels recounts his enormous labor of seven years defending this description—translating all modern science, that is, into the terms of the Marxian dialectic. He concludes, somewhat pathetically, that the task has become too great for one man. In Lenin's Russia a whole coterie of men, constituting almost a professional revolutionary-philosophical priesthood, devoted themselves to it. A continual stream of abstruse volumes and a philosophical magazine of the highest technicality bore witness to their labors. It would be difficult to imagine a more futile employment of the human mind than this going over of the whole body of organized knowledge, restating every finding that cannot be doubted or otherwise disposed of, in the form of an analogy to the proletarian revolution. For that is what the process amounts to, once you have dispensed with Hegel's original and rather more practical purpose of "rising to God out of the empirical view of the world." Instead of issuing the command to contemporary science, "Give all you've got in the name of the working class!" the Bolshevik revolution issued the command, "Give nothing but the Negation of the Negation or we fire!"

All this incredible professorial hocus-pocus, associated so incongruously with the enterprise of revolution, was the result of fear. The fear was expressed by Lenin himself in an article which he wrote for that monthly magazine of philosophy when it was founded. Its task should be, he said, to find the answers to "those philosophic questions which are created by the transformation of natural science, and by way of which the intelligentsia, prone to worship bourgeois fashions, slips into the reaction." For this purpose he advised the editors to "organize a systematic study of the dialectic of Hegel from the materialist point of view." Is it not surprising that, in order to defend his revolution against modern bourgeois fashions arising out of the latest developments of science, Lenin should call in the help of a bourgeois professor whose reactionary disquisitions, based on the developments of science, were fashionable a hundred years ago? Lenin's opinion of bourgeois professors in general is this: "Not one of them . . . *is to be trusted to the extent of one word, once the question of philosophy arises.* . . . Professors of philosophy are the learned errand-boys of the theologians." And yet, because he cannot simply posit the existence of his own revolutionary purpose, Lenin has to fall back on one of the most loyal of these errand-boys of theology to defend the revolutionary plan of action. Lenin's will had no need of help from Hegel. It had no reason to fear science, nor the philosophic questions arising out of an attempt to generalize science. Once that revolutionary will is understood to reside in revolutionists, and not in the universe, the free and unlimited efforts of scientists to understand the universe can only be a help to it. These real efforts, moreover, can be distinguished directly, and without the aid of any study of the Hegelian dialectic, from the attempts of metaphysical professors to implant animistic purposes in the universe. Instead of fighting one form of animism with another, you can fight animism with science, and all the metaphysical professors—Hegel and the soviet priesthood with the rest—can be dismissed as a superfluity and a nuisance. In their place a corps of real teachers can dedicate themselves to the immortal revolutionary ideal of Bakunin—that science should become "one in fact with the immediate and real life of all individuals."

Religion and the Arts

An abandonment of the dialectic religion would make possible a sensible policy toward other religions. The Marxian policy is to root out all warm and personal religions, and at the same time destroy wonder and a sense of the world's mystery, by putting a cold and impersonal religion in their place. No human being not specifically and professionally occupied with the revolutionary struggle will accept such a religion as this of Dialectic Materialism. It has, therefore, no value whatever as an antidote to the "opium of the people." But a great many human beings—we do not know how many—will accept instruction in the distinction between animism and science, and will agree to adopt the scientific viewpoint, if you can show them what it really is. You leave them their freedom of feeling—which they will retain in any case—but you convince them that science and practical wit are the only forms of reasoned knowledge, and that the only way to get anything done is to do it.

Abandoning the Marxian philosophy would also make possible a wise attitude toward art and poetry. Since according to Marxism the class struggle is the essential general reality of life and history, there can be no really important art or poetry which is irrelevant to it. In other words, the creative arts, having with difficulty escaped from their bondage to religion, must enter into bondage to politics. They must be regarded as subordinate to a single practical enterprise. Nothing could be less consistent with the ideal of human freedom than this attitude toward sheer creativeness. Poetry and art may contribute vitally to purposive effort, but they are in their essence and definition distinct from it and independent of it. Their interest is in experience and not in purpose, in being and not in becoming. Even when a poet lends his art to an effort to change reality, the thing which he lends is a genius for experiencing and making others experience the qualities of reality as it is. That these qualities are of infinite variety is the very basis of the possibility of his art. To tell a sensuous poet that there is but one "reality" in matter—that expressed in the words "hydrogen nuclei and electrons"—is to deny the emotional validity of his poems. And yet such formulas are, after all, science and not metaphysics. To tell a poet of humanity that there is but one reality in contemporary social life and history, the class struggle, is fantastic. Whatever the poet may try to do with his opinions, his art by its very nature opposes and refutes all such formulas.

To recognize the depth and ultimateness of the distinction between poetry and science, between realization and adjustment, is in my opinion the way in which scientifically educated people can best retain their sanity. It is the way in which, unconsciously, they do retain it. Science has gradually built up a conception of the real world which deprives it of every quality that is humanly interesting. At the hands of Einstein and the higher chemistry, the "primary qualities"—shape, motion, impenetrability—are following the "secondary qualities"— color and sound and taste and fragrance—into the realm of the "unreal." The "reality," with these savants, is becoming little more than a set of mathematical formulas. By this route, science and the attempt to generalize science are arriving at a conception of the universe just as "idealistic" as that of the philosopher's, but without the personal qualities which make the philosopher's idealistic universe interesting. No complete and living man, who wishes to imagine what he knows, will be content to live in such a universe. He will find his way out. And there are, it seems to me, but two ways out. One is to jump the gulf which divides this cold idealistic universe of science from the warmer one of metaphysics. The metaphysicians will provide abundant tackle and scaffolding for the purpose of this jump, and we shall find ourselves back again in the animistic attitude to reality. Those mathematical formulas of Einstein will begin to speak with the tongues of angels, and their first word will undoubtedly be *Duty*. But there is another way out of that barren world offered to our imagination by science, and that is to declare the parallel and equal rights of poetry, or the pure experience of things.

When science denied the "tertiary qualities"—the qualities of spirit—to the material world, it opposed itself to religion. That opposition was ultimate and essential to the nature of science, because religion like science is concerned with adjustment and tries to accomplish things. But when science denied the "secondary qualities," it opposed itself to poetry—an opposition which is not ultimate, because poetry as such is not concerned with adjustment and only seeks to realize things as they are. Far from being an enemy of science, poetry is the one thing which can sanction it, and justify the violence which it does to the obvious qualities of experience. If the moment of realization is invalid, is there not a kind of absurdity in these intellectual contortions which are only by-products of the effort to achieve it?

If this viewpoint is just, or can even be plausibly defended, in regard to sciences of such high generality as physics and chemistry, its validity in regard to the specific scientific enterprise of social revolution can hardly be denied. The poetry of life, and its infinite variety, far from being subordinate to this enterprise, is the one thing which justifies it and gives it any command upon the energies of men, no matter to what class they belong.

Morals

A practical social science would also abandon the irresponsible Marxian generalizations about morals. Real morality, as the Greeks perceived, is intelligent judgment applied to the problems of conduct and the estimation of human character. Moral precepts will naturally vary, not only according to the maturity of the intelligence—the degree to which responsible judgment has replaced mere social custom—but also according to the conditions of each particular problem. In this science, as in other practical sciences, the truth is always concrete. And no set of moral ideals, no system of ethics, can relieve each society, each class, each individual, of the task of solving specific problems.

Marxism has wisely emphasized this fact; it has done its share to liberate mankind from absolute moral precepts. But it has very unwisely blurred the distinction between moral intelligence and mere customary judgment, and attempted to reduce the whole wisdom of personal life, along with all the other achievements of the human brain, to a mere reflection of social relations that are determined by the state of the productive forces. In the Marxian religion, all moral ideals change completely with a revolution in these forces and relations, the good becoming evil and the evil good. Indeed, according to the strictest Hegelian kind of Marxism, evil and good are but two aspects of a single dialectic process, the evil being the progressive and disturbing side—the natural dress and appellation of the revolution.

In my opinion religions frequently cherish moral irresponsibility more than they correct it. And this religion of Marxism is no exception to the rule. A revolutionist—and particularly a revolutionary leader—who believes that he is the mere expression of a change that is being taken care of by the "Productive Forces," is far less likely to be reliable than one who understands that he is guiding a revolutionary struggle in the direction of a new society. A more explicit reliance upon educated leaders was one of the changes adopted by Lenin in unconsciously abandoning the Marxian religion. Consciously abandoning this religion would increase the likelihood of their being reliable. It would make room for the instinctive sentiment and natural human opinion that a person who undertakes to lead a class struggle toward the goal of a better society has assumed an unusual moral responsibility. Wherever the word "ought" has a meaning, it will be affirmed that such a man ought to know his own motives, and be honest with those whom he leads. Anything that weakens that intelligent sentiment and conviction, weakens the resources of the revolution. Anything that strengthens it, strengthens the revolution.

Lenin was fully aware of this. Lenin was not in the least sentimental, and therefore he was free from that overcorrection of sentimentality which makes some Marxists hold themselves superior—in public discourse, at least—to the important problems of personal character. He was not afraid to say that it is necessary for a professional revolutionist to be "devoted," "heroic," "self-sacrificing," "honest."

"A demagogue," he said at the beginning of his career, "is the worst enemy of the working class. . . . A man can slip into demagogism through mere political naïveté, and I will never stop repeating that a demagogue is the worst enemy of the working class."

And at the end of his career he said: "Without a party possessing the confidence of all that is honest in the class in question . . . it is impossible to wage the struggle [of proletarian dictatorship] with success."

In short, while abandoning the illusion that the success of the revolution was metaphysically inevitable, Lenin declared that without honesty in the vanguard it was actually impossible. Marxists could well blot out most of their large talk about Ethics and the Materialistic Interpretation of History, and write in its place this simple statement of fact by a practical revolutionary engineer.

Bureaucratism

The chief enemy of the effort to make society more free and equal through any kind of organization is bureaucratism. In proportion as the effort succeeds, the leaders of the organization find themselves transformed from disreputable rebels to sovereign officials. A tendency to confirm and solidify their own power, not only at the expense of the masses, but of the rank and file of their own organization, is inevitable. Instead of going forward with the experiment, they tend to form a new dominant group in whose minds the revolutionary ideas —dynamic in the past—degenerate into ideological phrases. A pious repetition of these phrases replaces the arduous discipline of action and provides a cover for the rebirth of the old system.

That the Hegelian-Marxian metaphysics plays straight into the hands of this enemy needs no demonstration. Being a religion, it is the natural property of a priestly caste. Its pretense that science is something else besides a perfection of the natural process of thinking—that wisdom is, in fact, a mysterious art discovered in Germany by a professorial wizard entirely unintelligible to simple men—automatically divides the revolutionary culture into two parts. There is the esoteric doctrine, property of the few who have learned to "think dialectically," and there is the vulgar gospel for the common people. Hegel himself said that his philosophy presupposed "a higher level of culture than ordinary," and this view was substantially carried over into Marxism. "The art of operating with ideas," says Engels, "is not inborn, and it is not bestowed with ordinary everyday consciousness." And his American translator adds: "So removed is the point of view of the writer of these pages from that of the man in the street that it is doubtful whether it is possible for more than a comparatively few students thoroughly to grasp the significance of the dialectic and apply it in a satisfactory and effective fashion." Kautsky preached a distinction between Marxism as "cheaply and vulgarly understood," and the Marxism of those who have acquired sufficient knowledge and striven faithfully enough to "resolve the contradiction between the surface and the essence of things." Plekhanov expressly divided the Marxian theory "as it may be stated in popular speech" from the true doctrine. And even Lenin, who had little natural taste for the esoteric, was compelled to concede that an inferior discipline called formal logic "must continue to be taught, with amendments, to the lower grades in the schools."

All this mystification militates directly against the formation of a radically democratic society. It not only withdraws from the masses the right to understand their own revolution, but it withdraws from them the right to all scientific understanding. The simple-hearted reader, who would like to cherish the hope of mastering a little science some day, may imagine the nebulous empyrean into which that hope receded when the theories of Einstein had been translated by Soviet scholastics into the terms of the Hegelian dialectic. As a result of the greatest popular revolution in history, science was darkened and withdrawn from the people, instead of being popularized and made clear to them.

Education

Aside entirely from the problem of bureaucratism, the hopes of a democratic civilization stand or fall with the true education of the children. And true education can only be founded upon a true psychology. The instinctive position of Lenin in Russia was that of a "fraternal teacher of the people"—to recall again the eloquence of Bakunin—and in that he furnishes an example to all radical leaders. But in order to develop the full implication of that example, it is necessary to go beyond Lenin. It is necessary to understand how you think, and teach that, as well as the result of it, to those who follow you. It may be that a psychological science would have made little difference in the political strategy of Lenin; that locomotive genius had small need of self-analysis. But if Lenin had been conscious of his own intellectual method and position, he might have tapped an immense reservoir of revolutionary will and energy existing in sincere but immature minds, socialist-revolutionaries, and anarchists, whom he was compelled to dismiss as "revolutionary adventurers" because he did not know how to teach them. It is no accident that anarchism finds its best adherents among the French and southern European races, who love hard clear thoughts and prefer doubt to metaphysical consolation. Hegelian Marxism will never get a firm foothold in those countries. Any natural child of Montaigne or Machiavelli will always rather remain in a state of innocence than go to school to a German metaphysician. Approach an anarchist, not with the proposition that you know just what the universe is doing, having learned it from a Hegelian philosopher, but with the proposition that a great undertaking requires a great plan, and you have some chance of teaching him how to think.

Moreover, if Lenin had understood his own thinking he could have left in his place a body of men better trained to carry it forward than those he did leave—

condemned to the vain effort to reconcile his wisdom
with an antique animistic intellectualism which he ignored and trampled on from the beginning of his life
to the end. And still more important, the Commissariat
of Education in Lenin's Russia would have presented a
more thoroughly and systematically intelligent picture
than it ever did. Never before have so many modern
educative ideas been adopted on a large scale as in Lenin's
Russia; never have so many bold experiments in scientific education been made. And yet they were made
under the tolerance, rather than by the initiative, of the
revolutionary government. And that, it seems to me, is
an inevitable consequence of the Hegelian-Marxian
philosophy. So long as the very preservation of the new
regime was erroneously identified with the promulgation
of a set of ideas hostile to all psychological understanding, a thorough and systematic revolutionizing of education was impossible. So long as the proletarian party
issued pamphlets indoctrinating its members, on pain of
exclusion, with a belief that the sentence, "Workers of
the world, unite!" is not an exhortation to action but "a
reflection in the heads of Marxists of the fact of proletarian solidarity," it was impossible to teach even gram-
mar, to say nothing of the true art of thinking and being
a man. If "Workers of the world, unite!" means that
the workers are united, what does "The workers are
united" mean?

The example is typical of many absurd pronuncia-
mentos that were put out in the name of education by
the Doctors of the State Philosophy under Lenin. And
it shows, only a little more clearly than usual, the essential motive of this, as of other philosophies—to convince
the believer that the objective world is at one with his
aspiration. To me, the most unsatisfactory feature of

the socialist experiment as initiated by Lenin's party was the failure to establish a great system of education. They established in the place of it this great solemn fetish of Dialectic Materialism, which is nothing but the old shoes of the Almighty God.

Marxian Utopianism

A final enemy of all intelligent radicalism is the utopianism of Marx's own theory. Marx's scheme was a practical and realistic one only up to, and including, the establishment of a dictatorship of the proletariat which should expropriate the capitalists. The problems arising after that, Marx was inclined to regard, not as postponed problems greater in their complexity than that of capturing the power, but as problems which "history" would solve. The very doctrine of Marxism, indeed, was supposed to begin to die of contradiction and give place to a "higher unity," when this necessary process of which it was a reflection had been achieved. Marx's attitude to the subsequent course of history was, therefore, hardly distinguishable from the general attitude of the utopians. He believed that truly miraculous things would follow of themselves. That there might be a problem of preserving the new society, and preventing its relapse into capitalism, or into something more disastrous, never occurred to his mind.

The principal miracle which Marx anticipated from the proletarian revolution was a wholesale change in human nature. Marxism knows nothing of the distinction between hereditary instincts and acquired characters. That human nature in its fundamental and general outlines could only be systematically changed by an extended process of selective breeding, whether artificial or natural, is a point that Marx never learned from Darwin, and that he could not learn without breaking down his whole philosophy of history. For that philosophy requires that human nature should be regarded as a mere function of the evolution of the productive forces, an indefinitely variable factor. "The whole of history," Marx tells us, "is nothing but a continual transformation of human nature." And Plekhanov develops this essential thesis of Marxism as follows:

"According to the character of the means of production, men enter into such and such relations in the process of production (since this is a social process), and according to their *relations* in the social process of production, *their habits, their sentiments, their tastes, their way of thinking and acting, in short their nature* is modified. Thus it is not human nature which explains the historic movement, it is the historic movement which fashions human nature in different ways."

From this it follows that once an economic revolution is achieved and completed, the transformation of human nature necessary to sustain it will automatically follow. The problem of adjusting the forms of the new society to the original nature of man does not and cannot exist. Psychology as a science of human behavior has no more place in Marxism than psychology as a science of the mind. In building a model hen-house a Marxist would have the good sense to consider the instinctive nature of the hens, but in building an ideal social structure for mankind he is prevented by his religion from even asking a question about the natural tendencies of this animal.

The extent of the utopian dreaming which has been founded upon this myth of the indefinite changeability of human nature may be seen in the remark of Engels:

"Socialism will abolish both architecture and barrow-pushing as professions, and the man who has given half an hour to architecture will also push the cart a little until his work as an architect is again in demand. It would be a pretty sort of socialism which perpetuated the business of barrow-pushing."

Here it is evident that Engels is not a practical engineer, considering the problem of actually producing a socialist society and making it work. He is a dreamer, discoursing about an ideal state of things which must come in due course, if the universe continues its "endless ascending from the lower to the higher."

The indifference of Marx and Engels, and of all Marxists, toward the all-important problem of controlling population is another example of the utopianism inherent in their religion. For my part, I believe that a free and real human society will never be created by a people who ignore the necessity for intelligent control of the quantity, if not indeed in a negative way the quality, of the population. But it is very difficult for Marxists to see this problem or approach it with practical intelligence, because population is one of those things which are supposed to be especially in the divine care of the Process of Production.

A similar utopianism prevails among Marxists in regard to the problem of sex equality. Seeing that the dependence of woman is largely economic, and that her general independence, like that of man, can be attained only in a free and equal society, they jump to the conclusion that an economic revolution will automatically solve the problem of woman's independence. This great achievement, too, they leave in the hands of the Productive Forces. But if you face the actual psychological and physiological elements of the woman's problem, it is only too obvious that it will not be solved automatically, even by a social revolution. It will be solved by men and women, and particularly women, who devote their utmost intelligence and energy to its solution.

Another example of the Marxian utopianism is the theory of the automatic "dying away" of the state—a theory that has been reduced to such dreadful absurdity by the state capitalist tyranny of Stalin that we need not here discuss it.

Lenin himself of all Marxists was the least inclined to lean on history, or leave to that dialectic universe in which he tried to believe the tasks and responsibilities that belonged to him. And yet Lenin was not free from the utopianism inherent in the dialectic philosophy, as the following quotations will show:

"Capitalism inevitably leaves, as an inheritance to Socialism, on the one hand old professional and craft differences . . . and on the other trade-unions, which only very slowly and in the course of years can and will develop into broader industrial rather than craft organizations. . . . These industrial unions will in their turn lead to the abolition of the division of labor between people, to the education, training and preparation of workers who will be able to do everything."

"Under socialism all will take a turn at administration, and will soon become accustomed to the idea of no administration at all."

These statements have no support whatever in the facts of human nature. Only by completely ignoring the data of psychology, and putting a completely metaphysical faith in the place of this science, is it possible for a moment to believe them. Bertrand Russell in his most utopian phase had a far more realistic and practical approach than Lenin to this future problem.

"People will be taught," he said, "not only as at present, one trade, or one small portion of a trade, but several trades, so that they can vary their occupation according to the seasons and the fluctuations of demand. Every industry will be self-governing as regards all its internal affairs, and even separate factories will decide for themselves all the questions that only concern those who work in them. There will not be capitalist management, as at present, but management by elected representatives. . . ."

The contrast between these two statements is a contrast between practical possibilities and utopian dreams. And because they are problems of the future, it was the anarchistic utopian who was practical, and the "scientific socialist" who was dreaming.

Lenin was not affected in his practical character and activity by these dreams, because he knew how to keep them in the remote future. He used to recall his followers to the immediate task, and illustrate the practical-scientific realism with which it should be attacked, by means of the figure of a man who is pulling himself hand-over-hand along a chain. It is not enough, he would say, to believe in the ultimate goal of the historic process —one must be able to "find in the chain at each moment the link which it is necessary to seize with all one's force, in order to retain the chain as a whole and pass to the next link." There is a difficulty in imagining this picture. It really illustrates, better than anything else, the absurdity of mixing animistic faith with practical science. For if future history is a chain securely attached to the co-operative commonwealth, there is hardly more than one link within reach, and that is the next one. But this confused figure enabled Lenin to keep the millennium out of the present task, and that is what he used it for. There was perhaps a moment, just after the October revolution, when his faith in the purposes of "history" introduced an element of legend into his practical calculations. Trotsky tells us, at least, that in the early meetings of the Soviet of People's Commissars, Lenin continually asserted that "in six months we will have socialism." Only four of those six months had passed, however, when Lenin stated at a convention of his party that "The bricks are not yet baked with which socialism will be built."

"What socialism will be when it attains finished forms, we do not know and we cannot say. . . . Our program is a description of what we have begun to do, and of the next steps which we want to take. . . . The name of our party signifies clearly enough that we are going toward complete communism, that we present to ourselves such an abstract proposition as that each will work according to his abilities, and receive according to his needs, without any military control or violence. But it is early to talk about that. When has any state yet begun to die away?"

What had begun to die away here was the utopianism of the Marxian metaphysics. It will inevitably die away in honest minds when the real facts arrive. And the most important question we have to ask is: What shall take its place? The remarks of Lenin make clear the answer: A thoroughly experimental procedure. The aim will be defined at first very loosely and "abstractly," and held subject to redefinition in the light of the developing facts; the facts will be defined more exactly, but they also will be continually redefined in their relation to the aim and the redefinition of it; and the hypothesis, the plan of action, will be kept in a state of development and living relevance both to the facts and to the aim. Doubt will be given its due place, and thinking will be done as it is done by scientific minds.

PART SEVEN

TROTSKY DEFENDS THE FAITH

TROTSKY DEFENDS THE FAITH

LIKE ALL religions, Dialectic Materialism rests fundamentally not on investigation and rational calculation, but on the will to believe. As Gisors says in André Malraux's novel: "Marxism is not a doctrine, it is a *will* . . . you must be Marxists not in order to be right, but in order to conquer without betraying yourselves." Trotsky has said a more extreme thing: "The will to revolutionary activity is a condition indispensable [even] to understanding the Marxian dialectic."

It is doubtful whether either of these authors realized the full import of what he was saying. It is a frank avowal that the pretense of Marxism to be an objective analysis of history and society, its pretense to the authority of empirical science, is a bluff. Marxism is not a valid account of the real world, but a system of ideas to be adopted—and to be understood!—only by those within the real world (whatever it may be like) who are actuated by a certain passion and striving to effect a certain change.

Although not so frankly avowed, this fact about the Marxian philosophy is evident in the very first paragraph of those *Theses on Feuerbach* in which it took its rise. For the discussion there is not about what reality *is*, but how reality "is to be conceived." If you will try to imagine Trotsky, when preparing for the seizure of power in October, asking himself, not whether the garrison of

Petrograd *is* revolutionary, but whether the garrison "is to be conceived" as revolutionary, you will realize how remote this attitude of mind is from that of objective inquiry.

It is, however, a very human attitude of mind, more native to most men than scientific skepticism because grounded in the psychology of the savage, and more imposing to those dwelling east of the Rhine because employed to build up such stupendous temples of intellectuality by the German transcendental philosophers. Santayana has a passage on German philosophy which ought to be used as a preface by those who wish to understand its legitimate if slightly wayward child, Dialectic Materialism. He says:

"Dominated as this philosophy is by the transcendental method, it regards views, and the history and logic of views, as more primitive and important than the objects which these views have in common. The genial Professor Paulsen of Berlin (whose pupil I once had the advantage of being) had a phrase that continually recurred in his lectures: *Man kann sagen*, as much as to say, Things will yield the following picture, if one cares to draw it. And he once wrote an article in honor of Kant very pertinently entitled: *Was uns Kant sein kann*. . . . To take what views we will of things, if things will barely suffer us to take them, and then to declare that the things are mere terms in the views we take of them—that is transcendentalism."

In the case of Dialectic Materialism, it is not only a question of taking the view "one will" or drawing the picture one "cares to." It is a question of taking the view and drawing the picture presented as indispensable to the transformation of human society from a thing of cruelty and woe and exploitation to a paradise on earth. The will to believe for the soul's sake is subtle, shifty, inwardly evasive; it could not be kept up if the believer made clear note of the point at which judgment abdicates and choice steps in. The will to believe for revolutionary action's sake is equally subtle and evasive, but it is also violently combative. The believer maintains his belief with lusty blows both of logic and empirical demonstration. He maintains it on objective grounds, and with even more than the usual disdain of his opponents —they cannot even *understand* because they have the wrong volition!—but he is impermeable as though clad in supernatural armor to any similar blows from them. I had experience of this on a visit to Trotsky in Prinkipo island, where I spent the better part of two weeks vainly attempting to get his momentary attention to any one thing that I had to say about Dialectic Materialism. He had received some time previously a copy of the French edition of my book, *Marx and Lenin,* and this had been his comment:

"I am terribly sorry that you have taken so unacceptable and theoretically erroneous a position on the question of Marxism. I am afraid that we shall have to have a fight. I do not know of one case in the history of the revolutionary movement of the last thirty years where a rejection of Marxism did not ruin a revolutionist politically also. I repeat: not one case. Moreover I know scores of *outstanding* cases where people began with a rejection of dialectic materialism, especially historic materialism, and ended . . . in a reconciliation with bourgeois society. I have as yet only leafed over your book and will read it in the near future. In my next book I will have to devote a short chapter to you: political friendship demands clarity above all."

The hauteur of the remark, "I am sorry you have taken so unacceptable and erroneous a position. . . . I have as yet only leafed over your book," is more characteristic perhaps of Trotsky than of Marxists in general. Some of them at least are more tactful. But the underlying attitude is typical of all believers in Dialectic Materialism. They have only to "leaf over" a volume and spot one new idea that conflicts with the old religion and, without a moment of curiosity or interested inquiry, they gird their loins for a fight in defense of the faith.

Lenin's reactions were even more violent. "I could not control myself," he writes to Petressov after reading books by the Neo-Kantians, Struve and Bulgakov. And when Lunacharsky and others became interested in the efforts of Ernst Mach to find a common standpoint for physics and psychology, he wrote to Maxim Gorky:

"They assure the reader that 'belief' in the reality of the external world is 'mysticism,' mix up materialism and Kantianism in the most disgusting manner, preach a variety of agnosticism (empirio-criticism) and idealism (empiriomonism),—teach the workers 'religious atheism' and the 'worship' of man's highest potentialities—declare Engels' teachings about dialectic to be mystical—dip up from a stinking source some kind of French 'positivists'—agnostics or metaphysicians, the devil take them, with their 'symbolic theory of knowledge!' No, this is too much! Of course we rank-and-file Marxists are uneducated in philosophy, but why on that account insult us by handing us this stuff as the philosophy of Marxism? I'd rather be drawn and quartered than agree to participate in a journal or a school with people propagating such stuff."

That was the mood in which Lenin decided to educate himself in philosophy, his avowed purpose being to exterminate these "exterminators of dialectic materialism." It may seem strange to call so furious a state of mind scholastic, and yet, if scholasticism is "an effort

to reconcile lay knowledge with theology," that is what
the better part of Lenin's *Materialism and Empirio-
criticism* is. That is the whole concern of Engels's seven
year labor, *Dialektik und Natur*. It is the major concern
of Plekhanov's theoretic writings, and of Bukharin's.
There is no other concern in what has been written on
the subject by Stalin's "theoreticians." George Sarton,
from whom I borrowed the above definition of scholasticism, points out that this drag upon scientific progress
was not confined to Christendom, but that it afflicted
Mohammedan science as disastrously and was equally
rife among the Chinese, the Buddhists, and the He-
brews. A demonstration that Marxism has all the defining attributes of a religion would be incomplete without
a warning against its own peculiar brand of scholasticism.

II

Trotsky in the past has never given himself heartily
to these sterile exercises. He has, for one thing, been less
the victim of Teutonic influences than the "vast majority of the Russian intelligentsia" who, as Plekhanov re-
marked, "in so far as they have any interest in philosophy trail along after German teachers." In the process
of being banished from one country to another Trotsky
has acquired a very cosmopolitan culture. For another
thing he has no aptitude for philosophic speculation and
little knowledge of philosophy. I have always felt that
prudence was one of Trotsky's motives for failing to
cross swords publicly with his philosophic opponents—
with John Dewey, at least, whose devastating reply to
Their Morals and Ours was left hanging in the air like
the words of an oracle.[1] But Trotsky has also a vast gift

[1] *The New International*, June and August, 1938.

of impatience, and has no doubt been influenced in avoiding scholastic disputations by the natural wish of a man of dynamic thought and action not to be bothered with intellectual rubbish.

Only in recent times, when Stalin's tyranny has made the plan-of-action embodied in the Marxian religion seem so obviously impractical, has Trotsky felt obliged to fall back upon the religion itself to defend the plan. He has himself denounced the regime which issued from the October seizure of power in such unmeasured language that any man of good sense, to say nothing of scientific intelligence, inevitably infers that the plan should be changed.

"The realities of Soviet life today," he says, "can indeed be hardly reconciled even with the shreds of old theory. Workers are bound to the factories; peasants are bound to the collective farms. Passports have been introduced. The freedom of movement has been completely restricted. It is a capital crime to come late to work. . . . The frontiers are guarded by an impenetrable wall of border-patrols and police dogs on a scale heretofore unknown anywhere. To all intents and purposes, no one can leave and no one may enter. Foreigners who had previously managed to get into the country are being systematically exterminated. The gist of the Soviet constitution, the 'most democratic in the world,' amounts to this, that every citizen is required at an appointed time to cast his ballot for the one and only candidate handpicked by Stalin or his agents. The press, the radio, all the organs of propaganda, agitation and national education are completely in the hands of the ruling clique. During the last five years no less than half a million members, according to official figures, have been expelled from the party. How many have been shot, thrown into jails and concentration camps, or exiled to Siberia, we do not definitely know. But undoubtedly hundreds of thousands of party members have shared the fate of millions of nonparty people. It would be extremely difficult to instill in the minds of these millions, their families, relatives and friends, the idea that the Stalinist state is withering away. It is strangling others, but gives no sign of withering. It has instead arrived at a pitch of wild intensity unprecedented in the history of mankind."

On reading these words from the organizer of the October revolution, one exclaims almost irresistibly:

"Surely then, after getting this result, you are not going to do the very same thing over again!"

This is so obviously a sensible reaction, that a good many people think Trotsky's stubborn hostility to it is due to pride in his own life's work, or ambition to get back to Russia and be a power again. They fail to realize the degree of Trotsky's consecration to the cause of socialism, a prodigious phenomenon, and they fail to realize the rigor of his philosophic faith. To Trotsky the Russian revolution was not, except in its details, an experiment. It was part of a grand historical process determined by the very nature of the material out of which the world is made, a process which he conceives as sweeping on through no matter how many such "contradictions"—nay, by the very "motor force" contained in contradictions—to final triumph. He is therefore unable, without revising himself and the very universe in which his mind and feelings live, to revise his fundamental plan.

Trotsky is not only unable to revise his plan in view of its failure; he is unable, in the present circumstances, to admit that it is a flat failure. After so eloquently describing a state in which the workers have no voice, he goes on blandly to inform us that Russia is a "workers' state." And if we ask him why, his answer contains no allusion whatever to the workers. His answer is: Because the Russian state has nationalized the industries and instituted state planning. So long as these two conditions prevail, Trotsky tells us, the USSR must be conceived not as a bureaucrat's state exploiting the workers, but as a workers' state with bureaucratic degenerations. It must not only be so conceived intellectually, but all the practical inferences must be drawn. Stalin's Russia must be defended to the point of armed warfare, if necessary, by the workers of other states—and this even includes (although Trotsky is too sly to say so explicitly) the workers of ravished Finland.[2]

This position, fantastic to a man of practical judgment, flows with inexorable logic from Trotsky's dialectic religion. According to the terms of that religion a workers' revolutionary state is destined to expropriate the capitalists, take possession of the industries, and inaugurate a planned economy. Out of this situation is destined to emerge, through what other conflicts and contradictions cannot be foreseen, the society without class and without government. It would be quite possible, according to this religion, to admit that the Russian workers, or any other given workers, had made an effort and failed to achieve this historic mission. Hope would still be unbroken, faith be whole. But to admit that it was achieved not by a workers' but by a bureaucrats' state—or even to admit that parallel with the process of its achievement the workers' state *became* a bureaucrats' state—is to abandon the whole creed. A universe can do almost anything and still be dialectic; and

[2] Trotsky's New York followers were reckless enough to draw this inference in the first months of the invasion of Finland. But Trotsky, so far as I know, has let them bear the responsibility for this valid inference from his views.

therefore Trotsky is undaunted by any setbacks that can be invented by the Stalin regime. But a dialectic universe, having set out upon an upward procedure as nicely specified as the expropriation of the bourgeoisie by the proletariat and the establishment of a planned economy, cannot let *somebody else* expropriate the bourgeoisie and establish a planned economy without betraying its essential nature. That is why we find Trotsky, impatient and ironical of theological buncombe as he believes himself to be, defending the fantastic thesis that a state in which the workers have no power is a "workers' state."

It is a theological position, and naturally those in Trotsky's group who want to be a little more simple and sensible appeal to secular good sense and to the authority of science. As neither good sense nor science will have anything to do with such conceptions as a workers' state in which the workers have no power, Trotsky is compelled to fall back on the naked framework of his dialectic religion. He is compelled—tastes, training, natural gifts, and prudential considerations to the contrary notwithstanding—to become a scholastic. Accordingly we have, in the *New International* for March, 1940, a statement from Leon Trotsky as to what "the dialectic" is, in what mysterious ways it moves, and how superior it is to the logic used by laymen in "the daily problems of life."

Trotsky is able, of course, only to "sketch the substance of the matter in very concise form." And, strangely enough, that is all any dialectic materialist has ever been able to do. The whole of the literature on the Marxian dialectic consists of fragmentary remarks supposed to summarize a larger body of knowledge. But this larger body of knowledge, although as the essential science by means of which mankind is going to find his way to an earthly paradise it is certainly important above all other objects of attention, nobody has ever had time to present. In another number of the *New International* one of Trotsky's followers alludes to this fact, and remarks that probably nobody will ever have time really to expound the dialectic method—the revolution is coming too soon, and Marxists are so very busy! Let us be humbly thankful, therefore, that Trotsky has at last paused long enough to sketch for us the "ABC of Materialist Dialectics" in a few short paragraphs.

"The dialectic," he begins, is ". . . a science of the forms of our thinking in so far as it is not limited to the daily problems of life but attempts to arrive at an understanding of more complicated and drawn-out processes. The dialectic and formal logic bear a relation similar to that between higher and lower mathematics."

Now let us take that statement seriously and accept for the time being what it really means: *There are two kinds of human thought-process so different as to constitute the subject matter of two different sciences. . . .*
We shall have to ignore the fact that psychology, which studies thought-processes without regard to norms, has never found signs of these two distinct kinds of thinking, and that, strangely enough, Marxists have never suggested that they be made the object of psychological investigation. We shall have to put out of our minds such natural questions as: Just where do "daily" problems end and "drawn-out" problems begin? Some people, especially among the proletariat, find daily problems both complicated and drawn-out. Suppose, for instance, that a problem lasted a week and involved four-

teen different complications—would that require dialectic thinking? Would a month-long problem engender it?
Does the mere dwelling upon a problem bring it into
action, or does complexity itself in some mysterious
manner gear in that cerebral supercortex which we must
assume to underlie this distinct system of thought-forms?

To all these questions, quite obvious and inevitable
if one takes his initial statement seriously, Trotsky's sole
answer is the remark that "the dialectic and formal logic
bear a relationship similar to that between higher and
lower mathematics." As an analogy this would be faulty,
because higher mathematics rests upon the complete validity of lower mathematics and applies the same logic
either to more difficult problems or to solving the same
problems more simply. But, moreover, it cannot be employed as an analogy because mathematics is a branch
of logic, and if there is a higher kind of logic called dialectic, then higher mathematics would have to be dialectic, not something similar to it. To say that there are
two kinds of thinking, and they differ from each other
as do higher and lower mathematics, can make sense only
if mathematics is not thinking.

But let us ignore all these difficulties, and not only
accept Trotsky's definition of "the dialectic" but hold
fast to it while he goes on talking.

"The Aristotelian logic of the simple syllogism," he proceeds, "starts from the proposition that A is equal to A.
This postulate is accepted as an axiom for a multitude
of practical human actions and elementary generalizations.
But in reality A is not equal to A. This is easy to prove
if we observe these two letters under a lens—they are quite
different from each other. But, one can object, the question
is not of the size or the form of the letters, since they are
only symbols for equal quantities, for instance a pound of

sugar. The objection is beside the point; in reality a pound of sugar is never equal to a pound of sugar—a more delicate scale always discloses a difference. Again one can object: but a pound of sugar is equal to itself. Neither is this true —all bodies change uninterruptedly in size, weight, color, etc. They are never equal to themselves. A sophist will respond that a pound of sugar is equal to itself 'at any given moment.' Aside from the extremely dubious practical value of this 'axiom,' it does not withstand theoretical criticism either. How should we really conceive the word 'moment'? If it is an infinitesimal interval of time, then a pound of sugar is subjected during the course of that 'moment' to inevitable changes. Or is the 'moment' a purely mathematical abstraction, that is, a zero of time? But everything exists in time; and existence itself is an uninterrupted process of transformation; time is consequently a fundamental element of existence. Thus the axiom that A is equal to A signifies that a thing is equal to itself if it does not change, that is, if it does not exist." [3]

Now that is a cogent paragraph, and in its manner of rising to a philosophic climax in the last sentence, beautifully constructed. However, it contains no word which would have been news to Aristotle; it merely misunderstands in the manner of a schoolboy who has not done his homework what his logic is about, and what it means by saying that A is A, and that everything is either A or not-A, and nothing both A and not-A. Aristotle was not talking about existent things, but about consistent thinking. He was not writing in his organon a science of being, but of valid inference. The principle, A equals A, means that if you are going to be rational, or in other

[3] L. Trotsky, *The New International*, March, 1940, "A Petty-Bourgeois Opposition in the Socialist Workers Party," p. 37. I shall quote, with the exception of two small illustrative paragraphs, the whole of Trotsky's concise exposition of the dialectic.

words talk sense, the meaning of your terms must not shift while you are talking. You cannot even argue—as Trotsky does so skillfully in that paragraph—that all existence is a process, unless by existence you mean existence and by process process. You could not even state that a pound of sugar is always unequal to itself, unless the term *pound of sugar* remained identical in meaning with the term *itself.* That is what Aristotle perceived; that is what formal logic is about. Its principles are assumed by those who argue in favor of a "dialectic logic," just as they are assumed by those who argue about the price of sugar.

Surely this very problem about a dialectic logic is not a "daily" one—it is "complicated," it is "drawn-out." If higher thought-forms are apposite anywhere, they are apposite here. And yet Trotsky, like Marx before him, and like Hegel before Marx, presents the argument for a dialectic logic in the terms of the logic of A equals A. He could not do otherwise, of course, for no argument is possible in other terms, but he might at least have the circumspection to pretend to.

Trotsky begins his next paragraph with the remark that "at first glance" it might seem as though his "subtleties" about the pound of sugar are "useless." Which shows at least that he is dimly conscious of his clumsiness in the role of a scholastic. It is not, however, "at first glance," but upon reflection, that the total uselessness of his proof that a pound of sugar is not a constant entity appears. For if the axiom A equals A had, or was meant to have, any such existential reference at all, it would apply not only to pounds of sugar, but also to kaleidoscopes and moving pictures. His subtleties therefore not only seem useless, but they are so.

Ignoring this quite considerable bumper, or stumbling

hastily over it in loyalty to the needs of his religion, Trotsky hurries on to tell us more precisely in what circumstances we can safely operate with a logic which asserts that every pound of sugar, and every fickle maid, and every flying projectile, is in every respect and from every point of view and at all times constant. We can do it, he says—and the discovery is hardly overwhelming—"within certain limits." But let us have this, too, in his own words:

"To make use of the axiom, A is equal to A, with impunity is possible only within certain limits. When quantitative changes in A are negligible for the task at hand then we can presume that A is equal to A. This is, for example, the manner in which a buyer and a seller consider a pound of sugar. We consider the temperature of the sun likewise. Until recently we considered the buying power of the dollar in the same way. But quantitative changes beyond certain limits become converted into qualitative. A pound of sugar subjected to the action of water or kerosene ceases to be a pound of sugar. A dollar in the embrace of a president ceases to be a dollar."

Now I think any uninstructed person with a good head, on reading these statements about sugar, the sun, and the dollar, would be inclined to exclaim: "But that is all so obvious! Do you mean to say that Aristotle, the founder of three sciences and of literary criticism besides, the father of the scientific spirit, was such a fool as to write a system of logic which ceased to be valid when sugar was dissolved in water, or which assumed that sugar was still the same thing after it was mixed with kerosene!" And the uninstructed person would be quite right. It is not Aristotle's logic, but the dialectic critics of it, who are reduced to absurdity by these amateurish remarks of Trotsky. Trotsky has told us that the Aristotelian logic is all right for "daily problems," and yet he now asks us to believe that the Aristotelian logic is inadequate to the situation arising when the cook pours kerosene into the sugar, or the president takes forty-odd cents out of the dollar. The housewife and the financier would make a funny mess of daily problems if their "logic" were so frail. Logic has nothing whatever to say about sugar or about dollars, and the defenders of "the dialectic" are led inevitably into this nonsensical position by pretending that it has.

If Trotsky knew something about Aristotle's philosophy, he would not perhaps be quite so glib about his logic. He says later on that the Aristotelian logic was "founded in the period when the idea of evolution itself did not exist." The idea of evolution was familiar to Aristotle in the writings of Thales, Anaximander, Xenophanes, and Anaxagoras, all discussed by him in the first chapters of his metaphysics. Anaximander said that "man sprang from a different animal, in fact from a fish, whom at first he resembled," and based his opinion upon the fact that in the early phases of the struggle for existence an animal with so long a period of infancy would not have survived. Xenophanes based his theory of evolution on the evidence of fossils. It was Aristotle's interest in these biological problems, the problems of growth and development, as against Plato's delight in the unchanging truths of mathematics, that probably caused, more than any other one thing, their divergence in philosophy. And the essence of that divergence was Aristotle's refusal to regard being as something other than becoming. His entire philosophy may be described as an effort to explain how one thing can become another. If Aristotle had been unfamiliar with evolution— as unfamiliar as Trotsky is with Aristotle—he might indeed have written a science according to which dollars remain dollars and sugar sugar, no matter what happens to them in the world of change. But it would not have been logic, it would have been metaphysics. And it would not have been Aristotle's but Plato's.

However, let us pass over these difficulties too, and accept Trotsky's statement that beyond certain limits, and especially where quantitative changes "become converted into qualitative," we have to abandon the thought forms of ordinary logic and adopt a higher kind of thought forms. Might it not seem appropriate at this point, when we are certainly ready and willing to be saved from the disaster of confusing a dollar with fifty-nine cents, to go on and tell us what these higher thought forms are? It seems to me the only possible conclusion to Trotsky's argument up to the point where he says "A dollar in the embrace of a president ceases to be a dollar," would run like this:

"In our reasoning, therefore, we must not regard the term dollar as having even a fixed qualitative significance, to say nothing of its quantity. We must have a logic in which the term dollar itself is capable of shifting with the whims of presidents."

Instead of that, Trotsky forgets all about his promise to reveal the inner mystery of the dialectic logic, and draws—according to the Aristotelian logic—this simple practical inference from what he has just said about quantity and quality:

"To determine at the right moment the critical point where quantity changes into quality is one of the most important and difficult tasks in all the spheres of knowledge including sociology."

Yes, indeed! But where are the higher thought forms? You have not used them in telling us about presidents and dollars. You do not use them in drawing this inference from what you have told us. Are they to be used in *determining* that right moment and critical point? And if so, what are they? And where?

You might almost think that Trotsky had written this paragraph in order to make clear that the myth of a dialectic logic, apart from its religious function, has no function at all except to call attention to the fact that things change, and to the necessity of drawing the inferences which flow by ordinary logic from this important fact. He goes on, however, to make it still clearer:

"Vulgar thought," he says, "operates with such concepts as capitalism, morals, freedom, workers' state, etc., as fixed abstractions, presuming that capitalism is equal to capitalism, morals are equal to morals, etc. Dialectical thinking analyzes all things and phenomena in their continuous change, while determining in the material conditions of those changes that critical limit beyond which A ceases to be A, a workers' state ceases to be a workers' state."

Is it not surprising to learn that dialectic thinking, which has been defined as thinking which operates with the axiom that A is *not* A, turns out after three paragraphs to be thinking which determines the point at which A *ceases* to be A? Again we ask: Where are the dialectic thought forms? And we ask further: Where can they possibly be? For, is it not obvious that in the task of determining where A ceases to be A, a method of thinking based upon the assumption that A is not A would be of no use whatever?

I do not want to make this argument too complicated, but I cannot neglect to remark that no such thing as a change of quantity into quality occurs in nature. There comes a point when the quantitative changes in a dollar become so large that from our point of view it is a different thing. The same thing is true, although a little less obvious, when water becomes steam. The change is still quantitative, and is so expressed by science.[4] Physics, indeed, tries to express all changes in quantitative terms, and its whole effort would go to smash if quantities "turned into" qualities. That happens only in the idealist's universe. The survival of this formula in Marxism, like the attribution of motor force to "contradictions," proves, to anyone not wholly blinded by the will to believe, that Marx's alleged materialism is a fake. It proves nothing else.

Trotsky himself is apparently uneasy in the poor showing he has made as the expounder of a higher kind of logic, for in his next two paragraphs he carefully takes it all back. The first of these two apologetic paragraphs reads as follows:

"The fundamental flaw of vulgar thought lies in the fact that it wishes to content itself with motionless imprints of a reality which consists of eternal motion. Dialectic thinking gives to concepts, by means of closer approximations, corrections, concretizations, a richness of content and flexibility; I would even say a succulence which to a certain extent brings them close to living phenomena. Not capitalism in general, but a given capitalism at a given stage of development. Not a workers' state in general but a given workers'

---

[4] Sidney Hook has pointed this out in his criticism of Engels's *Dialectic and Nature*, and oddly enough Trotsky corroborates him. "When quantitative changes are negligible for the task in hand," he writes, "then we can assume that A is equal to A. . . . But quantitative changes beyond certain limits become converted into qualitative." In this unconscious *non sequitur* quantitative changes are assumed to become qualitative when they cease to be negligible "for the task at hand"—or in other words from our point of view.

state in a backward country, in an imperialist encirclement, etc."

In other words, dialectic thinking does not differ from vulgar thinking in using a different logic based upon "the axiom that everything is always changing." Dialectic thinking is thinking with the ordinary logic *about the fact* or *with consideration for the fact*, that everything is changing. People who become aware of this fact make constant "corrections" in the light of it; they do not rest in abstract judgments or large generalizations, but insist upon "concretization," upon making "closer approximations" to the particulars, and upon freedom to change their judgments when the changing factual complex makes this necessary—in other words upon "flexibility." This is what gives "richness of content" and even a kind of "succulence" to their thinking.

But this also requires that they should continually revise their thinking, making ever new decisions about the same evolving set of facts. Indolence is more than half the cause of dogmatism; people who think flexibly have to think often. It thus becomes possible to describe their thinking as composed of the same kind of judgments and inferences as those of dogmatic thinkers, but with a higher frequency. And that is what Trotsky does in his second and still more apologetic paragraph, which I will now quote:

"Dialectic thinking is related to vulgar thinking in the same way that a motion picture is related to a still photograph. The motion picture does not outlaw the still photograph but combines a series of them according to the laws of motion. Dialectics does not deny the syllogism, but teaches us to combine syllogisms in such a way as to bring our understanding closer to the eternally changing reality."

That is the end of Trotsky's concise sketch of the dialectic logic. This logic began by differing from ordinary logic as higher does from lower mathematics; it ends by differing as a rapid series of still pictures does from a single one. It began by employing different "forms of thought" because reality is eternally changing. It ends by employing the *same thought forms*—even to the much abused and admittedly artificial syllogism—but *combining them* in such a way as to *get closer* to the eternally changing reality. A more candid admission that there is no such thing as dialectic logic could hardly be framed. And it forms a fitting conclusion to Trotsky's "concise sketch," which is nothing from first to last but the reduction to absurdity by a reckless amateur of the whole theological construction.

There is no dialectic logic. There are no higher thought-forms. There is merely reflection which is wise enough to take account of the fluidity of its subject matter, reflection which understands that terms are not things, nor copies of things, and keeps coming back to things and making new judgments in proportion as the change requires it. Perhaps the best illustration of this wisdom is the reply of Solon—a century before Heraclitus ever announced that all things change—to someone who asked him what is the perfect form of government. Solon said: "For whom and at what time?"

Let us quote once more Trotsky's concluding sentence above, and draw the natural conclusion from it:

"Dialectics does not deny the syllogism, but teaches us to combine syllogisms in such a way as to bring our understanding closer to the eternally changing reality." . . . Therefore the pretense of dialectics to be a higher kind of logic operating with supersyllogistic thought-forms is the quintessence of cant.

That is not only the natural, but the only rationally possible conclusion of Trotsky's own confession about dialectics. Instead of drawing it, however, Trotsky suddenly catches his breath, sensing the danger to his "philosophy of optimism," snatches himself back, as it were, from the brink of the disaster of common sense, and mumbles—once more in complete *non sequitur*—the name of Hegel, and the pious formulas of the dialectic faith:

"Hegel in his *logic* established a series of Laws: change of quantity into quality, development through contradictions, conflict of content and form, interruption of continuity, change of possibility into inevitability, etc., which are just as important for theoretical thought as is the simple syllogism for more elementary tasks."

You need only apply to these Delphic utterances the advice given you by Trotsky in the sentences preceding —you need only make them *concrete* and bring them *closer to the facts*, in order to see what they mean, and what their function is.

"Change of quantity into quality" is similar enough to a frequent natural phenomenon to give plausibility and the appearance of mysterious knowledge to the whole series.

"Development through contradictions" means faith in the working-class struggle and its victory as the only and the inevitable outcome of social evolution.

"Conflict of content and form" means that the new society is ripening in the shell of the old.

"Interruption of continuity" means proletarian seizure of power.

"Change of possibility into inevitability" means that, if you have the "will to revolutionary activity," you can with a little casuistry believe both that proletarian victory is dialectically inevitable and that your activity is essential to its success.

"Etc." means that Trotsky, like all the other priests of this religion, is too busy to give you a forthright and complete account of it. "Etc.'s" function is to suggest mysteries within mysteries which he might expound to you, if he were not too busy with the practical end of the job. As a matter of fact, he has told you in these few paragraphs all that he knows about the Marxian dialectic, and, with some small omissions, all there is to it.

It may seem strange that a man of Trotsky's make, having plainly confessed that there is no such thing as dialectic logic, should continue to keep up the pretense that there is. A man so sarcastically impatient of devious locutions and conceptualistic bombast in the sphere of politics ought to have some limit of tolerance on philosophic questions too. Here, however, you have to remember the two things I pointed out in the beginning. First, that Trotsky committed himself in early life, and by an admittedly voluntary act, to belief in an optimistic religion. He lacks the mental toughness to face the changeful world as it is and simply try to make it change for the better—not personally, perhaps, but he grew up in a culture which lacked that toughness. He grew up kidding himself that the world is in process of making itself better—to be sure, by a process of tough struggle—and of himself as joining in that struggle on the winning side. Even now, after all these years of argument with western radicals dominated by the scientific point of view, he cannot repress a suspicion that the struggle against materialist dialectics expresses "a spark of hope for an after life"!

Secondly, you must remember that Trotsky is trying

to establish the thesis that a state in which workers have no power, and no share in the profits of industry, is a "workers' state." For this truly metaphysical purpose he has to fall back, as never before, on the naked framework of his voluntary faith. He has to make you regard the fact that workers have no power in a workers' state not as a logical contradiction in his definition, but as a dialectic contradiction in the material facts—a contradiction, moreover, through whose mystic force those very facts are destined to be overcome.

"It is not surprising—" he says, returning to the political theme of his article—"it is not surprising that the theoreticians of the opposition who reject dialectic thought capitulate lamentably before the contradictory nature of the USSR. However, the contradiction between the social basis laid down by the revolution and the character of the caste which arose out of the degeneration of the revolution is not only an irrefutable historic fact, but also a motor force."

In other words, the worse Stalin's regime becomes, the more certain we may be that the universe is with us in our efforts to overthrow it. Stalin employs the same argument with equal validity to justify his sitting tight:

"Any dialectic thinker must understand that in order eventually to wither away, the state must first grow stronger." (Speech at the 16th party congress.)

Such are the uses of a "philosophy of optimism." The new movement for a more free and equal society which will presumably emerge from this bloody miscarriage of the Marxian faith, will not, it is to be hoped, base itself either upon optimism or philosophy, but upon resolution and scientific intelligence.

NOTE: To my acute regret Trotsky died while these comments were in the press. I think he would have read this chapter.

ACKNOWLEDGMENTS

IN COMPOSING this textbook I have made a free and disrespectful use of my own previous writings on the subject. Part I is an echo from a speech I once made in Carnegie Hall on Religion and the Bolsheviks. Part II is drawn from my Introduction to *Capital and Other Writings*, an edition of Karl Marx that I prepared for the Modern Library. Part III originally appeared in *Artists in Uniform*, published by Alfred Knopf. Part IV is a revised text of all but the first two chapters of Part I of my book, *Marx and Lenin, the Science of Revolution*, published in 1926 by Allen & Unwin in London, and later in the United States by A. & C. Boni. The two essays in Part V, *What Science Is* and *The Seed of the Marxian Philosophy*, were written especially for this present volume, and they are the heavy artillery if anybody wants to attack it. Part VI is a revised and shortened text of the second Part of *Marx and Lenin*, again omitting two chapters, one on *Mensheviks* and one on *Revisionism and the Fabians*. The reader thus has here the whole revised text of that earlier book as I now wish to present it. In place of the first two chapters he has the two essays in Part V of the present volume, which treat more simply and maturely of the same general subjects, the nature of scientific thinking and the origin of the Marxian philosophy. In place of the two chapters on Mensheviks and Revisionism I can only offer him—for the present at least—my recent book, *Stalin's Russia and the Crisis in Socialism*. Part VI, *Trotsky Defends the Faith*, was newly written for the present volume. My appendix, *The Americanization of*

Marx, was published in 1934 as a pamphlet with the title "The Last Stand of Dialectic Materialism." I have changed the title, as there have been other "stands" since then. And as Sidney Hook has largely abandoned the stand I was criticizing, I have altered the introductory paragraphs. Otherwise I have left the pamphlet substantially as it was written, for I think that because of its polemical nature it provides, as though in a different key, a useful résumé of the whole subject of this book.

M. E.

NOTES AND REFERENCES

PAGE 23. Marx: *The Civil War in France*, sec. III.

PAGE 25. Engels: Speech at the grave of Marx.

PAGE 34. Aristotle: *Metaphysics*, 1004b 25.

PAGE 35. Abelard: Quoted by Henry Osborn Taylor in the *Mediaeval Mind*, vol. II, p. 379.

PAGE 41. Marx: *Zur Kritik der Hegelschen Rechtsphilosophie*, in *Aus dem Literarischen Nachlass*, p. 385.

The denunciation of Hegel is in *Die Heilige Familie* and the renunciation of philosophy in general in favor of empirical science in *Die Deutsche Ideologie*, *Marx-Engels Archiv*, vol. I, pp. 237 and 240.

PAGE 42. Engels: *Ludwig Feuerbach*, sec. 1.

Marx: *The Civil War in France*, sec. III. The word "noble" I borrow from Charles Longuet's French translation of the word "higher" in the same passage.

PAGE 43. Marx: *Die Heilige Familie*, chap. IV.

Benedetto Croce: *What Is Living and What Is Dead of the Philosophy of Hegel*.

PAGE 44. Lenin: His notes made when studying philosophy are to be found in vols. IX and XII of the *Leninsky Sbornik* (Lenin Collection). My quotations are from vol. IX, p. 69, and vol. XII, pp. 323-4-5.

PAGE 46. Hegel: *Logic*, p. 41.

Engels: *Anti-Dühring*, the chapter on *Dialectic*.

PAGE 48. Engels: Letter to Joseph Bloch, September 21, 1890.

PAGES 48-9. Marx: *The Eighteenth Brumaire of Louis Bonaparte*, p. 9; a letter to Amenkov, 1846, and a letter to Weydemeyer, 1852.

PAGE 53. "Bringing the proletariat a consciousness of its own destiny": This idea was first formulated by Marx in the correspondence published in the *Deutsch-Französische Jahrbücher* in 1843. "We will not then oppose the world like doctrinaires with a new principle. . . . We expose new principles to the world out of the principles of the world itself. . . . We explain to it only the real object for which it struggles, and consciousness is a thing it must acquire even though it objects to it."

PAGE 58. Socrates: "Although Socrates was doubtless sincerely interested in the reconciliation of the two sides, yet the fact that he
approached the matter from the side of matter-of-fact method
. . . was enough to bring him to the condemnation of death as
a contemner of the gods and a corrupter of youth." John Dewey,
Reconstruction in Philosophy, p. 14. In connection with this
chapter read also Thorstein Veblen's essay on "The Evolution of
the Scientific Point of View," *University of California Chronicle*,
vol. X, no. 4.

PAGE 60. "The true reason-world": Hegel's *Logic* (pp. 152, 153).

PAGE 61. "Marx's childhood was less churchly-religious": At the age
·of nineteen Engels wrote as follows: "I pray every day; almost
all day long I pray that the truth may be given me. I have done
this ever since doubts assailed me, but still I cannot return to
our faith. . . . I write these lines with tears in my eyes, it is
hard for me to control my emotion, but nevertheless I feel that
I will not be lost, that I will find God, toward whom I aspire
with all my heart." (I translate from a Russian text given by
Riazanov, *Essays on the History of Marxism*, p. 36.)

Doctor's Thesis: "The General Differences between the Nature
Philosophies of Democritus and Epicurus," written in 1841. (*Aus
dem literarischen Nachlass von Karl Marx, Friedrich Engels und
Ferdinand Lasalle, herausgegeben von Franz Mehring*, vol. I, p.
65.)

PAGE 62. "And that faith in the omnipotence of the Idea": The quotation is from "Schelling and Revelation: A Criticism of the
Latest Reactionary Attempt upon the Free Philosophy"—a
pamphlet long attributed to Bakunin, but written by Engels, and
published in 1842. (From the Russian text given by Riazanov,
Essays on the History of Marxism, pp. 40-41.)

PAGE 63. "Says Marx": In *Herr Vogt*. Compare also the following
statement of Marx in the correspondence published in the
Deutsch-Französische Jahrbücher, in 1843: "We will not then
oppose the world like doctrinaires with a new principle. . . . We
expose new principles to the world out of the principles of the
world itself. . . . We explain to it only the real object for which
it struggles, and consciousness is a thing it must acquire even
though it objects to it."

PAGE 64. "By means of all seeming accidents": The phrases quoted
are from Engels's *Feuerbach*, IV and I.

"It was not because of emotional dependence": I say this with so
much assurance, because of the paragraph in Engels's *Feuerbach*,
where he mentions in the most casual manner the scientific prediction of an end of life on the earth, and the probability that
there is, therefore, "in human history not only an ascending but

also a descending branch." In the face of this probability—which is an emotional, if not indeed an intellectual, reduction to absurdity of the whole philosophy of "an endless evolutionary progress of human society from the lower to the higher"—Engels nonchalantly remarks: "We find ourselves, at any rate, still at a considerable distance from the turning-point, where the history of society begins to go downward. . . ."

"Being a German philosopher": I mean, *Being a German philosopher of the classical or official tradition*. Schopenhauer was a German philosopher, and Schopenhauer first perceived that relation between impulse and intelligence which lies at the basis of modern psychology. But Schopenhauer was not an official German philosopher; he was not an "instructor of youth appointed by the state." Nietzsche perceived the significance of this fact. Nietzsche was far more Marxian than Marx in his attitude to the official German philosophy. "Experience teaches us," he said, "that nothing stands so much in the way of developing great philosophers as the custom of supporting bad ones in state universities. . . . It is the popular theory that the posts given to the latter make them 'free' to do original work; as a matter of fact, the effect is quite contrary. . . . No state would ever dare to patronize such men as Plato and Schopenhauer. And why? Because the state is always afraid of them. . . . It seems to me that there is need for a higher tribunal outside the universities to critically examine the doctrines they teach. As soon as philosophers are willing to resign their salaries, they will constitute such a tribunal. . . ." (*Schopenhauer als Erzieher*, translation by H. L. Mencken in *Nietzsche*.)

"The coincidence": I give this "Thesis" in the form found by Riazanov in Marx's notebook, and not as Engels gives it in his *Feuerbach*. ("Essays on the History of Marxism," p. 75.)

PAGE 65. Plekhanov: *From Idealism to Materialism*, II.

Rosa Luxemburg: From an article in *Vorwärts* on the twentieth anniversary of Marx's death, cited by Siemkovsky in his *Khrestomatia Marxisma*. (I translate from his Russian text.) In her speech at the Inaugural Congress of the Communist Party of Germany (Spartacus League) the emotional function performed by this idea in Rosa Luxemburg's mind is even more clear: "On November 10th our revolutionists allowed to slip from their grasp nearly half the instruments of power they had seized on November 9th. We learn from this, on the one hand, that our revolution is subject to the prepotent law of historical determinism, a law which guarantees that, despite all difficulties and complications, notwithstanding all our own errors, we shall nevertheless advance step by step towards the goal." (British *Communist Review*, September,

1921.) Here even the present failure is converted into an evidence of future success.

PAGE 66. Plekhanov: "History shows that even fatalism, not only does not always hinder energetic practical action, but, on the contrary, in certain epochs has been a psychologically necessary foundation for such action. In evidence we may cite the Puritans, surpassing in their energy all other parties in seventeenth-century England, and the followers of Mahomet, subjecting to their power in a short space of time an enormous strip of earth from India to Spain. They are greatly mistaken, who think that we need only be convinced of the inevitable arrival of an event of a given kind, in order to lose every psychological possibility of co-operating with or opposing it.

"Here all depends on the question whether my own activity constitutes a necessary link in the chain of necessary events. If yes— then so much the less do I waver, so much the more decisively I act." ("The Question of the Rôle of Personality in History," an article contributed by Plekhanov to a Collection entitled *After Twenty Years*.) Plekhanov speaks in a footnote of Moses and Cromwell. "All Cromwell's activities," he says, "were for him colored in advance with the hue of necessity. This not only did not prevent him from striving from victory to victory, but gave to his efforts an unconquerable power."

PAGE 67. "The definition of freedom": Read Sections 145, 46 and 47 of Hegel's *Logic*, and Section B of the second division of Part II of his "Lectures on the Philosophy of Religion" (translated by Spiers and Sanderson). And do not read them in the mood of filial piety that Marxists cherish toward Hegel. Do not mistake unintelligibility for wisdom. Remember that Marx too disliked Hegel until he had Hegel drilled into him at school.

Hegel says: "The link of necessity qua necessity is identity, as still inward and concealed, because it is the identity of what are esteemed actual things, although their very self-subsistence is bound to be necessity. The circulation of substance through causality and reciprocity therefore only expressly makes out or states that self-subsistence is the infinite negative self-relation—a relation *negative*, in general, for in it the act of distinguishing and inter-mediating becomes a primariness of actual things independent one against the other—and *infinite self-relation*, because their independence only lies in their identity.

"This truth of necessity, therefore, is *Freedom*."

Whatever that may mean logically, it is plain that science cannot bother with it, for the simple reason that science has too much to do. And what it means *morally*, and *politically*, Hegel takes pains to make as clear as his logical meaning is obscure:

"We may note in passing," he says, "how important it is for any man to meet everything that befalls him in the spirit of the old proverb which describes each man as the architect of his own fortune. . . . The other way would be to lay the blame of whatever we experience upon other men, upon unfavorable circumstances, and the like. And this is a fresh example of the language of unfreedom, and at the same time the spring of discontent. If man saw, on the contrary, that whatever happens to him is only the outcome of himself, and that he only bears his own guilt, he would stand free, and in everything that came upon him would have the consciousness that he suffered no wrong. . . . It is their view of necessity, therefore, which is the root of the content and discontent of men."

That is the Marxian doctrine of historic necessity, studied "from the standpoint of its origin." The meaning of it in plain language is this: "Speculative philosophy is too difficult for you, a simple artisan or perhaps a housekeeper, to understand. But I will tell you 'in passing' what you would learn from it, if you could understand. You would learn that it is right and proper for you to feel 'free'—to feel that your choices are real—so far as taking the whole responsibility for your misfortunes is concerned, but when it comes to doing anything to change your 'circumstances,' then you must recognize that your 'freedom' is only a consciousness of the necessity of everything's being just what it is."

"One of the most brilliant discoveries": Quoted from the article by Plekhanov above mentioned.

PAGE 68. "The thinking of Plekhanov about the doctrine of necessity": For example, the following paragraph from the same article: "A consciousness of the unconditional necessity of a given phenomenon can only strengthen the energy of the man who favors that phenomenon, and considers himself one of the forces producing it. If such a man should fold his arms, because he is aware of this necessity, he would thereby show that he knows little about arithmetic. Let us suppose that the phenomenon A must necessarily appear, if we have at hand a given sum of conditions S. You have proven to me that this sum of conditions is partly at hand already, and partly will be at hand at a given time T. Convinced of this I—a man favoring the phenomenon A—cry 'How nice that is!' and flop down to sleep right up to the joyful day of the event you have foretold. What comes of that? Just this: In your reckoning, into the sum S, necessary to the accomplishment of the phenomenon A, entered also my activity, equal, let us say, to a. Inasmuch as I took my little nap, at the moment T, the sum of conditions favorable to the occurrence of the given phenomenon will now not be *S*, but *S minus a*, which changes the whole state of affairs."

Any reader who has time to think, will see that if Plekhanov has proven anything here, it is the opposite of what he set out to prove. He has at least given an excellent illustration of the opposite thesis—namely, that all practical thought or argument implies that the future is *not determined*. You have to be able to say "If a man should . . ." and *mean it*, in order to talk sense about a practical problem.

In his preface to a Russian translation of Engels's *Socialism Utopian and Scientific*, Plekhanov has some more remarks of the same kind:

"The chief distinguishing feature of scientific socialism is now defined for us with complete clarity. Its advocates are not satisfied with the *hope* that the socialist ideals, thanks to their elevated character, will attract general sympathy and therefore triumph. No—they require *certainty* that this very attraction of general sympathy by the socialist ideals is a *necessary social process*. And they derive this certainty from an analysis of contemporary economic relations and the course of their development. . . . Certain writers, for example Stammler, remark that if the triumph of socialism is a historic necessity, then the practical activity of the social-democrats is *entirely superfluous*. Why help to create phenomena which will in any case inevitably appear? But this is a pitiful and ridiculous sophism. Looking upon historical development from the standpoint of necessity, the social democracy looks upon its own activity as a *necessary link* in the chain of those necessary conditions, the combination of which makes inevitable the triumph of socialism. A necessary link cannot be *superfluous*: its removal would break the whole chain of events."

Here again the alternative: *If* my activity is withdrawn, the whole chain of events will be broken. The only question then is: Can I, or can I not withdraw my activity? And if I can *not*, then what is the use of talking? What is the use of thinking? In a world which contained no genuine alternatives, thinking would never have arisen.

I give two more quotations from Plekhanov, as there is no better way to cure practical minds of a taste for Hegelian Marxism.

"The Marxists have succeeded in finding a bridge uniting ideals with reality. They have lifted themselves up to Monism. According to their opinion, capitalism in the course of its own development leads to its own negation and the realization of their . . . ideals. That is historic necessity. The Marxist serves as one of the instruments of that necessity, and cannot fail to serve as such, both because of his social situation, and because of his mental and moral character, created by this situation. That also is the side of necessity. But once his social situation has developed in him just this and not another character, he not only serves as an instrument of necessity, and not only cannot fail to serve as such, but he passionately desires and cannot fail to desire to serve. This is the side of freedom, or more truly, this is freedom identifying itself with necessity—it is necessity transforming itself into freedom." (*The Question of the Rôle of Personality in History.*)

"Engels dedicated his life to an extraordinarily high aim, the liberation of the proletariat. He also had his ideal, but it was not everlastingly separated from reality. His ideal was this same reality, but the reality of tomorrow, a reality which will come into being, not because Engels was idealistic, but because the attributes of the present reality are such that out of it, according to its own inward laws, must develop that reality of tomorrow, which may be called the ideal of Engels. Undeveloped people may ask us: if the whole thing lies in the attributes of reality, then what is the use of Engels? Why should he mix into an unavoidable historic process with his ideals? Cannot the business get along without him? From the objective side, the situation of Engels presents itself thus: In the process of passing from one of its forms to another, reality seized upon him, as one of the necessary instruments of the economic overturn. From the subjective side, it results that to Engels his participation in the historic movement is agreeable, that he considers this his duty and the great task of his life." (Remarks upon Engels's book *Ludwig Feuerbach*.)

Thus, after all the commotion and trumpeting about realism and materialism and atheism, and getting down to the hard business facts, we find ourselves in exactly the same position as the Apostle Paul. We are "seized upon" by an abstract "Reality," and made to "serve" as its "instruments," and we find it not only agreeable, but "our duty and the great task of our lives" to serve.

"When Engels says": *Anti-Dühring*, I, XI.

PAGE 70. "Marx and Engels repudiated": *Capital*, vol. I, ch. 13, footnote to p. 406 of Untermann's translation. *Feuerbach*, II. *Socialism Utopian and Scientific*, p. 38.

Trotsky's official reaction to my criticisms of Marxism was contained in the following letter to the Editorial Board of *The Militant*:

"Dear Comrades: Recently I have repeatedly had opportunity to convince myself of the fact that Max Eastman is carrying on a systematic fight against materialist dialectics, the philosophical foundation of Marxism and scientific Communism. In its content and its theoretical tendency this fight does not differ in any way from the other varieties of petty bourgeois revisionism, beginning with Bernsteinism (in its philosophical-theoretical parts). If Eastman while so doing keeps his warm sympathy for the October revolution and even for the Left Opposition this crying illogicality is subjectively honorable for him but does not raise by one iota the value of his criticism of Marxism.

"I could have left the Croton variety of revisionism silently to its proper destiny, if I had not been bound for a long time to Eastman himself by personal and literary ties. Eastman recently translated three volumes of my *History of the Revolution* into the English language. As is generally acknowledged, he has carried out this big task in an excellent manner. I have expressed to him my sincere thankfulness for this, and am prepared to repeat it here. But as soon as Eastman attempts to translate Marxian dialectics into the language of vulgar empiricism, his work provokes in me a feeling which is the direct opposite of thankfulness. For the purpose of avoiding all doubts and misunderstandings I consider it my duty to bring this to the knowledge of everybody.

"With Communist greetings,

"L. Trotsky."

In reply to this I wrote Trotsky that he was quite right in assuming I was carrying on a fight against dialectic materialism: "What else is the life of a writer but a fight for the ideas he believes in?" And I pointed out that through ignorance of my position he was helping me in my fight.

"If you had read my book," I said, "as I have repeatedly urged you to do before judging my position, you could not have been so glib with the word 'vulgar.' I argued that Engels, in describing the materialism of natural science as 'vulgar,' revealed himself to be defending a rationalistic metaphysics—that is, a religion in disguise. 'Whence indeed this word vulgar on the lips of a revolutionist?' I asked. 'It is the Marxian way of saying *profane*.' The only weakness in my argument lay in the ambiguity of the word *materialism*, which might be vulgar in another sense. You hand me the phrase 'vulgar empiricism' which can mean nothing to a thinking mind but thoroughgoing empiricism, courageous empiricism, radical empiricism—a plain man's belief that knowledge does actually come from experience and not from somewhere else—and thereby concede a rationalistic or a priori element in the dialectic philosophy. That is the best help you could give me in my effort to keep dialectic materialism out of America while bringing the Marxian science in."

PAGE 71. "The abolition of religion": The quotation is from Marx's *Zur Kritik der Hegelschen Rechtsphilosophie* published in 1844. (*Nachlass*, vol. I, p. 385.)

"Marx himself declared": See the Introduction to his *Critique of Political Economy*, published in 1859, and his letter to Lassalle,

February 22, 1858. "Hegel," he says in this letter, "first understood the whole history of philosophy, and you cannot demand
of him that he should make no mistakes in the details."

Engels made the same two contradictory assertions. In his Introduction to the English edition of *Socialism Utopian and Scientific*
(p. 37) he declares that philosophical ideas are "offshoots of the
economic relations prevailing in a given society." In his *Anti-
Dühring* (the chapter on Dialectic) he asserts that the whole
history of philosophy has been an independent dialectical process.

In an *Introduction to the Philosophy of Dialectic Materialism*, by
A. Deborin, a book which reached its third edition in Soviet
Russia, we have an explanation of the whole course of modern
philosophy as an independent dialectic development. But the
author apologizes in his preface for not having *also* explained
modern philosophy as a development determined by "social relations at the basis of which lies the evolution of the productive
forces!" Such a double-barreled history of philosophy seems to
Deborin the natural Marxian product, whose only drawback is
that it would require "an extended work of several volumes."

The way in which Marx fell into this inconsistency was undoubtedly as follows: Hegel considered social and political history to be
a self-development of the divine Reason in an alien form. Therefore, Hegel could describe the history of philosophy as an independent self-development of Reason, and yet at the same time
declare that the philosophy of any historic period is a reflection
of the social and political history of that period. "It is one Mind,"
as he says, "which manifests itself in and impresses itself upon
these different elements." Marx retained these two ways of viewing the history of philosophy through mere habituation, although
his substitution of the forces of production for the Divine Mind
as an explanation of history had rendered them inconsistent. (My
quotations here are from Hegel's *Lectures on the History of
Philosophy*, Haldane's translation, vol. I, pp. 5 and 115.)

PAGES 73-74. The quotation is from the Introduction to Marx's
Critique of Political Economy. (My own translation.)

PAGE 75. "The forces of production rebel": The quotation is from
Engels's *Anti-Dühring*, III, II.

PAGE 76. "*Condition* and *determine*": The German words are *bedingt*
and *bestimmt*. Plekhanov interchanges *condition* and *cause* in the
same way: "Social man himself creates his social relations. But if
he creates at a given time these and not other relations, this
happens, you may be sure, not without a cause; it is conditioned
by the state of the productive forces." (*The Question of the
Rôle of Personality in History*.) Engels, in his original outline
for the Communist Manifesto, defined communism itself as "the

science of the *conditions* of the emancipation of the proletariat."
(My italics.)

That Marx at his most Marxian really conceives of a positive and
detailed causation of the ideological superstructure by the economic basis, may be seen in a footnote in chapter 13 of the first
volume of *Das Kapital.* Here he suggests that one can infer religious ideas from the material relations of the society in which
they arise, and that this would be "the only materialistic, and
therefore scientific" method of studying religion.

Lafargue: In an essay on "Economics, Natural Science, and Mathematics."

PAGE 77. "The Marxian explanation of law and the state": I believe
it is true that this explanation is "usually expressed in a dynamic
form" at least by revolutionary Marxists, although in the classical
exposition of it the state appears to have arisen out of reasons
rather than causes. "The state," Engels says, "is the product of
society at a certain stage of its development. The state is tanta-
mount to an acknowledgment that the given society has become
entangled in an insoluble contradiction with itself, that it has
broken up into irreconcilable antagonisms of which it is powerless
to rid itself. And in order that these antagonisms, these classes
with their opposing economic interests, may not devour one
another and society itself in their sterile struggle, some force
standing seemingly above society, becomes necessary so as to
moderate the force of their collisions and to keep them within
the bounds of 'order.' And this force arising from society, but
placing itself above it, which gradually separates itself from it—
this force is the state." (*The Origin of the Family, Private Property and the State,* translated by Untermann, ix.)

This explanation is decidedly metaphysical and mystical, but it is
usually very quickly supplemented and made real and scientific by
adding some such statement as this: "The state is nothing but
a machine for the oppression of one class by another" (Engels's
Introduction to *The Civil War in France*), or "The state power
is nothing but an organization given to themselves by the ruling
classes—capitalists and landlords—in order to defend their social
privileges" (Engels's Letter to Kuno, January 24, 1872), or, The
state is "an organization for the systematic use of violence by one
class against another" (Lenin, *State and Revolution*).

Reformists, who wish to make the doctrines of Marx as mild as
possible, cling to the metaphysical statement of this theory, and
maintain on the basis of it that the state is an organ for the "reconciliation" of opposing class interests. Inasmuch as everything
in the world is supposed, according to the dialectic philosophy, to
be engaged in the process of reconciling opposites in a higher

unity, the reformists have rather the best of this argument, so long as the theory is stated in the metaphysical form. The first three pages of Lenin's book *State and Revolution* are therefore occupied with wriggling out of Engels's classical statement, and arriving at the revolutionary slogan that "The state is an organ of class rule," which "was created by the governing class." The whole first chapter of this book is a proof of the inappropriateness and inconvenience to a practical revolutionist of a metaphysical theory of history.

"The religious world": *Capital*, vol. I, ch. I, sec. IV. This viewpoint is developed by Engels in the concluding chapter of his *Anti-Dühring*. "Religion," he says, "is nothing but the fantastic reflection in the heads of men of those earthly powers which rule over their daily life, a reflection in which earthly powers take on the form of unearthly ones."

Compare with this glib statement James H. Leuba's work on *The Psychology of Religious Mysticism*.

PAGE 78. "Calvin's doctrine of predestination": The quotation is from *Socialism Utopian and Scientific*, Introduction, p. 21. In Engels's *Feuerbach*, IV, Calvinism appears as "the authentic religious disguise of the *interests* of the contemporary bourgeoisie." (My italics.)

In order to realize the remoteness of this sort of thing from exact science, the reader might compare with Engels's explanation of the doctrine of predestination, Pokrovsky's explanation of the doctrine of free will. Pokrovsky is the author of an excellent Marxian history of Russia. Science has proven, he declares, that all things are in a state of absolutely determined change, but the bourgeoisie, in order to make their class enemies believe that the present order of society is an exception to this rule, have invented the doctrine that man is free from causal determination!

Trotsky: *Literature and Revolution*, IV.

PAGE 80. "Principle of investigation": "Historic Materialism is not a finished system crowned with unalterable truth. It represents simply a scientific method for the investigation of the human process of development." Franz Mehring, *Concerning Historic Materialism* (Russian text).

"Our interpretation of life is chiefly an introduction to study. . . ." (Engels's Letter to Conrad Schmidt, August 5, 1890.)

"Classical philosophy": See Engels's Letter to Conrad Schmidt, October 27, 1890. The quotations are from his *Feuerbach*, V. See also the concluding chapter where he speaks of "that great theoretic mind," that "mind for pure scientific investigation, indifferent whether the results were practically profitable or not, contrary to the police regulations or not," which had been "the

honor of Germany in the period of her deepest political humilia-
tion." A more un-Marxian description of a cultural phenomenon
could hardly be imagined.

Hegel himself clearly perceived and frankly announced the reactionary and animistic mission of German philosophy in the modern
scientific world. "We shall see in the history of philosophy," he
said in his inaugural address at Heidelberg, "that in other European countries in which the sciences and the culture of the
understanding have been prosecuted with zeal and with respect,
Philosophy, excepting in name, has sunk even from memory, and
that it is in the German nation that it has been retained as a
peculiar possession. We have received the higher call of Nature
to preserve this holy flame, just as the Eumolpidæ in Athens had
the conservation of the Eleusinian Mysteries, the inhabitants of
the island of Samothrace the preservation of a higher divine
service. . . ."

How much truer than what Engels says about German philosophy!

"Feudal and bureaucratic despotism": The phrase occurs in "Revolution and Counter-Revolution in Germany," articles by Engels
published in the New York *Tribune* over Marx's name.

PAGE 82. Plekhanov: *The Question of the Rôle of Personality in
History.* Engels also, and in the same incidental way, acknowledges that an "understanding of the causes of economic and
political development and the conditions confronting the revolution" gives us additional assurance of its early success. (Letter to
Bebel, December 11, 1884.)

Marx: Letter to Kugelmann, April 17, 1871.

PAGE 83. Engels: Letter to Starkenburg, January 25, 1894.

Hegel: *Logic,* p. 265.

PAGE 84. Engels: *Feuerbach,* IV.

"Problems which trouble them the most": A good example of this
troubledness may be found in Riazanov's Preface to his excellent
"Essays on the History of Marxism." He makes on the first page
the following statement: "One may say—and from the theoretical standpoint it would be correct—that any historic process,
or any definite part of it, this or that change in the life of a
people, would have taken place without the co-operation of any
given historic personality."

Upon the page immediately after that, he makes the following statement: "One of the most interesting phenomena in world history
is the fact that the 'creative power' of ideas, and the deciding
rôle (sic) of historic personalities has nowhere appeared so fully
as in the lives of the two founders of the materialistic interpretation of history."

Engels: Letter to Starkenburg, January 25, 1894. "If there had been no Napoleon, another would have taken his place. That is proven by the fact that the man was always found as soon as he was needed: Cæsar, Augustus, Cromwell." (Except, we may add, when he was not found: absence at other important moments of Cæsar, Augustus, Cromwell!)

PAGE 85. Trotsky: Speech at the Ukrainian Communist Party Conference in Kharkov, April 5, 1923, reprinted in his book *About Lenin*.

PAGE 86. Kautsky: "What does the Materialistic Interpretation of History Ask, and What Can it Give?"—one of the articles in his discussion with the English socialist, Belfort Bax, published in *Die Neue Zeit* in 1896. "We ought not to protest against the 'reproach' that we have leaders. Yes, we have leaders, and it depends to a considerable degree upon the qualities of our leaders whether our road to victory will be long or short, whether it will be comfortable or covered with thorns." Engels also speaks of the "end-result" in discussing the manner in which "history" operates (Letter to Joseph Bloch, September 21, 1890).

PAGE 87. Bernstein: *Die Voraussetzung des Socialismus und die Aufgaben der Sozial-democratie*, translated into English under the title *Evolutionary Socialism*.

Jaurès: I have in mind his debate with Paul Lafargue on the Idealist and Materialist Interpretation of History.

Croce: *Materialismo storico ed economia Marxistica*.

Simkhovitch: *Marxism Versus Socialism*.

Seligman: *The Economic Interpretation of History*.

Bernstein: *Evolutionary Socialism*.

Kautsky: *Bernstein and the Materialist Interpretation of History*.

Engels: Letter to Joseph Bloch, September 21, 1890, and to Conrad Schmidt, October 27, 1890. (My translations of the second letter are from a Russian text.)

PAGE 89. Kautsky: "The Materialistic Interpretation of History and the Psychological Factor"—his first article in the discussion with Belfort Bax, referred to above.

"It was Marx, and not History": That Marx was also a product of history, and his purposes and ideas conditioned by the age and society in which he lived, does not alter this fact or contradict it. We do not know the degree in which Marx's purposive ideas were conditioned by his place in history, and we do not know the positive concrete causes of those ideas at all. We shall never escape from metaphysics without ceasing to pretend to know everything.

PAGE 90. "Early Christians": "Delivered from capitalist slavery, from the innumerable horrors, barbarities, absurdities, and infamies of capitalist exploitation, people will gradually become accustomed to the observance of those elementary rules of social life, known for ages, and repeated for thousands of years in all maxims, to their observance without violence, without compulsion, without subjection, without the special apparatus for compulsion which is called the state." (Lenin, *State and Revolution*, V. 2.)

PAGE 91. "All past history": A statement often repeated by Marx and Engels and always in this sweeping form. The quotation here is from Engels's *Socialism Utopian and Scientific*, p. 41. The quotation at the end of the chapter is from the Communist Manifesto.

"Penetrated with unity": The phrase is from the article by Rosa Luxemburg, published in *Vorwärts* on the twentieth anniversary of Marx's death (Russian text, see note to p. 65). "Since Marx established in the sphere of philosophy, history and political economy the historical point of view of the working class, the thread of bourgeois investigations in these spheres has been broken. Natural philosophy, in the classical sense of the word, has ceased to exist. The philosophy of history has come to an end. Scientific political economy has come to an end. In historical investigations wherever an unconscious and inconsistent materialism does not prevail, the place of a complete theory is occupied by a many-colored eclecticism—that is to say, the idea of an explanation of the historic process penetrated with unity has been renounced, the philosophy of history has been renounced."

PAGE 92. "The predominating purpose": My quotations are from Marx's earliest exposition of his social theory, *The Poverty of Philosophy*, II, V, and from his "Zur Kritik des Sozial-democratischen Programms von Gotha," a letter written late in his life.

"Marx greeted Darwin's theory": Letter to Lassalle, January 16, 1861.

PAGE 93. Engels: Introduction to the Communist Manifesto (1888).

"Glorious corroboration": The phrase of Anton Pannekoek in his *Marxism and Darwinism*, the ablest and most original of all the writings on this subject.

PAGE 94. "Universal law of motion": This is in substance Engels's definition of the dialectic both in *Feuerbach* and *Anti-Dühring*.

PAGE 95. "In studying revolutions": From the Introduction to the *Critique of Political Economy* (see page 73 of this book).

"The law of development of human history": The phrase is from Engels's speech at the grave of Karl Marx.

PAGE 96. "He speaks of his doctrine": See, for instance, the Preface to the first edition of *Das Kapital*. "My standpoint, which views the development of the economic social formation as a process in natural history, holds the individual responsible less than any other for relations whose creature he remains, no matter how much he may raise himself subjectively above them."

PAGE 98. "Reflection in thought": *Socialism Utopian and Scientific*, p. 47.

PAGE 99. "General expression": "The theoretical conclusions of the communists . . . merely express in general terms actual relations springing from an existing class struggle, from a historical movement going on under our very eyes." (Communist Manifesto, II.) "The theoretical propositions of the communists are by no means founded on ideas and principles invented or discovered by this or that reformer of the world: they are merely a general expression of the class struggle" (Kautsky—Debate with Belfort Bax).

Rosa Luxemburg: Article in *Vorwärts* on the twentieth anniversary of Marx's death. (See note to p. 65.)

PAGE 101. Lenin: The quotations are from *Materialism and Empirocriticism*, and *One Step Forward, Two Steps Back*.

Trotsky: *Terrorism and Communism*.

Plekhanov: From his Preface to the Russian translation of Engels's *Socialism Utopian and Scientific*. (Complete Works, vol. XI, p. 88.)

PAGE 102. Bukharin: *Historic Materialism*: To this book belongs the distinction of reducing Hegelian Marxism to a complete absurdity. Bukharin does not understand the tricks of metaphysics. He does not realize that, in order to establish a dialectic philosophy over and above science, it is necessary to accept the mechanical laws of motion just as they are given by the sciences, but at the same time insert into these mechanical laws a set of "speculative" laws, showing that motion is logical at the same time that it is mechanical, dialectic at the same time that it is dynamic. To put it in Hegel's own words: "The relation of speculative science to the other sciences may be stated in the following terms. It does not in the least neglect the empirical facts contained in the several sciences, but recognizes and adopts them; it appreciates and applies towards its own structure the universal element in these sciences, their laws and classifications; but besides all this, into the categories of science it introduces and gives currency to other categories. . . ." This clever device for the preservation of animism Bukharin does not understand. He thinks that the dialectic laws are themselves mechanical like Newton's laws of motion, or Kepler's or Einstein's laws. Thus according to Bukharin we have two mechanical sciences side by side—one invented by Hegel and Marx, who perhaps never entered a laboratory, and the other developed by men who spent their lives trying to achieve an experimental understanding of mechanical motion. The absurdity of this position is obvious. And it reduces the whole dialectic metaphysics to absurdity, because it is in a sense the same thing naïvely and clumsily done. Bukharin is like the pupil of a magician, giving away the tricks of his master by trying to perform before he has quite learned them.

PAGE 103. Lenin: The quotations are from *Materialism and Empiro-criticism*, VI, 4; from a letter to Maxim Gorky published in *Pod Znamenem Marxisma*; from his *What to Do?*, II, 2; and again from *Materialism and Empiro-criticism*.

PAGE 104. "Semitheological jargon": See Engels's *Feuerbach*, I, and *Landmarks of Scientific Socialism*, p. 152. Also Lenin's *Materialism and Empiro-criticism*, the section on "Absolute and Relative Truth."

PAGE 106. I first indicated this view of the relation between Marxism and Freud's psychology in an article on "Wilson and Lenin," published in *The Liberator* in 1918.

"Infantry, Cavalry and Artillery": *Der Achtzehnte Brumaire des Louis Bonaparte*, III.

PAGE 109. Engels: Letter to Franz Mehring, July 14, 1893.

Marx: *Der Achtzehnte Brumaire des Louis Bonaparte*, III.

PAGE 110. Engels: Letter to Joseph Bloch, September 21, 1890.

PAGES 111-12. Engels: The quotation is from his letter to Conrad Schmidt, October 27, 1890. The second quotation is from *Feuerbach*, IV.

PAGE 113. "An early biographer": Scott, *Napoleon*, VI, 251. Before Napoleon the word ideology meant the science of ideas, and in France—strangely enough—it is this meaning which survives.

PAGE 114. The quotations are from Engels's *Anti-Dühring*, the chapter on Political Economy, secs. I and II.

The words "more magnificent" occur in the Introduction to *Anti-Dühring*. "The heavenly bodies like the formations of the organisms by which they are under favorable conditions inhabited, arise and perish, and the courses that they run, so far as is on the whole permissible, take on eternally more magnificent dimensions."

PAGE 115. "So often repeated": Read for instance Engels's Introduction to Marx's *Poverty of Philosophy*, and Marx's *Criticism of the Gotha Program*. This latter document reveals more clearly than any other the manner in which Marx projected his own purpose into the evolving "Economic relations."

PAGE 118. Marx: Letter to Engels, January 8, 1868.

PAGE 122. "Marx himself confessed": Preface to the second edition of *Das Kapital*.

"Famous subject of dispute": See Böhm-Bawerk's *Karl Marx and the Close of his System*. The reader will find a defense of Marx's position in Louis Boudin's book, *The Theoretic System of Karl*

Marx, V and VI. I recommend this book as the most reliable outline of orthodox Marxism in English. The book is conceived in a spirit of humorless and unconvincing sarcasm, which will repel the scientific reader—but this also belongs to the orthodox tradition. Marx's *Poverty of Philosophy*, Engels's *Anti-Dühring*, and Plekhanov's attacks upon Mikhaelovsky, were all weakened with this cocksure theological sarcasm. Lenin's polemics are more powerful, but also not always free from the flavor of the tirade.

PAGE 123. "A penetration": The quotation is from *Capital*, vol. III, p. 199 of Untermann's translation.

Engels: Introduction to Marx's *Wage, Labor and Capital*.

"Experimental humility before the facts themselves": A step in the direction of this change in Marxian economics was taken by Karl Renner in his book, *Die Wirtschaft Als Gesamt-Prozess Und Die Sozialisierung*. Conceding that Marx's theory is deductive and abstract in its mode of exposition, Renner undertakes to expound it concretely and empirically. So far so good. But until it is conceded that Marx's economics is abstract and deductive—and not only that, but Hegelian-animistic—in its essential intellectual structure, the empirical and practical good sense that is tangled up in it will never be made to emerge clearly.

PAGE 124. "Inner, hidden": See p. 84 of this book.

"Visible external movement": *Capital*, vol. III, p. 369, of Untermann's translation.

PAGE 125. "Independent of their consciousness and their wills": In his preface to the second edition of *Capital* Marx quotes with approval a Russian critic who says: "Marx regarded the social movement as a process of natural history governed by laws, which are not dependent upon the will, the consciousness or the designs of men, but rather the contrary, which determine their wills, their consciousness and their designs." Marx himself said the same thing in a letter to Annenkov, December 28, 1846. See also *Feuerbach*, IV.

It is surprising how many studious and scientific people have made the mistake of imagining that Marxism rests upon the concept of the "economic man"—Bertrand Russell, for instance (*Roads to Freedom*, p. 47), Paul Howard Douglas in *The Trend of Economics*, p. 154, and the Russian economist, Tugan-Baranovsky. Usually I think this is a result of mere hasty reading. But Tugan-Baranovsky's error was the outcome of a serious effort to understand Marx's mind. He failed in this effort because he took the "Theses on Feuerbach" to mean all that they seem to mean. On the basis of these "Theses," and of a similar remark in *Die Heilige Familie*, he assumed that Marx had abandoned the Hegelian view of the relation between will and understanding, and that "on

this decisive psychological point Marx was at one with Schopenhauer and not Hegel." Having thus erroneously assumed that
Marx recognized the primacy of the will, Tugan-Baranovsky naturally proceeded to discover Marx's fundamental error in the fact
that he "ignored the many-sidedness" of this will. "Out of all the
variegated web of human motives he took into consideration one
only, economic interest in the narrowest sense" (*Theoretische
Grundlagen des Marxismus*, ch. II, p. 40). Marx did not really
take "economic interest" into consideration at all, and therefore
Tugan-Baranovsky's whole book is entirely beside the point. Every
effort to understand the mind of Marx will be beside the point,
which fails to understand that the "Theses on Feuerbach" were a
step back toward Hegel, and not forward with the development
of a scientific attitude.

PAGE 126. The translation is from *Die Heilige Familie*, ch. IV.

PAGE 128. The translation is from the next to the last chapter of the
first volume of *Das Kapital*.

PAGE 130. "Hegel's philosophy": See vol. III, p. 55, of his *Lectures
on the History of Philosophy*.

PAGE 131. "An association which excludes": *Das Elend der Philosophie*, II, 5.
"Leap from the kingdom of necessity": *Anti-Dühring*, III, II.
"Most adequate expression": Engels's Preface to the first English
translation of *Das Kapital*.

PAGE 137. Hegel: The quotation is from his *Philosophy of Religion*.
Engels: The quotations are from the chapter on "Dialectic" in his
Anti-Dühring.

PAGE 138. "In another passage": *Socialism Utopian and Scientific*, II.

PAGE 139. A good example of the baser uses to which the idea of a
dialectic method can be put, will be found in Engels's Introduction to the third volume of *Capital* (p. 24 of Untermann's translation). He is discussing the fact that Marx's theory of value,
which appears in the first volume to be a definition and explanation of the actual normal rates at which commodities exchange
on the market, turns out in the third volume to be a penetration
beneath such superficial phenomena into the "internal essence and
inner form of the capitalist process of production" (p. 199 of the
same volume). What Engels says about it is this:
"It is a mistaken assumption . . . that one may look at all in
Marx's work for fixed and universally applicable definitions. It is
a matter of course that when things and their mutual inter-
relations are conceived, not as fixed, but as changing, that their
mental images, the ideas concerning them, are likewise subject to
change and transformation; that they cannot be sealed up in rigid

definitions, but must be developed in the historical and logical process of their formation."

What seems to me "a matter of course" is that so long as you have a philosophy which permits you to dodge out of difficulties in this irresponsible fashion, real and reliable science is impossible.

For another example of this employment of the idea of "dialectic thinking" to dodge a difficulty, see the paragraph of Engels's letter to Conrad Schmidt, October 27, 1890, beginning, "What these gentlemen lack is dialectic," and ending, "For them Hegel never existed."

PAGE 143. Lenin: "Once More about the Trade-Unions." Complete Works, vol. XVIII, part I, p. 60.

PAGE 144. The quotation is from Lenin's article entitled "Concerning Our Revolution," Complete Works, vol. XIII, part II, p. 117.

Years before this, when studying Hegel, Lenin made a marginal note which shows how instantly, in his practical mind, the idea of dialectic identified itself with the idea of mental flexibility, of adroit conceptual maneuvering among evolving facts. I quoted this note from memory on p. 261 of *Stalin's Russia*. Here is the complete text:

"Conceptions which seem dead, Hegel analyzes and shows that there is movement in them. Final? It means moving to an end. Something? It means not this but another. Being in general? It means such indefiniteness that being equals non-being. An all-sided, universal flexibility of conceptions, flexibility going to the point of an identity of opposites—that is the essence of it. That flexibility applied subjectively is eclecticism and sophistics. Flexibility applied objectively—that is, reflecting the all-sidedness of the material process and its unity—is the dialectic, is the correct reflection of the eternal evolution of the world." (Leninsky Sbornik, Vol. IX, p. 71.)

PAGE 145. Marx: Letter to Kugelmann, June 27, 1870.

Engels: Preface to the second edition of *Anti-Dühring*.

Plekhanov: "Cant versus Kant," Complete Works, XI, p. 41.

PAGE 160. Bertrand Russell: *The Scientific Outlook.*

PAGE 161. Ernst Krieck: Dispatch in the New York *Times*, July 1, 1936.

PAGE 162. Einstein: *Religion and Science*, New York *Times* Magazine, Sept. 9, 1930.

PAGE 173. Darwin: *Life and Letters of Charles Darwin*, by Francis Darwin, vol. I, p. 71.

PAGE 195. As an addendum to this chapter on the mystic origins of the Marxian philosophy, let me warn those interested in the effort to make revolutionary thinking scientific, not to be too much upset or awe-struck when solemnly informed that they do not "understand" Marxism. Marxism, in so far as this means the dialectic philosophy, is similar to all other schemes designed to read the ideal into the real, the satisfaction of your voluntary nature into your definition of objective facts. Like these other schemes, it cannot convince you by mere appeal to the facts. It rests upon, and in part consists of, the decision upon your part to enter the scheme, the will to believe. When a skilled dialectic materialist looks at you, therefore, with a lofty pity in his eye, and regrets that you do not seem to be able to "understand" Marxism, remember that he is a direct, if cooled-off, descendant of those who have said with the same high complacence throughout the ages: "You do not yet grasp the doctrine of the atonement. You must meditate longer upon the mercy of Jesus." It is not only understanding, but the voluntary assumption of an attitude that he asks of you. It may well be that you do not understand Marxism, for Hegel's "dialectic" scheme for making the universe support the prepossessions of a ruling class was certainly the most ingenious and complicated one ever invented, and when Marx turned the thing otherside up in the interests of the proletariat, it did not become any less complicated. On the other hand, however, it may be, especially if you were brought up in the matter-of-fact traditions of Anglo-Saxon thinking, that you understand it all too well. In either case do not be disheartened when they fix you with that look of withering pity.

PAGE 201. "Carry it forward": This does not mean, of course, that Marxians can "make revolutions," in the catastrophic sense of the word. It would be truer to say that revolutions are a natural force like the tide or the lightning, and just as electrical engineers may be said to have "harnessed the lightning," so revolutionary Marxists seek to harness revolutions and make them serve the highest interests of mankind. Lenin indicated the natural limits of reasonable effort, so far as concerns action in a crisis, in the following words, which he called the Fundamental Law of Revolution:

"Only when the masses do not want the old regime, and when the rulers are unable to govern as of old, only then can a revolution succeed. This truth may be expressed in other words: Revolution is impossible without an all-national crisis, affecting both the exploited and the exploiters."

PAGE 204. Plekhanov: Anarchism and Socialism. (My translation is from the French text, p. 22.)

PAGE 205. Kropotkin: Modern Science and Anarchism, VIII.

"Ignored the contribution of psychology": The conclusion of Köhler, for example, in his painstaking study of the behavior of the chimpanzee, that "Mutual obstruction is more frequent than co-operation," has a more decisive bearing upon the problem than all of Kropotkin's more general biological data put together. (*The Mentality of Apes*, by Wolfgang Köhler.)

PAGE 206. "Bakunin's early protest": Mehring's *Life of Marx*, V, 7. "Bakunin . . . wrote his share": See, for instance, *God and the State* (p. 32 of the New Edition, published by the Freedom Press, 1910): "Whatever human question we may desire to consider, we always find this same essential contradiction between the two schools. Thus, as I have already observed, materialism starts from animality to establish humanity; idealism starts from divinity to establish slavery and condemn the masses to an endless animality. Materialism denies free will and ends in the establishment of liberty; idealism, in the name of human dignity, proclaims free will, and on the ruins of every liberty founds authority. Materialism rejects the principle of authority, because it rightly considers it as the corollary of animality, and because, on the contrary, the triumph of humanity, the object and chief significance of history, can be realized only through liberty."

Marx: *Das Elend der Philosophie*, II, I.

PAGE 207. Kropotkin: *Modern Science and Anarchism*, XIII and XV. For another clear statement of what he thinks the science of economics ought to be, see his preface to *Fields, Factories and Workshops*.

PAGE 209. The three quotations are from Kropotkin's *Modern Science and Anarchism*, IX, XIV, and XII.

In Kropotkin's history of the French Revolution, the reader will see even more clearly the absence of any scientific plan, the reliance upon magic, upon a mystic virtue supposed to reside in what he calls "the people," to save other revolutions from going the way of this one. He makes it plain that the organization of a centralized state by the middle classes was what prevented the lower classes from gaining any of their ends. But his plan for preventing such a catastrophe in a future revolution is not to organize a corresponding power for the lower classes. His plan is simply and literally to *wish* away that organization of the middle classes.

"Any more than the other anarchists": I dwell upon Kropotkin because, of all the anarchists, he makes the best claim to be considered scientific. The belief in magic is so obvious in the writings of other revolutionary anarchists that I think it is hardly worth while to demonstrate it. One has only to seek out in each of them the particular event, or idea, or formula, to which he ascribes an occult virtue capable of producing the desired miracle. For Bakunin it was the very idea of "science" taken abstractly which possessed this high potency.

"The major part of the natural laws connected with the development of human society . . . have not been duly recognized and established by science itself.

"Once they shall have been recognized by science, and then from science, by means of an extensive system of popular education and instruction, shall have passed into the consciousness of all, the question of liberty will be entirely solved. The stubbornest authorities must admit that there will be no need either of political organization, or direction, or legislation" (from *God and the State*).

PAGE 211. George Sorel: The quotations are from *La Décomposition du Marxisme*, VI, and *Réflexions sur la Violence*, IV, III.

PAGE 212. "The longest backward step taken by any genuinely revolutionary theorist": A longer backward step, and a somewhat similar one, was taken by Hendrik de Man in a book called *Zur Psychologie des Sozialismus*, but de Man cannot be described as a genuinely revolutionary theorist. Sorel worked out a metaphysical consecration of the present motive in order to get the support of the universe in his revolutionary purpose. De Man has worked out a similar, although more mystical, consecration of mere motive, in order to get religious support for his abandonment of the revolutionary purpose.

"The older I grow," he confesses, "the more I feel myself a revolutionist, but the less I believe in the revolution. I am a revolutionist: that means that the transformation of capitalism into a socialist order is to me a psychical motive. . . . The present motive, not the future goal, is the sole essential. . . . I am a socialist, not because I believe in the superiority of the socialist image of the future over any other ideal, but because I have the conviction that the socialist motive makes better and happier men. . . . It is a perspectival delusion of our will which, so to speak, sifts out socialism from the activities of the present moment, in order to misplace it as a 'goal' in the future. Goals are only imaginary points of a future horizon, upon which we project the desired end of our volitional tendency. . . . If socialism as a movement has any general meaning, it is to make the men who take part in this movement happier. . . . The essential thing in socialism is the struggle for it. . . . I believe still only in the revolution which transforms our Self. This conception corresponds as well to the demands of real-political opportunity as to those of the moral law. . . . This same conviction that the ethical motive is at the same time the best and only real-politic, guides me when I emphasize the necessity of a regeneration of the socialist attitude through the moral-religious consciousness. . . . There is nothing more real in man than the divine power of the moral law."

It is needless to prove that this talk is not scientific, since it quite frankly declares itself religious. What I am moved to say about it is that it is immoral. All that there is in me which corresponds to those words "ethical motive," "moral law," etc.—namely, a strong sense of what is good and praiseworthy in human character and conduct—finds this abandonment of purposive intelligence in behalf of mere emotional motive, bad and weak and sickly, and to be condemned unconditionally by every person who loves humanity or has any hope of its development.

PAGE 213. "Reason, hopes and the perception": *Réflexions sur la Violence*, IV, p. 181.

PAGE 217. Lenin: *What to Do?*, IV, 3.

PAGE 218. The quotation is from Lenin's Introduction to the first edition of a collection of articles entitled *After Twelve Years*, written in 1907.

"Official history": *A History of the Russian Communist Party*, by Gregory Zinoviev, p. 71, of the Russian Edition, Moscow, 1923.

PAGE 219. "Lenin repeatedly declared": In *What to Do?* the statement occurs three times. My quotation is from ch. IV, sec. 3.

PAGES 220-222. The quotations are all from *What to Do?*

PAGE 222. Plekhanov: "The Working Class and the Social Democratic Intelligentsia," an article in *Iskra*, No. 71, August 1, 1904. Plekhanov's citation from Marx is from *The Holy Family*. Lenin's tribute to Plekhanov's philosophical writings is in the article already cited, "Once More about the Trade-Unions," and his response to Plekhanov's attack appears in the Introduction to *After Twelve Years*.

PAGE 224. "Midwife of Revolution": "We are not utopians . . . we are men of science, we do not devise new social forms, but only offer to capitalist society the service of midwife, when the hour comes for the birth of a socialist society." (Paul Lafargue in a Debate with Jaurès.)

PAGE 225. "Better that ten workers": The quotation is from the official report of the second convention of the Russian Social-Democratic Workers' Party, in London, 1903 (p. 251).

PAGE 226. "Attempted to define them": Karl Radek describes this change in Lenin's way of thinking as an advance in scientific accuracy. He says that Lenin "did not at first understand the social significance and social sources" of Menshevism. For that reason he first emphasized the distinction between "reasoners and fighters" within the working class. Subsequently he learned to identify Menshevism with the new layers of the petty bourgeoisie which are constantly entering the proletariat. And at a still later date he regarded it as "the politics of that part of the working class which can find satisfaction for its interests inside the frame of bourgeois society"—that is, the aristocracy of labor. Radek fails to note that Lenin never abandoned his original psychological definition, but kept it going *alongside* of these new economic ones. How strongly it survives in authoritative circles may be seen in the statement of Clara Zetkin at the Fifth Congress of the Communist International, that "the organizational and political superiority of Bolshevism . . . is the principle that a revolutionary party cannot tolerate merely paying members, that every member must be an active, working, fighting member." (My quotations are from Radek's articles on "The Scientific Organization of Labor in the Perspective of the Further Development of the Revolution," beginning in *Pravda*, No. 41, 1924.)

"Work, according to the definition of Marx": *Das Kapital*, vol. I, sec. 3, ch. V.

PAGE 230. The quotation is from *What to Do?*, IV, 3.

PAGE 231. "He was seriously attacked": Speech of Akimov in the Second Congress of the Russian Social Democratic Labor Party in 1903. The quotation immediately following is from Lenin's pamphlet "The Infantile Disease of Leftism," VI.

"Veritable tribunes of the people": These quotations are also from *What to Do?*

PAGE 232. "Marx also recognized the peasants": In a letter to Engels, often cited by Lenin himself, Marx wrote: "The whole cause of Germany will depend upon the possibility of reinforcing the proletarian revolution with a kind of second edition of the Peasants' War, then all will be well." (Translated from Lenin's text.)

"Policy of sharp turns": The expression is used by Trotsky in *The New Course*.

PAGE 235. "Pausing to write a tribute to Lenin": Bukharin's *Lenin, Marxist* is a fair example of these orthodox writings. After a conscientious but pale account of certain modifications introduced by Lenin in the Marxian theory, Bukharin casually mentions his "teaching upon the organization and structure of the party, the relations among the party, the working class, the masses, the leaders, etc.," calling this a "secondary question."

A pamphlet of Karl Radek, "About Lenin," contains some marked contrasts to this orthodox way of approaching Lenin. "The principal science of Lenin as a political leader preparing the conquest of power by the proletariat, was his science of the significance of the proletarian party." "The greatness of Lenin consisted in the fact that no formula composed yesterday ever prevented him from seeing the changing reality, that he had the courage to abandon yesterday's formula if it prevented his grasping today's reality."

PAGE 236. The quotation is from "The Infantile Disease of Leftism."

PAGE 238. The quotation is from Lenin's article "Concerning Our Revolution," Complete Works, vol. XVIII, part 2, p. 118 ff.

PAGES 238-239. The quotations from Marx are to be found in the Introduction to the Critique of Political Economy, The Poverty of Philosophy, II, 5, the Criticism of the Gotha Program and the Preface to the first edition of Capital.

PAGE 241. The passage from Cardinal Manning is quoted by Lytton Strachey in his Eminent Victorians.

"Truth is always concrete": A favorite maxim with both Lenin and Plekhanov, quoted from Chernishevsky, who first introduced the Hegelian philosophy into Russian revolutionary circles.

PAGE 242. "Marx says": Letter to Weydemeier, March 5, 1852.

"Lenin says": State and Revolution.

"In Lenin the scientific thinker": The doubleness of Marx's mental character, and the singleness of Lenin's were both observed by those who knew them. H. M. Hyndman described most vividly the interplay between the purposive thinker and the metaphysical professor in Marx. "The contrast," he wrote, "between his excitement in moments of strong indignation and the peaceful transition to an exposition of his views on contemporary economic events was most striking. He passed without visible effort from the rôle of prophet and flaming prosecutor to the rôle of tranquil philosopher. . . ." (Retranslated from a foreign text.) Compare what Trotsky says about Lenin: "This great engineer of history, not only in politics, but in his theoretical works, in his philosophical speculations, in the study of foreign languages, and in conversation with people, was continually possessed by one and the same idea—the goal."

PAGE 243. Engels: Anti-Dühring, I, XI. "How young is all human history, and how ridiculous it would be, to wish to ascribe any absolute validity to our present views, may be inferred from the simple fact that all history up to now may be described as the history of the period from the practical discovery of the transformation of mechanical motion into heat, until that of the transformation of heat into mechanical motion."

Lenin: Materialism and Empiro-criticism, VI, 2. The second quotation is from What to Do?

PAGE 244. The quotation is from Materialism and Empiro-criticism, VI, 2.

PAGE 247. "Partisan": Materialism and Empiro-criticism, VI, 4, and "Conclusion."

PAGE 251. "Hegel himself said": Logic, p. 18.

PAGE 252. "Desultory empirical observations": The student should examine section 81 of Hegel's *Logic* (p. 147 in Wallace's translation); then the chapter on "Dialectic" in Engels's *Landmarks of
Scientific Socialism* (A translation of the substance of his *Herrn
Eugen Dühring's Umwälzung der Wissenschaft*, called *Anti-
Dühring* for short); and then, if possible, a letter written by
Engels to Conrad Schmidt on November 1, 1891. This will be
enough to convince him that the dialectic "law of motion" is
not a definable and verifiable empirical generalization, or anything
remotely approaching it. Starting with the assertion that "Everything that surrounds us may be viewed as an instance of Dialectic," Hegel proceeds to tell us about some sufficiently peculiar
matters in which we can find ."illustrations" of it, and "traces of
its presence." Here are two of them: "In political life, as everyone
knows, extreme anarchy and extreme despotism naturally lead to
one another." "The perception of Dialectic in the province of
individual ethics is seen in the well-known adages, Pride comes
before a fall: Too much wit outwits itself." Engels in his *Anti-
Dühring* adds some equally casual illustrations from the sphere of
chemistry and mathematics, and in his letter to Conrad Schmidt,
who was trying to convince himself of the dialectic philosophy,
he makes the following suggestion (I translate from a Russian
text):
"You as a bridegroom will find a clear model of the inseparability
of identity and difference in yourself and your bride. It is absolutely impossible to determine whether sexual love is a joy in the
fact that there is identity in difference, or that there is difference
in identity. Throw out the difference (in this case, sex) or the
identity (the humanity of both) and what have you left?"—which
shows a remarkable innocence of the varieties of sexual experience,
but which will certainly not pass for science in these days.
Such illustrations of an aphorism parading as proofs of a law would
not have convinced anybody, even in Hegel's time. For convincing people, the dialectic philosophy relied entirely upon rationalistic devices, of which two examples will suffice. One of them is
the difficulty about making physical motion seem logical—the
paradox, or conundrum, discovered by Zeno. I have discussed it
in my chapter on "The Dialectic Method." The other consists of
building up a great mystification about the general idea of "being." You arrive at general ideas by dropping out of your con-
notation the concrete and real attributes of things, and when you
arrive at "being," the most general idea which is possible, you
find that all the attributes are gone, and the idea really *means
nothing!* This may amuse you a little, but it will soon strike you
as more interesting to think about *something*. . . . That is a

simple and natural, and also in the rough state, a *scientific* way of stating the principal fact upon which Hegel builds up his dialectic mystification. I will quote his own words in *The Science of Logic*, Part I, Ch. I. (Here I have to take the responsibility for the translation.)

"A.—Being.

"Being, pure being—without further definition. In its undefined immediacy it is only equal to itself, and also is not unequal compared with anything else, has no distinction within itself, nor without. By any definition or content, which might be distinguished in it, or through which it might be put in distinction to something else, it would fail to be grasped in its purity. It is pure undefinedness and emptiness.—There is nothing to contemplate in it, if one can speak here of contemplating, or it is only this pure empty contemplation itself. There is likewise nothing to think in it, or it is just only this empty thought. Being, the undefined immediate, is in fact nothing, and neither more nor less than nothing.

"B.—Nothing.

"Nothing, pure nothing; it is simple equality to itself, complete emptiness, absence of definition and content; undistinguishedness in itself.—In so far as contemplation or thought can be mentioned here, it is considered a distinction, whether something or nothing is contemplated or thought. To contemplate or think nothing has thus a meaning; the two are distinguished, thus nothing is (exists) in our contemplation or thought; or rather it is empty contemplation and thought itself; and the same empty contemplation or thought as pure being.—Nothing is consequently the same definition, or rather lack of definition, and thus the same in general as pure Being.

"C.—Becoming.
"The Unity of Being and Nothing.

"Pure being and pure nothing are just the same. What the truth is, is neither being or nothing, but the fact that being—not passes over—but has passed over into nothing, and nothing into being. But in the same way the truth is, not their undistinguishedness, but that they are not the same, that they are absolutely different, but nevertheless undivided and indivisible, and each immediately vanishes in its opposite. Their truth is, thus, this motion of immediate vanishing of one in the other; becoming; a motion in which both are distinguished, but through a distinction, which itself has just now immediately been dissolved."

The most significant passage in Hegel's *Logic*, for those who understand the functions of the mind, is that in which he cautions the reader against taking the statement that "being and nothing are the same" for a joke (*Logic*, p. 163). It is a joke, in the most technical sense of the term—although it is not a very good one. (See my *Enjoyment of Laughter*.)

"As he once contemplated doing": See his letter to Engels, January 14, 1858.

PAGE 253. Lafargue: *Le Determinisme Economique de Karl Marx.*

Plekhanov: *As to the Question of the Development of a Monistic View of History*, p. 103 of the Soviet edition. "In order to escape from ignorance covered up in a more or less learned terminology, we must pass from the study of human nature to a study of the nature of social relations."

Kautsky: *Karl Marx and His Historical Significance*, II. In an essay on "Social Instinct in Marx and Darwin," Kautsky does broach the question of the relation between genetic psychology and Marxism, but only to remark that this science corroborates the "Theses on Feuerbach."

Lenin: In quoting a passage from Engels's *Feuerbach*, Lenin translates the German words *Gedanken-Abbilder* as "mental photographs." "Things which seem changeless, and likewise ideas, their mental photographs made by the head, are in a state of continuing change" ("Karl Marx, A Short Biographical Essay with an Exposition of Marxism," p. 13). In his *Materialism and Empirocriticism*, Lenin makes the following similar statements: "Matter is a philosophic category for the designation of an objective reality, which is given to man in his sensations, which is copied, photographed, reflected by our sensations, existing independently of them" (p. 142 of the first edition). "Materialism in general recognizes an objectively real existence (matter) independent of the consciousness, sensation, experience, etc., of humanity. Historic materialism recognizes a social existence independent of the social consciousness of humanity. Consciousness in both cases is only a reflection of existence, at the best an approximately true (adequate, mentally exact) reflection of it" (p. 394). "A recognition of the objective orderedness of nature, and the approximately true reflection of this order *in the head of man* is materialism" (p. 175). "To recognize the necessity of nature and infer from it the necessity of *thought* is materialism" (p. 189). "*Knowledge* can be biologically useful . . . only in case it reflects an objective reality, not dependent upon man" (p. 155).

I give these different quotations with my own italics, in order to show the complete lack of psychological science, or the conception of such a thing, in Lenin's mind. "Sensation," "thought,"

"consciousness," "social consciousness," "knowledge," "experience," "ideas"—any names that happen to occur to him for anything that exists or takes place "in the head of man"—are lumped
together without examination or discrimination as automatic photographs of the material environment. This is not materialistic
philosophy; it is mere negligence of psychological facts and distinctions. Lenin's "materialism" is satisfied by his assertion that
"matter, nature, existence, the physical, is primary, and spirit, consciousness, sensation, the psychical, is secondary" (p. 164)—a
statement which seems to him, because he has no conception of a
psychological science, practically interchangeable with these other
statements.

"Consciousness in general": *Materialism and Empiro-criticism*, p. 391.

PAGE 254. The phrases quoted are all from Hegel's *Logic* (pp. 50, 51, 149).

PAGE 255. "Hegel had a well-founded phobia": *Logic*, p. 69: "One
word on the relation of rational to empirical psychology," he
says. "The former, because it sets itself to apply thought to
cognize mind and even to demonstrate the result of such thinking,
is the higher; whereas empirical psychology starts from perception, and only recounts and describes what perception supplies."
In short it only tells us the facts!

Hegel pretends to study an evolution of the mind, but it is in reality a resurrection of God that he is studying. It is a coming back
to its "true and unadulterated self" of his *rationalistic conception*
of the mind, after having been "alienated from itself" in matter.
Such a study of its genesis obviously does not, and cannot, affect
the conception. Hegel's attitude to a real genetic psychology may
be inferred from the fact that he begins his *Encyclopedia of the
Philosophical Sciences* by making a fixed distinction between man
and the animals upon the ground that man "thinks," and he re-
curs to it ten times in the first one hundred pages. His *Lectures
on the Philosophy of Religion* begin with the same assertion: "It
is through thought . . . or more definitely, it is by reason of his
being Spirit, that man is man."

PAGE 256. Hegel: *Logic*, p. 103.

PAGE 257. Lenin: *Pod Znamenem Marxisma*, No. 2, and *Materialism
and Empiro-criticism*, VI, 4.

Bakunin: *God and the State*, p. 44.

The statement that "Religion is the opium of the people" occurs
in Marx's *Introduction to a Criticism of Hegel's Philosophy of
Law*. (*Nachlass*, vol. I, p. 385.)

PAGE 260. In connection with this page I will mention another slight
advantage which may accrue to revolutionary art from a disestab-
lishment of the religion of Marxism. A certain liberty of opinion

may be allowed as to whether Marx himself was a great artist. Franz Mehring—a person of general literary culture and discrimination—says in his biography (VIII, 2) that "Marx might compete in striking figurativeness of language with the great masters of comparison, Lessing, Goethe, Hegel." And among orthodox Marxists this is a very general opinion.

Here is an example of the way in which Marx used comparison— one of the worst examples, to be sure, but still taken from his mature, and not his youthful writings. He is speaking of the allotment of land to the peasants in France.

"The bourgeois order, which at the beginning of the century had placed the state as a sentry before the newly arisen allotment and dunged it with laurels, has become a vampire, which sucks out its heart's blood and brain-matter and throws it in the Alchemist's retort of capital." (Der Achtzehnte Brumaire des Louis Bonaparte, pp. 101-102, of the third edition.)

Nobody who knew the first principles of the art of comparison could have written this sentence. Marx had in his head the materials of which great literature is composed, but he lacked the fineness of imaginative perception and feeling to make any consistent use of them. He did indeed write some great sentences— but only a few, and never when he tried to.

PAGE 262. Lenin: The quotations are from What to Do? and "The Infantile Disease of Leftism."

PAGE 263. Hegel: Logic, p. 51.

Engels: Preface to the second edition of Anti-Dühring.

"His American translator": Austin Lewis (see Landmarks of Scientific Socialism, Appendix, p. 261).

PAGE 264. Kautsky: Three Crises in Marxism. "For the understanding of Marx," he says, "a certain knowledge is required, and a tireless striving to penetrate deeper and deeper. At first acquaintance one always understands Marxism cheaply and vulgarly; it is necessary continually to increase the stores of one's knowledge, and with the newly acquired knowledge tackle again and again the study of Marx's works, for only then is it possible to understand and solve the contradiction between the surface and the essence of things, between their superficially apparent and their profound relations." (From a Russian text.)

Plekhanov: "A new condition of the productive forces brings after it a new economic structure, as well as a new psychology, a new spirit of the times. From this it is evident that only in popular speech is it permissible to speak of economy as the primary cause of all social phenomena. Far from being the primary cause, it is itself a consequence, a 'function' of the productive forces." As to the *Question of the Development of a Monistic View of History*, V.

Lenin: "Once More about the Trade-Unions," Complete Works, vol. XVIII, part I, p. 60.

PAGE 265. "The eloquence of Bakunin": *God and the State*. "It is time," he says, "to have done with all popes and priests; we want them no longer, even if they call themselves Social-Democrats."

PAGE 266. "Reflection in the heads of Marxists": The quotation is from a pamphlet by Sarabianov entitled "Historical Materialism."

PAGE 268. Marx: *The Poverty of Philosophy*.

Plekhanov: *Anarchism and Socialism* (from the French text, p. 22).

PAGE 269. Engels: *Landmarks of Scientific Socialism*, p. 221.

PAGE 270. Lenin: "The Infantile Disease of Leftism," VI, and *State and Revolution*, VI, 3.

Bertrand Russell: *Roads to Freedom*, VIII. Although he gave his book this very promising title, *Roads to Freedom*, Bertrand Russell never for the length of one sentence took the viewpoint of a man standing in a defined position in the present, and asking the scientific question: With what forces, and by what method of their employment, can I begin actually moving in the desired direction? His book, like all anarchistic writings, is about "Programmes of Freedom"—a valuable contribution to that discussion, indeed the first contribution which shows the influence of modern psychology. But Bertrand Russell's "programmes" are left hanging in the air, as though they might realize themselves by the mere act of their promulgation. That is why I describe him as an extreme utopian from the point of view of method.

A similar thing is to be said of Thorstein Veblen's book *Engineers and the Price System*.

PAGE 271. "Confused figure": My translation is from the French of Victor Serge, who quotes this sentence in his *Lenin—1917*. It is amusing to note that Trotsky's more visual mind is troubled by this figure, and in reproducing it from memory he instinctively tries to improve it. "Lenin, I think, first expressed in 'Iskra' the thought that in the complicated chain of political activity one must know how to pick out the link that is central for the given moment, so that seizing it one may give direction to the whole chain" (*About Lenin*, V). Trotsky's improvement consists of detaching the chain from its fastening in the future, and converting it into something more in the nature of an armored car! Trotsky, as I have shown, is none too orthodox. He makes a more scrupulous effort to be orthodox than Lenin did. He lacks the philosophic self-confidence of his leader, and he is more conscious of the intellectual difficulties in their position. Also he finds the true theological way out. "The will to revolutionary activity," he says, in a pamphlet on Communism and Education, "is a condition indispensable to the understanding of the Marxian dialectic" —which is not far from saying, "All your doubts will disappear after you join the church."

PAGE 272. "In six months": See Trotsky's About Lenin, V.

"What socialism will be": From the Stenographic Report of the Seventh Congress of the Russian Communist Party, Fifth Session, March 8, 1918.

INDEX

For Product Safety Concerns and Information please contact our EU
representative GPSR@taylorandfrancis.com
Taylor & Francis Verlag GmbH, Kaufingerstraße 24, 80331 München, Germany